A HISTORY
OF THE
THOMAS JEFFERSON
SCHOOL OF LAW

KENNETH J. VANDEVELDE

Published by The California Press
San Diego, California

ISBN: 0615658776
ISBN I3:9780615658773

Front Cover: Assisted by former Dean Mary Lynne Perry, the author confers an honorary degree on WSU President Jack Monks at the law school's 1996 commencement exercises at the Organ Pavilion in Balboa Park.

Back Cover: The law school's Old Town campus, which it occupied from 1983 until 2011. The Old Town campus was expanded in 1996 when the law school acquired the Gann Professional Building across the street and again in 2005 when the law school acquired the adjacent building of the Melhorn Construction Company.

Table of Contents

For my wife, Lidia, and our daughters, Jenny and Shelly, who over a period of eleven years sacrificed countless evenings and weekends with their husband or father while he participated in some of the events recounted here; and

For my friends and colleagues at the Thomas Jefferson School of Law, who gave their unstinting support to a quest for excellence that transformed a law school.

Acknowledgements

This account was possible only because a number of those involved in the early history of the Thomas Jefferson School of Law very generously assisted me in reconstructing that history. First, I was extremely fortunate to have had the opportunity to speak on several occasions with Ardiste Reis Ladin, the only surviving founder of Western State University College of Law (WSU). She provided information about the origins of the college that was indispensable.

Gary Woolverton, widely acknowledged to be the man responsible for the founding of the San Diego campus of Western State University, which became the Thomas Jefferson School of Law, spent a day with me while in San Diego attending the funeral of a family member. His account was invaluable. Jim Hennenhoefer, who attended the law school during its first year of operation, agreed to an interview at the very moment he returned to his office after a lengthy trial. He provided both a student's perspective on the law school's first year of operation and much useful information.

Mel Sherman, who passed away in December 2011 only days before I was scheduled to call him for a final interview, very graciously invited me to his home in Palm Desert in 2006, where we were joined by Art Toll, Dick Leavitt, and Joel Goodman for a day of reminiscing about the history of the law school. Mel, Art and Dick purchased WSU from the founders in 1977 and owned it during the years when the San Diego campus separated from the rest of the college, became the Thomas Jefferson School of Law, and gained provisional and full ABA approval. Joel served in a variety of administrative roles and as their close advisor during the years following their acquisition of WSU. The recollections of these four men were critical to this project and I structured much of this account around my notes from our session. Mel also assisted me in locating Art, Dick and Joel after I had lost touch with them. All four kindly consented to additional telephone calls to remedy gaps in my information.

Hadley Batchelder, who taught at the law school from 1969 to 2003 and who served as dean from 1985 to 1988, provided some very critical details about the beginnings of the law school as well as the events of the 1970s and 1980s, including WSU's unsuccessful 1986 application for ABA approval. Karla Castetter, Joy Delman, Thom Golden, and Bill Slomanson, all of whom joined the faculty in the 1980s, gave generously of their time to tell me about the events of that decade. In addition, when he learned of this project, Bill kindly gave me a number of documents that he had collected over the years. Mary Lynne Perry, who joined the faculty in 1986 and who served as dean from 1990 to 1994, described for me the remarkable years of her deanship, during which the San Diego campus emerged from the consequences of the failed 1986 application for ABA accreditation and then grew strong enough to launch a successful accreditation application as an independent law school in 1995. Through his daughter, I asked Ross Lipsker, the first dean of the San Diego campus of WSU, for an interview, but received no response. George Kraft, who served as acting dean from 1988 to 1990, passed away before I had the opportunity to interview him (although I did have the pleasure of working with him on the faculty). This account thus draws upon the recollections of three of the five individuals who served as dean from the founding of the law school through 2005.

Jennifer Keller, who first worked at the San Diego campus in 1969 and, except for a few months when she returned to her native state of

Missouri, remained at that campus continuously until 2005, gave me the benefit of her extraordinary memory of the law school's history. She also had saved numerous documents that she generously donated to the law school library, where they were available for my use. Jason Curtis, Leigh Inman and Patrick Meyer of the law library were extremely cooperative in providing me with a quiet place to review all of the law school's historical documents. The always wonderful Lori Wulfemeyer gave me access to the photo archives of the law school's Communications Department and Diana Mikesell assisted me with finding and cropping some of the photographs.

Marybeth Herald, who was my co-conspirator in everything from the moment we both joined the faculty in 1991, read and commented upon the first draft of the entire manuscript, offering her invariably sage advice and saving me from what would have been some unfortunate choices. Julie Greenberg, who served as an extremely active and effective faculty chair during the pivotal year in which the shareholders decided to permit the San Diego campus to apply for ABA approval, helped me reconstruct some of the events of that important time.

I owe my deepest thanks to all of these individuals for their generous assistance. I apologize to them for any errors that I committed in my recounting of their stories. As anyone who has ever attempted to construct a historical narrative knows, recollections about past events often differ. In some cases, very clear recollections were contradicted by documents dating from the time period in question. I endeavored to describe events as they occurred, but my efforts to reconcile conflicting accounts may not have always met with success. I hope that the final product nevertheless provides some assurance that the time spent assisting me was well used.

Sadly, Max Boas, Beatrice Boas and Burt Reis, three of the four founders of WSU, and Bill Lawless and Jack Monks, the first two presidents of WSU, all passed away before I was able to interview them for this project. I never met Max or Beatrice Boas, Burt Reis or Bill Lawless and I regret that their important voices are absent from this account, apart from the thoughts that they left behind in a few documents. I was fortunate to have had numerous conversations with Jack Monks about the law school between 1990 and 1996. My work on this history only reminded me of his enormous contribution to our success.

The year 2011 marked the tenth anniversary of the Thomas Jefferson School of Law's receipt of full ABA approval and its conversion to a not-for-profit law school. It marked the fifteenth anniversary of the law school's separation from Western State University College of Law and its receipt of provisional ABA approval. This history is written in honor of the occasion.

Introduction

History is especially important at the Thomas Jefferson School of Law because few law schools have struggled so mightily with theirs. This was a law school founded with a very specific vision that, over time, proved increasingly difficult to realize. The essential dilemma was that the vision rested on a tension between two goals: providing access to a legal education for the broadest range of potential students and creating a highly-regarded law school that would confer a well-respected degree. The 36 year history sketched here is to a large extent a story in which the law school over time came to recognize the irreconcilable tension between these goals and in which the first goal gradually was eclipsed by the second. A quest for students became a quest for excellence.

The Thomas Jefferson School of Law is distinctive in that for much of its history it was a proprietary institution, *i.e.,* one owned by private individuals who operated it as a profit-making enterprise. One of the most important developments in the history of the law school was its transformation from a proprietary to a not-for-profit institution. As will be seen, the status of the law school as a proprietary institution complicated, but did not fundamentally change, the basic tension between its aspirations to provide access to legal education for a broad range of applicants and its aspirations to build a widely-respected school of law. The proprietors recognized that an open admissions policy would increase tuition revenue and thus enhance the law school's profitability, but they also believed that building the law school's academic quality and reputation similarly would promote their long term financial interests. Thus, the tension that pervaded the law school's mission for much of its history also pervaded the proprietors' own strategic planning.

No history can address every aspect of its subject. This is an institutional history, one that traces all of the major events in the evolution of the law school from its founding until 2005, although it focuses particularly on the events through which the 26 year old San Diego campus of a for-profit, state accredited, Orange County law school, within the space of six years, became an independent, nonprofit law school accredited by the American Bar Association (ABA). Apart from the law school's founding, these were the most significant events in its history, both because they radically transformed the institution from what it had been during its first 26 years of existence and because they created the conditions that would shape all that would come later. In tracing these events, this history recounts some of the ways in which the Thomas Jefferson School of Law moved beyond the circumstances of its origins as well as some of the ways in which its early history shapes it still.

When I began this project, I expected that the final manuscript would be no more than a hundred pages long. Including the photographic images that I decided to add, the final manuscript is four times that length. I believe that I can say with confidence that this account includes more about the history of the law school in greater detail than virtually anyone will want to know. After completing the manuscript, I identified a large number of passages that could be excised without significantly detracting from the core narrative, but then decided not to excise them. Over the years, I have been asked a lot of questions about a wide variety of aspects of the law school's history and I realized that, while not everything in this account would be of interest to every reader, everything would be of interest to at least some readers. Some may want to read, for example, about the founding of the law school, while others may be more interested in how we became the first for-profit law school to obtain ABA approval, or how we converted to a nonprofit law school, or how we increased admissions applications more than tenfold in a decade, or how we doubled our bar passage rate. Rather than choosing portions of the account to eliminate, I decided to divide the account into a large number of chapters and to subdivide the chapters into short topical sections. In that way, readers can select the passages that interest them and disregard the rest.

Although this account focuses on a series of institutional changes, particularly those in which I happened to be involved, the most penetrating history of the law school would not be an account of a few major institutional changes, but the story of faculty and staff members working hard on a daily basis to create and disseminate knowledge and to prepare students for the practice of a noble and learned profession. This account does not and cannot describe each class that was wonderfully taught, each book or article that was insightfully written, or each instance where someone cheerfully worked overtime to ensure that a project or program was a stunning success. Yet, it is precisely these unsung moments of excellence and commitment on which the institutional changes described here rested. The revolution at the Thomas Jefferson School of Law had many heroes and I regret that they cannot all be mentioned individually.

Nor was it possible to include photographs of all of the major contributors to our success. Consistent with the idea that this was an institutional history, I tried to include photographs, to the extent that they were available, of those who founded the law school, owned it during its years as a for-profit, or served as president, dean, associate dean, assistant dean or chairman of the board. I also included a few photographs relating to events or programs that were particularly significant to the institutional history. In addition, I sought to ensure that the photographs included at least a few images of the staff, faculty and students, the latter of whom generally appear as alumni. Because of my particular focus on institutional change, some of those at the law school whom I admire the most or whose contribution to the academic program or to the administration of the law school has been the greatest are not pictured.

In writing this account, I have drawn extensively on knowledge that I acquired from my direct involvement in many of the institutional changes described. I was privileged to serve as the associate dean of the law school from 1992 to 1994 and then as the dean from 1994 to 2005, a time during which the law school separated from its former parent, Western State University College of Law, obtained ABA accreditation, expanded its campus, and was converted to a nonprofit institution. My direct involvement has enabled me to recount many aspects of the law school's history that otherwise would have remained obscure, a fact that has prompted me both to write this account and to end it with my departure from the dean's office. As the reader will readily see, the account of the years after 1990 is as much a personal memoir as it is an institutional history.

While drawing on my personal experience has enabled me to tell a story that otherwise could not have been told, it has also placed me at the center of many of the events. It describes these events as I experienced them and as I understood them. My individual perspective, however, can never provide an account that corresponds entirely to the events as others experienced and understood them. I hope, therefore, that this narrative will inspire others to record their own recollections, from which will emerge a more complete history of the Thomas Jefferson School of Law.

Part One

Western State University
College of Law
of San Diego

1968-1995

1

Founding Western State University College of Law

The Thomas Jefferson School of Law originated with four people seated around a dining room table in Orange County, California, in 1966, dreaming of the founding of a successful, nonprofit, ABA approved law school. Thirty-five years would pass, however, before the law school that they created would finally realize their dream.

In 1964, a 42 year old Orange County businessman named Burton Reis and his wife, Ardiste, had started a school that trained medical and dental assistants. Burt served as the director of the school and Ardi, who had a degree in economics, was the chief financial officer. The school was an immediate success.

The school's success was particularly noted by Maxwell Boas, at that time a 47 year old Los Angeles attorney. Boas was well acquainted with Burt and Ardi Reis because his wife, Beatrice, was Burt Reis' cousin. Inspired by the success of the medical and dental assistants' school, Max Boas proposed that the four of them open a law school.

The two couples began to research the legal requirements for operating a law school. From the beginning, they intended that their law school would obtain accreditation from both the California Committee of Bar Examiners (CBE) and the American Bar Association (ABA). At that time, neither the CBE nor the ABA allowed the accreditation of law schools that were operated for profit. Thus, they organized their law school as a nonprofit corporation. The resources that they could commit to the venture would not be sufficient to meet ABA standards at the time of the law school's founding, but they planned to raise standards gradually so that their school eventually would qualify for ABA accreditation.

Max Boas proposed the founding of WSU and served
as its first dean from 1966 to 1981.

One aspect of founding their law school was selecting a name for the school. The founders wanted a name that would allow maximum flexibility with respect to the future evolution of the institution. They finally settled upon the name "Western State University College of Law." The use of the word "university" contemplated the possibility that the institution would offer programs in disciplines other than law. The use of the word "state" reflected their intention to attract students from throughout the state, rather than the Orange County region alone.

They chose for the location of their new college a building in a strip mall located at 1717 South Brookhurst Street in Anaheim. The first floor of the building housed the medical and dental assistants' school owned by Burt and Ardi Reis, while the law school was located on the second floor. Max Boas joked at the time that the two schools, taken together, already constituted a university.

Classes commenced in August 1966 with 138 students enrolled, far more than the founders had anticipated. Tuition was $25 per unit. Burt Reis served as the executive director, while Ardi Reis was the chief financial officer of the college, essentially the same positions that they held at the medical and dental assistants' school. Given the surprising success of the law school and the demands that it was placing on their time, they decided to sell their medical and dental assistants' school. Max Boas left the practice of law and became the dean of the college.

Burt Reis was one of the four founders of WSU and served as its executive director from 1966 to 1981.

WSU very quickly outgrew its campus. In 1969, the college began to lease classroom and office space in the Palomar Building, a three story office building located at 800 South Brookhurst Street. On January 1, 1970, the college acquired the Palomar Building. Max Boas and Burt Reis retained their offices on the original campus and the library and two classrooms remained as well. The campus thus was divided between two buildings located approximately nine blocks apart.

In December 1974, in order to consolidate its operation in a single location, the college relocated the campus to a custom built, 54,000 square foot building on a four acre tract in Fullerton, where it remains today. The original campus now houses the West Coast Islamic Center, while the Palomar Building is an office building.

The college soon became such a success that the founders decided to reorganize it as a for-profit corporation. As long as it was a nonprofit, they could receive only reasonable salaries for their work at the college. If it were a for-profit, they could receive salaries in the amounts that they designated, a distribution of any profits, and the proceeds from a sale of the college. By 1970, WSU had become a proprietary college.

Ardi Reis, left, and Beatrice Boas, two of the founders of WSU, pose with a drawing of the new WSU campus in Fullerton.

While in the process of converting WSU to a proprietary college, the founders urged the CBE to change its rules to permit the accreditation of proprietary law schools. In 1971, the CBE acceded to their wishes and modified its rules to allow the accreditation of a for-profit law school, although the new rule stated that a law school "preferably" would be organized as a nonprofit. A year later, the Anaheim campus received provisional CBE accreditation. The founders knew that the ABA rules continued to preclude the accreditation of a proprietary law school, but they believed that they would be able to persuade the ABA to change its rules, as the CBE had done. As time would show, they were right.

Establishing a Campus in San Diego

Meanwhile, in fall 1968, Max Boas and Burt Reis received a telephone call from a young law student in San Diego named Gary Woolverton. Gary had recently moved from Sacramento to San Diego, where he was starting a new job as a real estate appraiser at the First National Bank of Southern California. In Sacramento, he had been enrolled at the McGeorge School of Law, which was in the process of obtaining ABA accreditation. Gary had enrolled at McGeorge expecting that it would be ABA accredited by the time he graduated from law school, as indeed it would be, although the process was not yet completed when he relocated to San Diego. Because McGeorge was not yet ABA approved, Gary's two years of course work would not transfer to either of the two ABA approved law schools in San Diego, the University of San Diego School of Law or California Western School of Law. Accordingly, he enrolled in a law school not accredited by the ABA, Cabrillo Pacific University College of Law.

Max Boas hands Ardi Reis a pair of scissors at the ribbon cutting ceremony for the WSU campus in Fullerton.

Cabrillo Pacific, at that time, operated out of the second floor of an abandoned medical facility. Its enrollment totaled only about 25 students and the law school had no full-time faculty or staff other than the dean. Gary was disappointed with the quality of the instruction, which was well below the standards set at McGeorge. He decided that the only way that he would be able to obtain a rigorous legal education, one worthy of ABA accreditation, was to found a new law school.

Gary telephoned three law schools operating to the north, hoping that one of them would be willing to establish a branch in San Diego. These were the Beverly Rubens School of Law, the University of West Los Angeles (UWLA) School of Law, and Western State University College of Law. He left messages at each school indicating the nature of his proposal. Beverly Rubens, the dean of her eponymous law school, never returned his phone call. Wally Frank, the dean of UWLA, did return his call, as did Boas and Reis. Gary met with Frank, Boas and Reis. Frank did not pursue the matter further. Boas and Reis, however, told Gary that they were interested in further discussion. A number of students at WSU were commuting to Anaheim from San Diego and thus Boas and Reis recognized that a market existed for another law school in San Diego.

Boas and Reis imposed two conditions on Gary before they would commit to opening a branch campus in San Diego. First, they required him to assemble an executive board of distinguished community leaders who would be willing to lend their names to the new law school, giving it credibility. Gary's wife, Donna, worked for Clair Burgener, who was then a state senator and who later would become a congressman from San Diego, and Burgener agreed to serve on the board. Through Senator Burgener, Gary recruited additional community leaders who, in turn, brought still more local luminaries onto the board. By the time the campus opened, the executive board included, in addition to Burgener, Howard S. Dattan, the fomer dean of the University of San Diego School of Law; State Assemblyman Wadie P. Deddeh; Municipal Judge Richard J. Donovan; Municipal Judge Earl B. Gilliam; Imperial County District Attorney James Hamilton; former Superior Court Judge Edgar B. Hervey; San Diego County Clerk Robert B. James; Imperial County Superior Court Judge George R. Kirk; Chief Deputy County Clerk Jesse Osuna; and the Director of Legislative Representation for the City of San Diego, Charles E. Porter.

Law student Gary Woolverton proposed that WSU open a campus in San Diego.

The second condition imposed by Boas and Reis was that Gary find a campus. He located a vacant building at 1067 Front Street, at the corner of

Front and C Streets. The building previously had served as a Greyhound bus station and was adjacent to the existing bus station.

That area of San Diego at the time was a classic sailor's port of call, with bars, brothels and tattoo parlors all around. Yet, Gary's choice was a logical one. The county courthouse was across the street to the west and the county law library was across the street to the north. The building had a reception area, two offices, space for a single classroom, and a work room for office equipment.

The founders traveled to San Diego to inspect Gary's proposed campus. Burt Reis was skeptical about the venture and initially opposed opening a branch in San Diego. Max Boas and Ardi Reis, however, saw the potential and persuaded him that the college should open the new branch.

Donna Woolverton provided the connection to State Senator Clair Burgener that enabled Gary Woolverton to recruit a distinguished Executive Board.

At that point, Boas and Reis authorized Gary to recruit faculty for the San Diego campus. He advertised the positions and interviewed those who applied. Two men appointed to the faculty at the time the San Diego campus opened would have long associations with the campus. One was Judge Earl B. Gilliam, who would become the first African-American to serve on the superior court in San Diego and, later, the first African-American to be appointed to the federal bench in San Diego. Judge Gilliam used his extensive contacts to assist Gary in finding other faculty. He would teach as an adjunct at the San Diego campus until the late 1990s and would serve on its governing board following its separation from WSU. The other was Hadley Batchelder, who would teach continuously at the law school first as an adjunct and then as a full-time faculty member until 2003 and who would serve as dean from 1985 to 1988.

The founders authorized Gary to recruit a student body as well. He placed advertisements in local newspapers to attract entering students. He also informed his classmates at Cabrillo Pacific that WSU would be opening a branch campus in San Diego that would be state accredited and eventually ABA approved.

At his first meeting with Boas and Reis, Gary had told the two men that his proposal was to found a campus in San Diego that would provide a rigorous legal education and that would obtain ABA approval at an early opportunity. Had he merely wanted to obtain a degree that would qualify him to sit for the bar exam, he could have remained at Cabrillo Pacific. Boas and Reis assured him that they concurred in his desire to obtain ABA approval, although they cautioned him that the process would take some time. From the beginning, in recruiting the executive board, prospective faculty members and prospective students, Gary advertised the law school as one that would eventually seek ABA approval.

The prospect of attending an accredited law school was attractive and all but a couple of the Cabrillo Pacific students transferred to WSU. Soon after the campus opened, the students were surprised to learn that the founders had transformed the college to a for-profit entity, something that none of them had anticipated. Further, at least some students were disappointed that the college did not immediately apply for ABA approval.

College of Law facilities in San Diego

The original San Diego campus at Front and C Streets
was formerly a Greyhound Bus station.

The new San Diego campus commenced operations on December 9, 1968. Tuition by that time was $30 per unit, meaning that students would have paid about $660 per year. Classes began on February 17, 1969, with 119 students enrolled. Because the one classroom in the building occupied by the law school was insufficient, the school also rented space in the Charter Oil Building, located one block to the east, at 110 West C Street, at the corner of C Street and First Avenue. WSU shared the space in the Charter Oil Building with a school that trained court reporters. The Charter Oil Building was one of the first high rise buildings in San Diego and today is known as the Chamber Building.

By 1970, the law school had left its space in the Charter Oil Building and was renting space in the Union Bank Building, at 525 B Street. The space in the Union Bank Building included a law library, a bookstore and four or five classrooms.

During its first semester of operation, the San Diego campus offered first year courses identical to those being offered at the WSU campus in Anaheim. Courses offered included Criminal Law, taught by Boas; Introduction to Law, taught by Judge Donovan; and Criminal Procedure, taught by Jesse Osuna. Upper level courses included Conflict of Laws, Corporations II and Wills. In the early years, Boas would poll the upper level students each semester to determine which courses they wanted the college to offer. Classes were held in the evenings, Monday through Friday, from 7 to 10 p.m. and on Saturdays from 9 to 12 and from 1 to 4.

The college hired Gary to administer the campus on a part-time basis with the title "administrative assistant." Gary was responsible for all aspects of the administration of the law school, including student recruitment. He was also elected president of the Student Bar Association (SBA) for the spring 1969 semester. In October 1969, James A. Hennenhoefer, a student who had transferred with Gary from Cabrillo Pacific and an active duty naval intelligence officer, was elected to a full year term as SBA president. After graduation, Hennenhoefer would become a prominent divorce attorney in San Diego.

Hadley Batchelder was among the first faculty members hired by Gary Woolverton. Hadley was a talented musician who performed professionally while in law school.

Gary was assisted by a single staff member, a secretary named Janice Zimmerman. After a few months, Zimmerman was succeeded by Pat Brown, who soon advanced to the position of registrar and who, by 1973, was the director of admissions and records. Pat was a smart, energetic and charismatic young woman whose influence was much greater than her title would imply. As a practical matter, she created and managed the administrative apparatus of the campus and she served as the face of the San Diego campus to both the students and the community. At the end of the decade, ready for a new challenge, Pat relocated to northern California, where she became the first woman to serve as president of the San Jose Chamber of Commerce. Years later, the college would acknowledge publicly that she was critical to the early success of the San Diego campus.

In 1970, Pat would hire as the law school receptionist Jennifer Sublett, who had worked at the law school temporarily in 1969 and who, after her return in 1970, would remain at the law school until 2005, rising to the position of assistant dean. She would change her surname to Keller following her marriage to a college alumnus, Phil Keller.

Reis traveled to San Diego once a week to inspect the operation. While administering the law school, Gary attended classes and continued to perform real estate appraisal work for the bank.

Pat Brown managed the administration of the San Diego campus during the 1970s.

The tension between creating a highly regarded law school and offering admission to a wide range of applicants emerged very early at the San Diego campus. At the time the campus was founded, Gary managed it in ways that he believed would establish high academic standards and prepare the law school for ABA accreditation. Boas and Reis, however, directed him to recruit a hundred students for the first entering class, a goal that necessitated that the San Diego campus admit the great majority of those who applied. The weak credentials of some members of the entering class would impede the law school's efforts to graduate students who could pass the bar exam and thus to establish a strong reputation for its academic program.

Nevertheless, the San Diego campus did have an auspicious beginning. Its first graduate was Rodney Johnson, who sat for the bar exam in August 1969 and passed, giving the San Diego campus a 100 percent pass rate on its first bar exam.

Following his graduation in June 1970, Gary took a leave of absence to prepare for the August 1970 bar exam, while Professor Hadley Batchelder took his place as administrative assistant. In August 1970, Gary Woolverton, Jim Hennenhoefer and seven other classmates who had transferred from Cabrillo Pacific to WSU with them sat for the bar exam. Six of the nine, including Gary Woolverton and Jim Hennenhoefer, passed.

Gary returned in the fall as administrative assistant and as a member of the faculty, teaching Legal Analysis and Legal Writing, while also serving as the manager of the real estate services branch of the bank where he worked. Gary was offered a job in the real estate litigation section of Gray, Cary, Ames & Frye, then San Diego's largest law firm, but wanted to move to northern California and open his own practice. In the spring of 1971, he resigned from WSU and moved to Eureka, where he joined a 75 year old law firm to be known as Cooreia, Bacon and Woolverton. As Gary's departure became imminent, the student newspaper of the San Diego campus, *The Western Restater* (renamed *The Restater* in 1974 and *The Advocate* in 1994), hailed him as "the man largely responsible for bringing WSU to San Diego." Gary would later serve as a deputy district attorney in Eureka for a couple of years and then open his own practice in Susanville. In 2006, he would be elected district attorney for Modoc County. Gary was succeeded as campus administrator by Kenneth Lowe, who was succeeded after a couple of years by Frank Otto.

Jennifer Sublett (later Keller) was hired by Pat Brown in 1969 and, except for a few months in 1969-70, worked continuously at the law school until 2005, rising to the position of assistant dean of admissions, record and financial assistance.

Initially, the San Diego campus was regarded as merely another campus of the law school in Anaheim. In 1972, WSU designated San Diego as a coordinate campus, a move driven at least in part by the desire of the CBE to avoid confusion between the Orange County campus, which by 1972 had provisional CBE accreditation, and the San Diego campus, which at that time had only preliminary CBE accreditation. Thereafter, while the two schools were owned by a single corporate entity, they were known publicly by slightly different names: Western State University College of Law of Orange County and Western State University College of Law of San Diego. In 1972 as well, both campuses became eligible to participate in federally insured student loan programs.

2

The Early Years

In its early years, WSU operated, in effect, as a family business. As has been noted, Max Boas served as dean and was responsible for academic affairs, while Burt Reis held the title of executive director and supervised the administration of the college. Ardi Reis served as the chief financial officer. The two men, who were often referred to collectively as the "duumvirate," were regarded as coequals. They managed the college so informally that, at least during its first years of operation, it did not even have a formal budget. Reis explained that a budget was unnecessary and would merely require a lot of "cumbersome" paperwork.

Academic Program

WSU initially offered only a part-time, four-year program and employed no full-time faculty. All courses were taught by adjunct faculty. The college began to acquire a full-time faculty during the 1968-69 academic year, when John Morrison, who had taught Constitutional Law and Equity as a part-time instructor, became the first full-time member of the Anaheim faculty. Upon becoming a full-time faculty member, Morrison added Contracts and Community Property to his course load.

In order to maintain some measure of quality control over a predominantly part-time faculty, the administration supervised the academic program very closely. All faculty members teaching the same course on either campus were required to use the same textbook and the same syllabus. Each faculty member drafted proposed exam questions, which were submitted to Boas. Boas would create the final exam in each course by selecting from among, and often modifying, the questions drafted by the faculty. The exam in a particular subject would be administered on the same day and at the same time on both campuses. As WSU explained in a 1972 policy statement on faculty assessment, "[a]n individual instructor in a large institution can not be left entirely to his own devices."

As a result of this method of exam administration, no faculty member ever knew in advance the questions that would be asked on the final exam. The students' exam answers in each course, written in small booklets called bluebooks, were mixed together and randomly distributed to paid graders, who often were WSU alumni. Graders were required to have a law degree, but were not required to have passed the bar exam. Those who failed the California bar exam two or more times, however, were not retained as graders. Each grader was given a maximum of 100 exam answers to a single question and allowed one week to grade them. Graders were paid 75 cents per exam. The average grade awarded typically fell between a C+ and a C- and graders were required to write comments on any exam receiving a grade of D or lower. The operation had considerable magnitude. In 1977, for example, a total of about 30,000 bluebooks were graded each semester. Because of the use of outside graders, members of the faculty normally did not see their students' exam answers, except when a student appealed a grade.

The rationale for this system was that it provided a mechanism for evaluating the faculty. The grades of students from each section were compared and used as a measure of teaching effectiveness. Because the instructors never knew what would be tested on the exam, they could not try to boost their own students' performance (and thus their own apparent value to the college) by concentrating on the material to be tested on the exam. Using outside graders also reduced the burden on the faculty, most of whom had other, full-time employment.

Accreditation inspection teams visiting the campus early in its history noted that the faculty at other institutions would have seen this system of exam administration as an impermissible infringement on academic freedom. Indeed, the college itself acknowledged in a 1976 report submitted to the Western Association of Schools and Colleges (WASC), the regional accrediting agency for institutions of higher education in California, that, for those unfamiliar with the system, "it may have a superficial aura of 'Big Brother.'"

The curriculum in the early years was a spare one, dedicated mainly to preparing students to pass the California bar exam. In its first fall semester of operation, the fall of 1969, the San Diego campus offered Introduction to Law, one section of which was taught by Michael Dessent, who later would serve as dean of California Western School of Law; Legal Writing, taught by Max Boas; Contracts, including one section taught by Howard Dattan, the former dean of the USD law school; Torts, one section of which was taught by Hadley Batchelder; Real Property; Constitutional Law; Evidence; Income Tax; and Equity.

Judge Earl Gilliam began teaching at the law school during its first semester and taught continuously until the late 1990s. Visible in this picture is the original classroom furniture purchased in 1969 that the law school would use for the next 30 years.

In spring 1970, the San Diego campus offered Introduction to Law, Legal Analysis, Advanced Legal Analysis, Criminal Law, including sections taught by Mike Dessent and Judge Gilliam, Criminal Procedure, Contracts II, including a section taught by Judge Gilliam, Torts II, Constitutional Law II, Evidence II, Real Property, Conveyances, Agency, and Equity II. As these schedules indicate, the early curriculum featured almost exclusively courses that taught foundational legal skills or subjects tested on the California Bar Exam.

A site inspection conducted during the fall 1973 semester as part of the process of obtaining full CBE accreditation for the San Diego campus found that most of the teaching was "adequate." The inspection report elaborated that "[s]ome was only barely adequate, some was very good, and some was poor." Much class time was spent reviewing material covered in prior classes.

Some sense of the academic culture of the college in those days comes from memoranda generated during accreditation inspections, when college administrators feared how the school would be perceived by outsiders. In October 1970, two representatives of the CBE visited the Anaheim campus. Following the visit, Boas sent students a notice in which he reported that, during the visit, in one class six students in a row answered "unprepared," in a second class four students in a row answered "unprepared," in a third class a student sitting in front of the chairman of the CBE was reading aloud from a canned brief, and in a number of classes "students were reciting in an inaudible mumble that could not be heard three rows behind them." The notice from Boas observed that the college had always been cognizant of the special problems of part-time students. He went on to say, however, that the faculty and administration "have worked too long and too hard to build a reputation (envied by educators and attorneys alike) for Western State to blithely tolerate the impingement of such reputation because of the laziness, apathy or untenable work habits of some students." He threatened that "[i]f it becomes necessary to drop students who simply do not have the time and/or interest to prepare for classes, this will be done without hesitation." He also told the students that instructors were being requested to notify him if any student answered "unprepared" more than three times in a semester or if canned briefs were ever observed in a classroom. In a separate memorandum to the instructors, Boas noted that, during the visit, one instructor had been "considerably late" in starting class, while another attempted to end the class early.

He asked the instructors to "[p]lease keep after your mumblers to recite properly."

A memo sent by Kenneth Lowe to the students in San Diego in anticipation of a 1972 CBE inspection noted a different set of concerns. The memo urged students, "Please be especially quiet during breaks [so as not to disrupt other classes]. Do not straggle into class at the beginning or after breaks. Observe starting times scrupulously. Do not leave classes early. Be prepared to recite if called upon and participate actively in classroom discussion."

In the 1970s, WSU awarded three degrees. Students with an undergraduate degree would receive the degree of Juris Doctor (J.D.). Those who completed the same course of study, but were admitted to WSU without an undergraduate degree, would receive a Bachelor of Laws (LL.B.) degree. In addition, those who were admitted with at least 60 units of undergraduate work could transfer those units to WSU and, upon completion of 42 units at WSU, they would be awarded a Bachelor of Science in Laws (B.S.L.) degree. Upon completion of all of the required units, these students would be awarded a J.D. degree as well. Thus, the students in the B.S.L. program, which began in 1969, could earn both an undergraduate degree and a law degree from WSU and it is not uncommon to encounter WSU graduates from the 1970s and 1980s who earned both degrees. The LL.B. degree would be discontinued in October 1978, an action that was consistent with the general movement in American legal education away from conferring that degree. Thereafter, those who would have received an LL.B. degree in the past were awarded a J.D. degree. WSU would continue to offer the B.S.L. degree, however, until 1993.

The college held its first commencement ceremony at the Disneyland Hotel on August 13, 1969. Fourteen graduates received B.S.L. degrees at that ceremony. As will be discussed below, the Apollo 10 astronauts were selected as speakers at the ceremony.

The college held the first commencement ceremony at which it awarded professional degrees in the Chapman College auditorium in June 1970. California Supreme Court Justice Stanley Mosk spoke. A total of 52 graduates received degrees, including Gary Woolverton and seven other graduates of the San Diego campus. Graduating second in the class was Carol Boas, who was both the youngest graduating student and the daughter of Max and Beatrice Boas. She recently had graduated *cum laude* from UCLA, where she completed her final two years of undergraduate work while also enrolled in her first two years of law school.

The San Diego campus held its first separate commencement ceremony on July 7, 1973, at San Diego State University. The speaker was San Diego Mayor Pete Wilson and 78 graduates received their degrees. That ceremony also marked the first time that degrees were conferred upon graduates who had completed their entire four-year program at the San Diego campus.

Meanwhile, in February 1973, the San Diego campus relocated to better facilities in the Bank of California building, at 1333 Front Street, which is the corner of Front and Ash Streets, with a dedication ceremony led by Mayor Wilson. The original San Diego campus, at the corner of Front and C Streets, today houses the offices of a couple of bail bondsmen. For a time, WSU alumnus Kerry Steigerwalt operated a law office on the site.

Max Boas hands a pair of scissors to Pat Brown at the ribbon cutting ceremony for the second San Diego campus, at Front and Ash Streets, while Mayor Pete Wilson, third from right, watches.

The new building was two blocks from the county law library and the courthouse. The building had a large lecture hall, eight classrooms, a seminar room, a student lounge, offices for faculty, staff and student organizations, a library with seating for approximately 150 students, and a bookstore. For the first time, students could park in the building where their classes were scheduled, although they complained that the parking was too expensive.

WSU inaugurated a full-time program of study on the Orange County campus in 1973 and on the San Diego campus in 1974. The same year that it started its full-time program, the San Diego campus began to hire full-time faculty, including Joel D. Goodman, Arthur Schaffer, and James Wade. In 1976, the San Diego campus appointed Judy DiGennaro to its full-time faculty, the first woman to hold a full-time faculty appointment on that campus (although women already taught on the adjunct faculty). Known by students as "Judy D," she would remain on the faculty until the spring of 1987. In 1977, two members of the faculty who would later serve as dean, Hadley Batchelder and George Kraft, both joined the full-time faculty.

Many of the full-time faculty were experienced practitioners. Art Schaffer had served as deputy district attorney in San Francisco, where he was the prosecutor in the trial of famed comedian Lenny Bruce on obscenity charges. Schaffer later said in an article published in the *Western State University News* that he was "an avid friend and fan" of Bruce. He said that he "presented the evidence fairly" but "didn't try to get a conviction." Bruce nevertheless was convicted.

In 1976, Judy DiGennaro became the first woman appointed to the full-time faculty.

Moise Berger, who joined the full-time faculty with Judy DiGennaro in 1976, had served as county attorney for Maricopa County, Arizona, from 1969 to 1976 and as chief assistant county attorney in the mid 1960s, when the office prosecuted Ernesto Miranda for rape in the celebrated case that led to the Supreme Court's decision in *Miranda v. United States*. Moise joined the WSU faculty at the end of his second term as county attorney and remained on the faculty until 1993.

Occasionally, members of the faculty left to pursue other careers. Abbe Wolfsheimer, for example, who began teaching real property on the San Diego campus in 1974, resigned from the full-time faculty in 1985, when she was elected to the San Diego City Council, where she would serve two consecutive terms.

Student Body

Enrollment at WSU grew rapidly. Boas and Reis had timed the founding of their college perfectly because applications to law schools nationally were surging in the early 1970s. For example, in 1968-69, the Law School Admissions Council (LSAC) administered approximately 60,000 Law School Admission Tests (LSATs). By 1971-72, just three years later, the number of LSATs administered had doubled. It would peak in 1973-74 at just under 140,000, before beginning a long term decline that would continue until 1985-86. In the early 1970s, the nation was teeming with young men and women who wanted to attend law school.

Further, the Vietnam War provided a steady stream of discharged draftees with veterans' benefits that would pay for law school. Veterans' benefits were approved for the Orange County campus in 1968. Boas and Reis believed that the approval in Orange County would apply to San Diego as well and the college advertised that veterans who attended the San Diego campus would be eligible for veterans' benefits. By the time that Boas and Reis discovered that their understanding was incorrect, a substantial number of veterans had enrolled. Gary Woolverton proposed that the college allow the veterans to attend free of charge. Boas and Reis agreed and veterans were not charged tuition in San Diego until 1971, when that campus was approved for veterans' benefits.

Under these circumstances, WSU's enrollment quickly exceeded the founders' expectations. As early as July 1968, Boas announced that the college enrollment was six years ahead of projections. In 1969, when the San Diego campus opened, WSU already enrolled more than 450 students. By 1970, a year after the San Diego campus was founded, WSU was California's largest law school, with a combined enrollment of 1271 students. The majority of these students, of course, were in Orange County.

Enrollment soon exploded in San Diego as well, however. By the fall of 1973, enrollment on the San Diego campus had reached 936 students, many of them veterans. For example, in the fall 1972 entering class, 33 percent of the students were receiving veterans' benefits, while, in the spring 1973 entering class, 42 percent of the students were receiving veterans' benefits. By 1976, WSU was the largest law school in the nation and the San Diego campus was the largest law school in San Diego.

The college administration encouraged enrollment growth. At a November 1972 staff retreat held at Palm Springs, admissions counselors were cautioned not to make "unnecessary" comments that might tend to discourage entering students. While it was appropriate to be realistic about the rigors of law school, counselors were told, the emphasis should be on inspiring the student.

The growth of the college in the early years was attributable not only to the explosion in applications nationally and to the availability of veterans' benefits and other federal financial aid programs, but to lax admissions and retention standards. The college prided itself on applying a "whole person" admissions policy, under which admissions decisions would rest on many factors in addition to, or other than, scores on the LSAT or undergraduate grade point averages. Indeed, students often were accepted for admission without an undergraduate degree and without having taken the LSAT. In mid 1972, on the eve of a CBE accreditation inspection, a WSU administrator sent Boas and Reis a memorandum lamenting the poor condition of the admissions files. He complained that the "special students," those admitted without an undergraduate degree, had been admitted "without even a pretext of compliance" with CBE rules. Further, some students who had performed poorly on their exams and who should have been dismissed under the college's retention policies nevertheless had been allowed to continue. He complained that these students were "*not* qualified by any standard." "The sad truth of the matter," he continued, "is that they are wasting their time in law school since they simply do not meet the requirements for being in any California Law School." Anticipating the scrutiny of the CBE inspectors, he worried, "I cannot imagine any reasonable answer to a charge that we have allowed some students to continue on probation for semester after semester when the detailed evidence is in our own transcript files."

WSU saw its typical student as a college graduate with a C+ undergraduate grade point average and an LSAT score close to the national mean. As the college explained in a 1976 report to WASC, the WSU academic program was "designed to produce competent general practitioners from a student body of 'average' law students."

The students could be free-wheeling and irreverent. As early as 1971, the administration insisted on censoring the student newspaper, after it published articles critical of the college. The chief concern of the administration was articles that cast the college in a bad light. It otherwise allowed the students great leeway. For example, when Georgina Spelvin, the star of a well-known sexually explicit film, "The Devil in Miss Jones," began performing at the Pussycat Theatre in San Diego in 1975, *The Restater* sent a reporter to interview her about her indictment in Memphis on obscenity charges. The student newspaper published the resulting story along with two photographs of Spelvin topless in her dressing room. A few months later, when the Classy Cat Theatre in La Mesa began to feature nude male dancers, *The Restater* sent a reporter to interview the dancers and the club. The resulting story included a few references to the law, briefly mentioning that legal restrictions required that the dancers maintain a distance from the audience, and was accompanied by a photograph of two nude men dancing on stage.

Nor were the students easily cowed by the administration. For example, in the spring of 1975, Carol Boas, the daughter of Max and Beatrice Boas, offered a bar review course on both campuses. Her course apparently was allowed the exclusive right to post notices on college bulletin boards and was promoted by the faculty during class time. As it happened, only 29 students registered for the course in San Diego, prompting the cancellation of the San Diego course three days before it was scheduled to start. Students accused the WSU administration of giving preferential treatment to the course and then abandoning the WSU students who registered for it when enrollment did not meet expectations. Boas responded to a letter of complaint from SBA President Jennifer Messersmith, the first woman to serve in that position, by noting that course cancellations for lack of enrollment were a common practice and that he had offered to give free lectures on bar related subjects to students who had registered for the course. Boas added that he was "offended and shocked" at "student ungraciousness and a 'what-have-you-done-for-me-lately' attitude." He concluded by assuring Messersmith that the course would not be offered in San Diego again.

In 1974, Jennifer Messersmith became the first woman elected president of the Student Bar Association.

The arrival of a full-time student body in 1974 changed the atmosphere of the college. SBA President Susan Johann, a member of the last class admitted to the San Diego campus composed exclusively of part-time students, observed in 1975 that, in the past two years, she had noticed a decrease among students of "destructive criticism" and "impatience with growth not keeping pace with expectations" and an increase in energy and enthusiasm.

The presence of full-time students also enabled the San Diego campus to develop a wider range of extracurricular activities. In the spring of 1975, for example, the San Diego campus announced the creation of its student-edited law review, the *Criminal Justice Journal*, published annually and completely self-supporting. Before the establishment of a law review on the San Diego campus, San Diego students were permitted to work on the *Western State University Law Review*, published on the Orange County campus. The name of the law review on the San Diego campus originally was to have been the *Western Legal Journal*. At the time that the formation of the journal was announced, the students intended to devote the first issue to criminal law. By the time that the first issue appeared in spring 1976, however, the students had decided to devote all of the issues of the journal exclusively to criminal law and they had adopted the name *Criminal Justice Journal*. Future San Diego District Attorney Bonnie Dumanis served as book review editor during the journal's first year. The *Criminal Justice Journal* would become a semi-annual publication in 1979.

Because of its exclusive focus on criminal law, the journal at times would have difficulty attracting a sufficient number of submissions. In 1993, as the faculty advisor to the law review, I would recommend that it broaden its focus and the students would accept my recommendation. At that point, the students would change the name to the *San Diego Justice Journal,* a name suggested by Bill Slomanson. The law review would change its name to the *Thomas Jefferson Law Review* in 1996, at the time that the San Diego campus separated from WSU.

Bonnie Dumanis, the book review editor of the first issue of the Criminal Justice Journal, would later serve as superior court judge and San Diego district attorney. She is pictured here, left, in 1994 at the law school's 25ᵗʰ anniversary celebration with alumna Jonna Spilbor. A 1992 graduate, Jonna was president of the Alumni Association at the time of the celebration. Today, Jonna practices law in New York, writes a newspaper column on legal affairs and appears regularly as a legal analyst on CNN, Fox News and Court TV.

The WSU student body in the early 1970s reflected the male domination of the legal profession. Donna Woolverton had founded a sorority called Sigma Beta Alpha, also known as the "law wives." Membership was open to the wives of male law students. As the student newspaper, the *Western Restater*, explained in its February 1974 edition, "Many men who attend WSU don't have the time or energy to devote to running the school. . . . Whenever help is needed the law wives are there."

Yet, WSU in the early 1970s also reflected the changes that were occurring with respect to women in the legal profession. On February 9, 1974, the law wives held a membership tea (complete with yellow flowered centerpieces, sandwiches, tea and cookies) at which the group president announced that the association had formally changed its name to the Law Spouses Organization. The first law husband to join the organization was a Lieutenant Commander of the Navy, Jim Ryals, who joined in the fall of 1975. Meanwhile, in the spring of 1974, the students for the first time elected a woman, Jennifer Messersmith, president of the Student Bar Association. She was immediately succeeded by the second woman to serve as SBA president, Susan Johann. In 1974 as well, the college added to its catalogue a statement headed "Women at WSU," in which it said that the records of thousands of WSU students indicated that "on average, women are distinctly superior law students." A disproportionately large percentage of women graduated with honors. Accordingly, the statement said, the college "would welcome a higher percentage of women in its student body." In 1979, WSU created a Women's Law Institute that presented programs and course work deemed to be of special interest to women and that would promote women in the profession.

The student attrition rate in the 1970s was very high. In the early 1970s, typically, only 20 to 25 percent of the entering class graduated. Given the bar passage rates of the early 1970s, the net effect was that only 10 to 15 percent of the entering class ultimately graduated and passed the bar exam on the first attempt.

At the same time, however, the college took enormous pride in producing a number of highly successful graduates. Although the majority of those who enrolled did not graduate and many of those who graduated never passed the bar exam, the student body in those years included many exceptional individuals who would enjoy prominent careers as attorneys or public servants. For example, a partial list of graduates of the San Diego campus in the 1970s who have held public office includes Congressman Duncan Hunter, U.S. District Judge Roger T. Benitez, Superior Court Judge and District Attorney Bonnie Dumanis, State Assemblyman, State Senator and Superior Court Judge Larry D. Stirling, Superior Court Judge Lillian Lim, San Diego City Clerk Chuck Abdelnour, and California State Bar President Marc Adelman.

Particularly noteworthy as well was the family of attorney Jack Schall, who had five daughters – Kim, Lisa, Mindy, Victoria and Jill -- all of whom graduated from the San Diego campus. Jack had attended Loyola Law School and had passed the bar exam without having graduated. After practicing law for more than 30 years and watching each of his daughters attend WSU, he decided to complete his degree and to graduate with his youngest daughter, Jill, which he did. By the time he graduated, his daughter Victoria had already joined him as a partner in his practice. His daughter Lisa would be appointed to the municipal court in 1985 and to the superior court in 1989.

Martin Kruming, Class of 1977, is another notable alumnus from the 1970s. This photograph of Martin was taken in 1983, when he was appointed editor of the San Diego Daily Transcript. Martin later served as editor of the San Diego Lawyer Magazine. He remained active in law school affairs, serving on the 1986 dean's search committee and teaching Media Law for many years.

Reputational Enhancement

WSU sought from the beginning to build a strong reputation within the legal community. At the time of its founding, the college established an "Executive Board" composed of many distinguished Californians who served in an advisory capacity. As already noted, Boas and Reis required Gary Woolverton to establish a similar board in San Diego before they would authorize the opening of a branch campus there. In the early 1970s, the WSU board included, in addition to those already mentioned, Pete Wilson, a mayor of San Diego who later would serve as a U.S. senator and governor of California, and State Senator George Moscone, who would later be elected mayor of San Francisco and who would be assassinated in 1978 by Dan White, a member of the San Francisco Board of Supervisors. Over the years, other luminaries would join the board, including Congressman Duncan Hunter (a graduate of the San Diego campus); San Diego District Attorney Edwin Miller, Jr.; State Assemblyman (and later State Senator and Superior Court Judge) Larry D. Stirling; U.S. District Judge Earl B. Gilliam; California Court of Appeal Judge Gerald J. Lewis; and the well-known attorney, Melvin Belli. Many of the luminaries did not attend the meetings of the board, but the college sometimes polled the members by mail. In any event, the willingness of these men to lend their names to the enterprise indicates that WSU had sought and achieved a significant measure of credibility very early in its history.

The college took other steps to establish credibility. For example, at its first commencement ceremony, held in August 1969, the college awarded honorary doctor of laws (LL.D.) degrees to the Apollo 10 astronauts, Eugene A. Cernan, Thomas P. Safford, and John W. Young. Apollo 10 was the last manned mission to the Moon prior to the Apollo 11 mission, which landed Neil Armstrong and Buzz Aldrin on the Moon on July 20, 1969. The ceremony thus occurred less than a month after the first humans stepped onto the Moon, at a time when interest in the space program was at its apex. Thereafter, the college awarded an annual scholarship honoring the astronauts, known as the Apollo Scholarship. The scholarship was funded by a gift from the Theodore H. and Silvia Silbert Foundation.

The college carefully selected subsequent commencement speakers to enhance its credibility. Other WSU commencement speakers in the 1970s included U.S. Senator John V. Tunney; Counselor to the President (and former Secretary of Health, Education and Welfare and former Lieutenant Governor of California) Robert Finch; former U.S. Attorney General, former Secretary of Defense and former Secretary of Health, Education and Welfare (and later Secretary of Commerce) Elliot Richardson; former Watergate Special Prosecutor Leon Jaworski; former ABA President Chesterfield Smith; former FBI Director Clarence M. Kelley; and California Supreme Court Justice Frank Richardson.

WSU occasionally found other links to fame. For example, Bob Chandler, a wide receiver for the Buffalo Bills and then the Oakland Raiders, spent eight years during the 1970s earning his degree by attending classes only in the spring and the summer. He told the college that he had enrolled to prove that he was capable of doing something other than playing football. He graduated months after the Raiders won the 1981 Super Bowl, in which he caught four passes for a total gain of 77 yards. After his retirement from football in 1982, Chandler was a football commentator for NBC until his death from cancer in 1995.

Chandler was not the only professional football player to attend WSU in the 1970s. In 1973, WSU second year student Tommy Mason, a running back who had just ended his eleven year professional football career in 1971 as a player for the Washington Redskins and who previously had played for the Los Angeles Rams and the Minnesota Vikings, married well-known Olympic gymnast Cathy Rigby. Rigby had competed at the 1968 Olympics in Mexico City and the 1972 Olympics in Munich and was at the height of her fame as a gymnast. When, shortly after the marriage, Rigby appeared on the cover of a well-known fashion magazine, the college was quick to note the accomplishment of one of the "law wives."

3

Obtaining CBE and WASC Accreditation

From the beginning, the founders of WSU intended to obtain accreditation from both the CBE and the ABA. This was part of their vision of creating a law school that would offer a well-regarded program of legal education. As already noted, in both cases obtaining accreditation would necessitate that the college persuade the accrediting agencies to amend their rules to permit the accreditation of a law school operated for profit.

Obtaining CBE Accreditation

The CBE's modification of its rules in 1971 to permit the accreditation of proprietary law schools enabled the San Diego campus to obtain preliminary accreditation on July 1, 1972. In April 1973, the CBE notified Boas that the San Diego campus would receive provisional accreditation effective July 1, 1973, subject to certain conditions. The conditions imposed by the CBE included the appointment of a permanent, full-time dean for the San Diego campus, the acquisition of certain books for the law library, and a reduction in the number of four-hour class sessions. The CBE also required the San Diego campus to discontinue its Legal Analysis course, which was deemed to be of poor quality, and to review carefully its Introduction to Law course. The complaint about the Legal Analysis course was that it was largely a review of material covered in other courses. The college complied with each of these conditions. On January 19, 1976, the CBE notified the San Diego campus that it had received full accreditation.

WSU announces provisional CBE accreditation of the San Diego campus in 1973.

One important advantage of both provisional and full CBE accreditation was that students no longer were required to pass the California First Year Law Students' Examination (FYLSA), administered by the CBE, in order to continue their studies beyond the first year. Another was that students, under the supervision of an attorney, could appear in court on behalf of clients.

To satisfy one of the CBE's conditions, the college in July 1973 transferred Assistant Dean of Students Ross Lipsker of the Orange County campus to the San Diego campus, with the title of assistant dean for academic affairs. He assumed responsibility for all academic affairs in San Diego, subject to Boas' direction. Lipsker thereby became the first full-time employee with faculty rank on the San Diego campus. As an assistant dean, he was teaching three courses on a part-time basis -- Introduction to Law, Legal Ethics, and Contracts -- and thus San Diego still lacked any faculty members with full-time teaching responsibilities. In fall 1973, Lipsker was promoted to associate dean for academic affairs, creating an organizational parity between the San Diego campus and the Orange County campus, which was supervised by Associate Dean Keith Snyder. Lipsker would assume the title of dean of academic affairs and director of the San Diego campus in 1978.

Meanwhile, in 1976, Boas announced that Jim Wade had been appointed the first assistant dean of the San Diego campus. Wade would become associate dean in 1979. As a result of Wade's promotion, Hadley Batchelder and George Kraft would be appointed assistant deans in 1980.

Ross Lipsker served as the first dean of the San Diego campus until 1985.

In the very early 1970s, WSU's first-time bar passage rate generally was below 50 percent. A CBE study conducted in 1975 found that between 1970 and 1972, 230 WSU graduates sat for the bar exam and 103 passed on the first attempt, for an average first-time bar passage rate during those years of 44.8 percent. The study aggregated the graduates of both WSU campuses because, at the time, the two campuses were considered separate campuses of a single law school.

By 1973, separate data for the San Diego campus were available. On the July 1973 bar exam, 16 of the 45 graduates of the San Diego campus passed on the first attempt, for a first-time pass rate of 35.6 percent. In the mid 1970s, however, the San Diego campus would sometimes see bar passage rates that exceeded 50 percent. On the February 1977 bar exam, the San Diego campus actually scored a first time pass rate of 71.7 percent, its best performance of that decade.

The grant of provisional and then full CBE accreditation appears, paradoxically, to have had a significant adverse impact on WSU. As already noted, acquisition of CBE accreditation eliminated the requirement that all WSU students pass the FYLSA before continuing past the first year. The elimination of this requirement meant that the college could allow students who were unable to pass the FYLSA to remain and to graduate. Because the FYLSA, in effect, was a bar exam on first year subjects, it was a good predictor of success on the California bar exam. By forcing WSU to dismiss those who could not write acceptable bar exam answers, the FYLSA had helped to raise WSU's bar passage rate. Once WSU's students no longer were required to pass the FYLSA, the college could retain more students who were destined to fail the bar exam, resulting in a decline in the bar passage rate that began in the late 1970s.

In 1976, Jim Wade became the first assistant dean of the San Diego campus. In 1979, he became the first associate dean of the campus.

The grant of CBE accreditation contributed to a lower bar passage rate in another way as well. In the years that the college was seeking CBE accreditation and was being regularly inspected, the admissions office made some effort to ensure that applicants met certain minimum qualifications imposed by the CBE. Once CBE accreditation was received and inspections were no longer scheduled on a regular basis, the college weakened its admissions and retention standards. The decline in these standards in the mid 1970s would also contribute to declining bar passage rates in the late 1970s.

Another event that likely contributed, again paradoxically, to a lower bar passage rate was the creation of a full-time program on the San Diego campus in 1974. The presence of full-time students who were able to commit themselves to the study of law without the distractions of the substantial employment (and, often, family) obligations borne by most part-time students might have been expected to raise the bar passage rate. Yet, the reverse appears to have occurred. WSU always was able to attract many talented part-time students who could have gained admission to a number of ABA approved law schools, but attended WSU because it offered a part-time evening program, which California Western School of Law did not. Full-time students, by contrast, if they were capable of completing a J.D. program successfully, potentially could attend a large number of ABA approved law schools because of their greater geographic mobility. Thus, one of the most common reasons that full-time students attended WSU in the 1970s was that they were not able to gain admission elsewhere, perhaps because they had already been dismissed from another law school. Accordingly, after the creation of its full-time program in 1974, the San Diego campus was deluged with applications from all over the country submitted by applicants who had been denied admission to the other law schools to which they had applied. Many of these applicants were at a very high risk of failing the bar exam. Because they usually were not also bearing work and family obligations, they were far less likely than part-time students to withdraw from law school voluntarily if their grades were marginal. Unless the college dismissed them, they would graduate and most of them would fail the bar exam. Further, as is discussed below in greater detail, after 1974 applications to attend law school declined nationally, meaning that in the late 1970s ABA approved law schools seeking to fill their classes lowered their admissions standards and accepted students that they would have rejected at the beginning of the decade. Accordingly, the pool from which WSU drew its full-time students became progressively weaker and the full-time students that it admitted were at an even higher risk of failing the bar exam.

By the second half of the 1970s, the classes that were admitted following the receipt of CBE accreditation and that included full-time students began to graduate and bar passage rates declined as a result. For example, in July 1976, when students admitted prior to the receipt of provisional CBE approval and the establishment of the full-time program sat for the bar exam, the first-time pass rate in San Diego was 54.9 percent. The bar passage rate slipped to 50.6 percent in July 1977 and then plummeted to 36.9 percent in July 1978. By July 1982, the first time pass rate had fallen to 23.5 percent. After 1978 and until the late 1980s, bar pass rates would fall consistently below 40 percent and sometimes below 30 percent.

Considering an Application for ABA Approval

As the process of obtaining CBE accreditation neared the end, Boas and Reis had begun to consider actively an application for ABA approval.

A major benefit of ABA approval was that it would permit graduates of the college to sit for the bar exam in all U.S. jurisdictions. It would also greatly enhance the college's reputation. The chief obstacle to obtaining ABA accreditation was a provision in the ABA standards for approval of law schools that prohibited approval of proprietary law schools.

The ABA prohibition dated from 1921, when the ABA began to approve law schools. Ironically, the first American law schools all had been proprietary. In early America, lawyers learned their profession by studying with a practitioner. Some practitioners started law schools, all of which were proprietary. In 1779, Thomas Jefferson persuaded the College of William and Mary to appoint a professor of law to its faculty. Other universities soon followed William and Mary's example and appointed professors of law. By the early 1820s, universities were creating separate law schools that competed directly with the proprietary law schools, a competition that continued for a century. In 1921, the ABA took the side of the universities in the competition and, in an effort to destroy the proprietary law schools, prohibited their accreditation.

The ABA justified this prohibition on the ground that experience had shown that proprietary law schools were mere diploma mills that admitted large numbers of unqualified students in order to exploit them economically, while providing an inferior education. ABA opposition to proprietary law schools, however, seems also to have been motivated in part by a desire to exclude from the profession immigrants, Jews and African-Americans, who were more likely to attend proprietary law schools.[1]

---

1   See Susan K. Boyd, *The ABA's First Section: Assuring a Qualified Bar* 16-19 (1993); Robert Stevens, *Law School: Legal Education in America from the 1850s to the 1980s* 99-103 (1983).

In 1973, ABA President Chesterfield Smith visited the WSU campus in Orange County while attending a meeting of the California State Bar Association. Smith met with Boas and Reis for an hour and toured the campus. Smith apparently was favorably impressed because, a couple of years later, he told Boas that he would be pleased to state publicly that the ABA should amend its standards to allow proprietary law schools to obtain ABA approval. In response to student questions following Smith's visit, Reis said that WSU had no intention of applying for ABA approval "in the near future" but was "moving closer to ABA standards of [its] own volition."

In 1975, Boas and Reis approached the ABA consultant on legal education, James P. White, about applying for approval. Jim did not encourage them, noting the prohibition on accrediting proprietary law schools.

As indicated by the student questions posed to Reis during Chesterfield Smith's 1973 visit, many students wanted the college to apply for ABA accreditation. In the May 1973 edition of the *Western State Dictum*, the student newspaper of the Orange County campus, Burt Reis wrote a lengthy article defending the college's reasons for not applying for ABA approval. He contended that ABA accreditation would require a bar passage rate in excess of 60 percent. Because bar pass rates were a product of admissions standards and dismissal rates, he argued, WSU would be able to achieve such a pass rate only by eliminating an unacceptably large portion of its student body. He also noted that ABA approval would require charging a much higher tuition and using fewer practitioners to teach classes, contrary to the college's educational philosophy.

In its March 12, 1976, edition, the student newspaper on the San Diego campus, *The Restater,* posed the question "Should

Western State attempt to obtain ABA accreditation even though it would probably mean a tuition increase?" The handful of students interviewed were divided between those who believed that WSU should seek the benefit of ABA approval and those who believed it more important to maintain a law school where those who lacked an undergraduate degree or who had been dismissed from another law school could obtain a legal education. A commentary published in the April 21, 1976, edition of *The Restater* observed that the "eternal topic of conversation" among Western State students seemed to be the possibility of obtaining ABA approval. The same edition provided a state-by-state analysis of the requirements for admission to the bar and identified 17 states where a WSU graduate was not entirely foreclosed by the college's lack of ABA approval from gaining admission to practice.

ABA accreditation was not the only issue on the students' minds. The March 12, 1976, edition of *The Restater* also published a straw poll of students that indicated that students preferred Morris Udall over Jimmy Carter for the Democratic nomination for president and preferred Gerald Ford over Ronald Reagan for the Republican nomination. San Diego Congressman Lionel Van Deerlin took the floor of the House three days later to tout the straw poll as proof of a Udall surge.

Obtaining WASC Accreditation

Unable to gain ABA approval, Boas and Reis sought to obtain accreditation instead from the Western Association of Schools and Colleges (WASC), which was the federally recognized regional accrediting agency for higher education in California. Neither WASC nor any other regional accrediting agency had ever accredited an independent law school, that is, a law school unaffiliated with a university. In the 1970s, the Council on Post-Secondary Accreditation had imposed a moratorium under which regional accrediting agencies were asked not to accredit any types of institutions other than those that they had accredited in the past. In 1975, the moratorium was lifted, allowing WASC, if it so chose, to accredit WSU without violating the moratorium. The question was whether WASC would choose to consider WSU's application.

The ABA strongly opposed WASC accreditation for WSU. The ABA argued that its standards for approval of law schools established the minimum requirements that every law school should meet and that law schools should be evaluated according to ABA standards rather than WASC standards. It contended that WASC standards were not tailored to the particular circumstances of law schools and might not be demanding enough in some respects. The ABA also argued that prospective students might be confused by indications that a law school was WASC accredited and might infer incorrectly that graduates of WASC accredited law schools would be entitled to sit for the bar exam in states where graduation from an ABA approved law school was required. The Association of American Law Schools (AALS) echoed the ABA's concerns and also opposed WASC accreditation of WSU.

In November 1975, WASC decided to disregard the objections of the ABA and the AALS and announced that it would entertain an application from WSU. WASC explained that to permit all institutions to pursue accreditation would be in the best interests of higher education because the accreditation process generally improves the quality of an institution. To exclude independent law schools from the accreditation process would deny to students of such law schools the benefits of the process, which WASC believed would not serve the public interest. Although WASC seemed to agree that the ABA was better equipped to accredit law schools, the ABA was unwilling to accept an application from WSU. WASC later confirmed that it probably would not have considered accrediting an independent law school, if the ABA had been willing at an earlier time to consider an application by WSU.

On April 14, 1976, Jim White wrote a letter to the deans of all ABA approved law schools in California and Hawaii expressing the ABA's "concern and unhappiness" about WASC's decision to permit WSU to apply for accreditation. A week later, Millard Ruud, the executive director of the AALS, wrote a letter to WASC explaining that he and others in legal education were "troubled very much" by WASC's decision. Ruud noted that his advice had been sought by law professors around the country who had been asked to serve on the WASC accreditation inspection team. He had advised these individuals that the WASC decision had left them with two objectionable alternatives. If the team wrote a report that resulted in a denial of accreditation for WSU, the team would be accused of conspiring to prevent WSU from obtaining accreditation. If the team wrote a report that resulted in a grant of accreditation to WSU, the public would be confused about the implications of regional accreditation for a law school. Ruud told those who sought his advice that he did not know what he would do if he were asked to serve on a WSU site inspection team.

Reis and Boas interpreted Ruud's letter as an attempt to dissuade law professors from participating in the WASC accreditation process. They considered submitting a complaint to the U.S. Department of Health, Education and Welfare about what they regarded as attempts by Jim White and Millard Ruud to "interfere" with their efforts to obtain WASC accreditation.

Others, including the executive director of WASC, counseled against a complaint. One WSU administrator argued to Reis and Boas that WSU was acquiring a reputation of being cantankerous and that the reputation did not always serve its interests. He noted that the effect of the efforts by Ruud and White had been merely to discourage from participating in the WASC site inspection team those law professors who agreed with them. They thereby increased the probability that those who were on the inspection team would be sympathetic, or at least not hostile, to WASC's accreditation of WSU. In other words, the actions by the ABA and the AALS, if anything, had helped rather than hindered WSU's efforts to obtain WASC accreditation.

WASC decided to treat the two WSU campuses as separate entities for purposes of accreditation. By the time WSU was inspected in the spring of 1976, the enrollment of the San Diego campus had reached 1136 students, of whom 46 were considered undergraduates seeking a B.S.L. degree. Of those seeking the J.D. or LL.B. degree, 269 were full-time and 913 were part-time. The San Diego campus had three full-time faculty members. The library housed just over 13,000 volumes.

As WSU prepared for the arrival of the WASC site inspection team, the administration again urged the students to make a good impression. A memo to the students from Pat Brown stated that during the inspection "WSU hopes that attendance will be 100%, class participation stimulating, recitations brilliant, and attrition-at-the-break non-existent." Noting that members of the WASC team might attempt to engage the students in conversation, she observed, "Our hope is that such conversations will elicit a thoughtful, balanced, lawyer-like response, with due consideration as to where your long-term self-interest lies."

Boas sent a separate memo asking three things of students. First, they should make every effort to attend class. Second, they should not leave class during breaks. Third, they should not bring their commercial outlines to class during the inspection. Boas explained that, while WSU encouraged students to purchase commercial outlines as a supplement to the casebook, site inspectors who saw students with commercial outlines in class might misinterpret the situation.

Indeed, the use of commercial outlines was a sensitive subject on campus. In the late 1970s, the college did not renew the contract of a professor who was known for assigning a commercial outline, rather than a casebook, as a required text for his course. The student newspaper, *The Restater,* covered the dismissal extensively and speculated that the dismissal was the result of the professor's disregard of the "holy of holies," the casebook.

Despite the opposition of the ABA and the AALS to a WASC inspection, WASC was able to include legal educators on its WSU inspection teams. The site inspection team that visited the San Diego campus included J. Lani Bader, a law professor from Golden Gate University School of Law; Ernie Friesen, the dean of the Beverly Rubens School of Law, which later would become Whittier Law School; and two professors of education.

WASC emphasized the importance of a clearly defined institutional purpose. In anticipation of the 1976 visit, the college adopted a mission statement, which read, "Western State University College of Law is dedicated to providing educational opportunity of the highest caliber, at the lowest possible cost, to all possible qualified candidates for law study, with particular emphasis on those students who are obliged to work while attending college or who are otherwise limited financially." This statement reflected explicitly the basic tension in the college's mission, the tension between providing a legal education of the "highest caliber" and employing a lax admissions policy. It would be reaffirmed with minor modifications in 1980, in anticipation of a 1981 WASC visit. As slightly modified, it would remain the law school's mission statement until 1999.

The WASC site inspection team began its report with criticism of the institution's name, noting that the reference to "state" suggested that the institution was public rather than private, while the term "university" implied the existence of multiple academic or professional schools. Western State University, however, had no affiliation with the state and, according to the WASC team, it was "a University in name only" because it taught only a single discipline. WSU defended its name by noting that the term "university" was appropriate for an institution that encompassed more than one college and enabled the institution to expand into other disciplines in the future, an idea that was under consideration at least until the 1980s. The college's defense of the name never mentioned the reference to "state."

The team's report focused on those aspects of WSU that were particularly distinctive: its structure as a proprietary institution and its admissions policy. The report described WSU this way. "The College is a single-purpose institution and pursues its purpose with a singleness of mind which rules out excess expenditures for 'frills' of any kind. The management is in control of all events including curriculum changes, and one can confidently assume that they will not occur without a careful cost evaluation." The college was earning an annual surplus before taxes of about $1.5 million on revenues of about $4 million.

The report noted that the college employed a "whole person" admissions policy, which considered a wide range of factors in addition to the applicant's undergraduate grade point average and LSAT score. The report observed that the whole person philosophy "means in essence that very few applicants are rejected for low LSAT scores, previous academic deficiencies, or on other traditional criteria." In one admissions cycle, out of 1305 applicants, only 18 were rejected, a rejection rate of about 1 percent. Sixty nine applicants did withdraw their applications before a decision was made. If those were counted as rejections, the rejection rate would rise to 7 percent. The median undergraduate grade point average of its student body was 2.7, while the median LSAT score was 483 (on a scale of 200 to 800, with 500 being approximately the national mean score). The LSAT scores of individual students ranged from as low as 203 to as high as 726.

According to the report, some members of the faculty were concerned that the college's admissions process was "not adequately weeding out marginal students." The college, however, quite candidly told the team that its policy was to admit high-risk students and then to dismiss those whose work demonstrated that they were not qualified. The report observed that "whether this is wise is at least questionable." It elaborated: "To give every applicant a change to study the Law is laudable – to accept a year's tuition from those whose chances of completing the program are almost nil could be questioned."

The report found that faculty members "have an exceptionally heavy work load, including carrying the bulk of all pre-admission, admission, and on-going counseling for the more than eleven hundred students." Following the issuance of the WASC report, the college transferred admissions counseling responsibilities to the admissions staff.

The report concluded that the quality of instruction was "adequate" in light of the college's mission. The instructors were prepared, but the depth of discussion was "marginal." The level of student preparation was mixed, but the report noted that this was true in all law schools. The students, in any event, gave "abundant evidence of being satisfied with the instruction and academic programs."

According to a memorandum prepared by Burt Reis, the WASC inspection team had noted while on campus that half of the faculty on the Fullerton campus had graduated from law schools that were state accredited or not accredited at all. The student-faculty ratio was 100 to 1 and the faculty was "grossly overworked." Faculty salaries were about a third less than the median at ABA approved law schools, notwithstanding that WSU faculty taught year round rather than for nine months as at other law schools, while administrators received salaries that were "extraordinary." WASC found "not one scintilla of evidence that research is even mildly being encouraged." The librarian was a recent graduate of the college with no prior experience working in a library. A single Westlaw computer was treated as "mostly a novelty."

The report also discussed institutional governance, focusing on the extent to which the central administration governed the college by fiat. The Fullerton campus appeared to be "administratively top heavy" and "create[d] an impression of all-pervasive control." The faculty met only twice a year. The report noted that "with only minute variations" college policies were "exactly the same" at both campuses. It recommended that the faculty, staff and students be offered greater involvement in campus governance.

The aspect of the college that most impressed the team was its physical facilities. The team described the quality of the facilities as "superior" and "first class." In particular, it noted that the facilities were both attractive and well-planned.

The second San Diego campus, at Front and Ash Streets, impressed the WASC site inspection team.

Although the WASC site inspection team expressed reservations about WSU's policy of admitting virtually every applicant and then dismissing those who were not qualified, the report found that WSU was effective at serving the mission that it had defined for itself. At a meeting held June 14-16, 1976, WASC fully accredited the San Diego and Orange County campuses of WSU. WASC evaluated and accredited each campus separately. The two campuses thus became simultaneously the first independent law schools to be accredited by any of the federally recognized regional accrediting agencies.

WASC's decision to accredit WSU prompted controversy. Sister Sally Furay, who served the University of San Diego as dean of the college of arts and sciences and later vice president, denounced the decision at a meeting of WASC liaisons. She said that for WASC to apply its own standards rather than those developed by the ABA demonstrated "incredible arrogance." Sister Sally's remarks were not those of an isolated dissident, but of an influential WASC insider. The year after WASC accredited WSU, she was selected to be the president of the WASC executive committee, a position she held from 1977 to 1979.

Challenging the ABA

The ABA was not unique among accrediting agencies in prohibiting the accreditation of proprietary institutions. In 1972, however, the Department of Health, Education and Welfare (HEW) began to question such prohibitions, arguing that any institution that could satisfy the accreditation standards should be accredited, regardless of its organizational structure. Between 1972 and 1977, the ABA appeared before HEW repeatedly to discuss its compliance with federal requirements for accrediting agencies. Representatives of WSU attended some of those hearings to testify on the issue of the ABA's refusal to accredit proprietary law schools. During those same years, most accrediting agencies abandoned their prohibitions on accrediting proprietary institutions. In 1975, with HEW threatening to revoke the ABA's status as a federally recognized accrediting agency, the ABA promised to conduct a study of the issue. The Section on Legal Education appointed a three person Committee to Study the Accreditation of Proprietary Law Schools in May of that year.

The committee decided that it would need to conduct a study of existing proprietary law schools in order to determine whether the reasons for the prohibition against their accreditation remained valid. The committee applied for, and received, funding from the American Bar Endowment to conduct a study during the 1976-1977 fiscal year.

The committee then contracted with the American Bar Foundation to conduct the study, under the supervision of Dr. Donna Fossum. In fall 1976, Dr. Fossum visited both WSU campuses, inspected the facilities and interviewed administrators, faculty, staff and students. In January 1977, she produced a 92 page study. The study found that there were 31 law schools located in Alabama, California, Georgia, Minnesota and Tennessee that either were proprietary or, though nominally organized as nonprofits, effectively operated as proprietary law schools. These 31 law schools enrolled about 4 percent of all of the law students in the United States. The average bar passage rate for graduates of proprietary law schools was 56 percent, compared with 84 percent for graduates of all law schools.

The study concluded that only one of the proprietary law schools even approached compliance with ABA standards. Although the study did not identify the law school, presumably the veiled reference was to WSU.

After reviewing the American Bar Foundation study, the committee concluded that to answer the question of whether a proprietary law school could provide a sound legal education was difficult without having the kind of detailed information that would become available to the ABA only if such a school applied for approval. Accordingly, the committee recommended that the ABA grant a variance for the next two years to allow a proprietary law school to apply and to demonstrate that it was capable of meeting all of the standards, except those relating to the prohibition on the accreditation of proprietary law schools.

At its February 1977 meeting, the Council of the Section on Legal Education effectively adopted the recommendation of the committee. It suspended for a period of two years, but did not repeal, the prohibition and invited any proprietary law school that believed that it substantially complied with the standards to apply for provisional approval. The ABA would repeatedly renew the suspension until 1995, when it repealed the prohibition.

In light of the opposition to WASC's accreditation of WSU, however, WSU questioned whether the ABA's professed willingness to consider proprietary law schools was sincere. Indeed, in July 1976, Reis had sent a letter to Ruud informing him that WSU would never seek ABA accreditation as long as the ABA and the AALS were led by "such recalcitrants as you and Professor White."

Despite the advice from the executive director of WASC and some of its own staff, the WSU administration eventually submitted a complaint about the ABA's treatment of proprietary law schools to HEW, which granted the ABA its status as a federally recognized accrediting agency. As it happened, representatives of the Council of the Section on Legal Education were scheduled to appear before HEW's Advisory Committee on Institutional Eligibility in January 1978, in connection with the ABA's petition for renewal of its accrediting authority. The committee included as part of its consideration of the renewal petition the question of whether the ABA had acted properly with regard to proprietary law schools. Max Boas, Burt Reis and Richard Leavitt (who, as discussed below, had recently acquired an ownership interest in the college) traveled to Washington and testified at the hearing, as did representatives of Antioch School of Law and the Alumni Association of International University. The ABA was represented by Jim White, former Harvard Law School Dean Erwin N. Griswold, and the chair and chair-elect of the council. By the time of the hearing, the ABA had suspended its prohibition on proprietary schools and WASC had accredited WSU. In the end, HEW renewed the ABA's status.

Notwithstanding his 1976 letter forswearing any future application for ABA approval, in the summer of 1978, Boas contacted Samuel Thurman, the chair of the Council of the Section on Legal Education, in an effort to gain specific data quantifying some of the ABA accreditation standards, such as the number of volumes and seats required in the library and the salaries that would need to be paid to the faculty. Students soon learned that the college was exploring an application for ABA approval. An article in the September 1978 edition of *The Restater* reported that the hottest issue on campus was whether the college would apply for ABA approval. The following month, *The Restater* interviewed Boas about the prospect of an accreditation application. Boas explained that the decision to investigate the requirements for ABA approval was consistent with the college's past practice of seeking all accreditations to which it was "justly entitled."

The second hottest issue on campus, according to the September 1978 edition of *The Restater,* was a new preparedness policy under which students would be withdrawn from a class for unpreparedness. Previously, instructors had discretion to lower the student's grade for unpreparedness, but the faculty feared that the principal consequence of that policy had been merely to place more students at risk of academic dismissal. The faculty regarded the new policy as providing a significant penalty for failing to prepare for class without ending a student's career. Students suspected that the new policy was an attempt to better position the college for an application for ABA approval. In an interview in *The Restater,* Dean Ross Lipsker denied that the policy was related to an application for ABA approval and said that the faculty had adopted the policy because students' failure to prepare for class was a chronic problem. He noted that some faculty members refused to teach certain courses where lack of preparedness was especially prevalent and he said that he received more complaints from students about unpreparedness than about anything else, except smoking in the library. According to Lipsker, students complained that unprepared classmates asked too many irrelevant questions.

In the February 1979 edition of *The Restater,* Boas reported that he still had not received the quantitative information that he had requested from the ABA. Boas said that the ABA's refusal to provide the requested information caused him to question the "good faith" and "sincerity" of the ABA. In any event, Boas added, WSU would persevere in trying to obtain the information needed to assess whether or not the college should apply for ABA approval. Meanwhile, the college administration continued to study the ABA standards and the extent of the college's compliance with them.

The ABA's policy was not to provide precise quantitative indicators of compliance with its standards. Thus, Boas would never receive the data that he wanted. With the dawn of a new academic year, students seem to have surmised that no ABA application was likely. In its February 1980 edition, *The Restater* published an interview with Burt Reis. The reporter conducting the interview did not even ask about ABA approval, although Reis was asked about the preparedness policy, which clearly still rankled many students.

Students were also concerned about WSU's poor bar passage rate and they understood that the bar pass rate was largely determined by the strength of the entering class. In the same February 1980 edition of *The Restater* in which Reis was interviewed, Ross Lipsker was asked whether he believed that there was a trend toward poorer bar results at WSU. The reporter also asked Lipsker whether any decline in the bar passage rate was the result of falling admissions standards.

Lipsker denied that admissions standards had changed, although in fact, for reasons already discussed, the strength of the entering class had declined after 1974 and the bar results in the late 1970s and thereafter reflected those weaker classes. Students at the end of the 1970s recognized that the college's bar passage rate was in decline and they understood the reasons for the decline.

4

Changing Ownership

As early as 1972, WSU began a process that would lead to its first change of ownership, one of only two such changes in the history of the San Diego campus. The next change in ownership would not occur until almost 30 years later.

The college by 1972 was very successful financially and its reorganization as a proprietary entity was complete, allowing the founders to profit from a sale. When the founders started the college, they had not remotely expected it to succeed so well so quickly. Building an institution that in just four years had grown from nothing to the largest law school in California with two campuses and an enrollment of over 1200 students, however, had exhausted them. Burt and Ardi Reis had sold their medical and dental assistants' school after only a very few years of operation, at a time when it was very successful, and the founders decided to investigate a sale of WSU.

They hired a broker, who identified as a potential buyer a company called Educational and Recreational Services. The name of the company suggested to the broker that the company operated proprietary schools. In fact, the company, founded by a businessman named Mel Sherman, operated school buses. At its peak, the company owned some 600 buses that operated all over the United States.

As it happened, Mel had sold the company that year to ARA Services, although he would remain as president of the company until 1979. The broker approached Mel and asked whether he would be interested in acquiring WSU. Mel offered the deal to ARA Services, which turned it down. In the course of selling his own company to ARA, Mel had dealt with an ARA employee named Bill Siegel. Mel asked Siegel if he wished to participate in the purchase of WSU. He also invited Richard Leavitt, who had been his attorney since 1967, to participate as well. Dick Leavitt, in turn, invited his law partner, Arthur Toll, to participate.

Mel Sherman was approached by a broker representing the Reis and Boas families concerning a possible purchase of WSU. With Bill Siegel, Dick Leavitt, and Art Toll he would acquire WSU in 1977. He is pictured here at the law school's 25th anniversary celebration in 1994.

The four men were drawn to the proposal because WSU enjoyed a good reputation in Orange County, where a large portion of the practicing bar consisted of WSU graduates, and because the investment appeared to involve relatively little risk. In fact, they found a bank willing to finance 100 percent of the purchase price, meaning that they would not need to advance any of their own funds for the acquisition and that Mel could have purchased the college by himself. Dick Leavitt and Art Toll believed that, as attorneys, they had the knowledge needed to oversee the college. Sherman, Siegel, Leavitt and Toll reached an agreement with the Boas and Reis families to purchase WSU. The college was purchased for an amount in excess of $4 million and the new owners assumed a mortgage on the Orange County campus in excess of $3 million.

At the time that the founders converted the college to a for-profit entity, the Internal Revenue Service had raised questions about the tax consequences of the conversion. To settle the matter with the IRS, the founders established the Western State University Foundation, to which they made a substantial donation. The foundation established a revolving student loan program and provided scholarships to students, many of whom attended the University of Southern California. Meanwhile, the parties to the sale decided to defer execution of the sale until the tax issues were resolved.

Dick Leavitt was one of the four men who purchased WSU from the Boas and Reis families in 1977. Dick is pictured here at the law school's 25ᵗʰ anniversary celebration in 1994 with Jennifer Keller, left, the assistant dean of admissions, records and financial assistance, and Shari O'Brien, right, the assistant dean of administration.

By 1977, the tax issues had been resolved and, on August 24, 1977, the Boas and Reis families sold WSU to a corporation called Western State Enterprises, which was owned by Sherman, Siegel, Leavitt and Toll. Western State Enterprises owned the Orange County campus and the college, which was separately incorporated as Western State University of Southern California, Inc., and which leased the Orange County campus from its parent corporation. Recognizing that the college had become a great financial success under the management of Boas and Reis, the new owners signed a management contract with Max Boas, Burt Reis and Ardi Reis that left them in the positions that they had held since the college's founding.

Declining Fortunes

No sooner had the sale been completed, however, than WSU entered a period of decline. First, consistent with national trends, enrollment began to fall. The number of LSATs administered nationally had peaked during the 1973-74 academic year and then had begun to shrink annually, a trend that would not end until 1985-86. The explosion in applications that began in the 1960s had been caused by baby boomers wanting to attend law school, but by the mid 1970s the number of baby boomers in their early twenties was declining. The problem for WSU was compounded by the end of the Vietnam War in the mid 1970s, which curtailed the large and steady supply of applicants seeking to attend law school using their veterans' benefits. Thus, enrollment at the San Diego campus peaked in fall 1977, when it reached 1302 students. Five years later, in fall 1982, enrollment had plunged to 788 students, a drop of 40 percent in five years. It would continue to fall every year until the spring of 1988, when it would reach 319 students. The San Diego campus thus would lose three-fourths of its enrollment in a decade.

Second, as already noted, after 1977, WSU's bar passage rate declined sharply. The WSU administration understood that the poor bar passage rates were related to the composition of the student body. One solution was to raise admissions standards and to admit smaller, better qualified classes. The college, however, maintained its commitment to virtually open admissions and adopted an alternative strategy. It sought to achieve a satisfactory bar passage rate by adopting strict dismissal policies that would eliminate prior to graduation those students who were not capable of passing the bar exam. This strategy, however, would prove to be ineffective because, particularly in a time of declining applications and enrollments, the levels of attrition necessary to achieve the desired bar passage rate would have reduced enrollment to a level unacceptable to those who owned the college.

As time would show, Boas and Reis had developed a business model that was workable only under the special circumstances of the era in which they founded WSU. That era was a time of exploding demand for legal education, which enabled the college to combine lax admissions policies with high attrition rates to yield a student body that would generate sufficient revenue to operate the college profitably and achieve a bar passage rate adequate for the college's purposes. The shrinking enrollment after 1977 undermined this business model. By the time the enrollment peak had ended, however, Boas and Reis had sold the school. The new owners immediately faced the dilemma of operating a law school founded on large entering classes in an environment where far fewer applicants were available.

In an effort to reverse declining enrollments, the new shareholders in December 1980 hired Joel H. Goodman as director of planning and development, a position that gave him responsibility for marketing and admissions. Joel had been an assistant director of admissions at Stanford University as well as manager of admissions services at DeVry University. He held a master's degree in history from Stanford and a master's degree in teaching from Harvard. He had also taught at Beverly Hills High School. Joel would be promoted to dean of admissions in 1983 and then vice-president of administration in 1984, a position that he would hold until his retirement.

Joel had been hired just as the management contracts between the college and Max Boas, Burt Reis, and Ardi Reis were about to expire.

Joel suggested that WSU replace the duumvirate with a president and the shareholders agreed.

Max Boas retired in January 1981, while Burt Reis retired the following September. Ardi Reis retired at the end of the year. Boas would pass away in 2006, at the age of 87. Beatrice Boas is also deceased. Burt Reis' life following his retirement is obscure, although he too apparently has passed away. Ardi Reis, at the time she retired from WSU, was the president of the Orange County chapter of the American Cancer Society and she continued to work with that charity for many years, serving on the board of the statewide organization. As of this writing, she is active with Planned Parenthood and resides in Newport Beach.

Max Boas, at the podium during his retirement party in 1981. The man seated to the left is Art Toll, one of the four men who purchased WSU from the Boas and Reis families in 1977. Also pictured are Art Toll's wife, Charlotte, far left, and Beatrice Boas, seated to the immediate left of Max Boas.

Restructuring College Governance

The retirement of the founders was a critical moment in the history of the college. From its founding until 1981, the college had been essentially a family business. Even after the college was sold in 1977, Boas and Reis continued to manage it subject to only very general oversight by the new shareholders. The sale of the college seems not to have been announced publicly or even internally. WSU publications in the late 1970s never referred to, or published photographs of, the new shareholders. To all appearances, nothing had changed. Boas and Reis continued to manage the institution and to speak as its authoritative voice. One member of the faculty from that era later recalled being stunned to learn, when Boas and Reis retired, that the college had been sold to others years before.

The new shareholders could have continued the tradition of direct management of the college by the ownership, particularly given that Dick Leavitt and Art Toll both had law degrees and Mel Sherman and Bill Siegel both had business management experience. They possessed collectively the same skills that Max Boas and Burt and Ardi Reis had brought to the management of the college. Yet, they chose not to do so. Dick and Art were partners in a successful law practice and neither Mel nor Bill Siegel had a law degree. The change in ownership would change college governance profoundly.

The shareholders decided that they wanted a president with national stature. The school hired an executive search firm to find a president and the firm found William B. Lawless, a man with an excellent resume. A native of Tonawanda, N.Y., he served as president of the Buffalo City Council from 1956 to 1960. In 1960, he was elected justice of the New York Supreme Court. In 1968, he was named dean of the Notre Dame Law School. During the three years that Lawless served as dean, Notre Dame became one of the first law schools to operate a study abroad program. In 1971, Lawless left Notre Dame and joined the New York law firm of Mudge, Rose, Guthrie and Alexander, the firm where then-President Richard Nixon had been a partner prior to his election to the presidency. In January 1982, Lawless assumed his new duties as president of Western State University College of Law.

Bill Lawless served as WSU's first president from 1982 to 1987.

The decision to appoint a president with national stature reflected the institution's longstanding and continuing desire to create a strong, well-regarded program. A month after Lawless' appointment, on February 17, 1982, the board of directors adopted a resolution to "formally express the official policy of the University to be that the long term interests of the shareholders, staff, faculty and students is best served by enhancing the academic quality of the University and by maintaining the very highest quality of training commensurate with the expressed mission of the institution." The resolution recognized the tension that pervaded the college's mission, but expressed the shareholders' view that the tension could be resolved. They believed that a law school could provide a high quality legal education while continuing to provide access to a very broad range of students.

Lawless almost immediately signaled that the college was changing. His single greatest concern was the college's poor bar passage rate. As already noted, the bar passage rate would fall to 23 percent during his first year as president, a dismal result that obviously reflected policies adopted long before his arrival but that surely was humiliating nonetheless. Lawless understood that the solution lay in making greater investments in people. He called for raising admissions standards and improving the quality of the faculty. He also spoke publicly about meeting ABA standards and perhaps applying for ABA approval.

At the same time, Lawless did not call for any fundamental change in the college's commitment to serving a broad range of students. He told students that he had accepted the appointment as president because he was drawn to the idea of a law school that taught second career students. He said that the improvements in the college since its founding gave him reason to believe that further improvements in quality were possible.

To that end, Lawless proposed a couple of changes in policy. The college long had followed a "whole person" admissions policy, but its experience had demonstrated that the LSAT was the best available predictor of success in law school. Accordingly, in his effort to improve the strength of the entering class and raise the bar passage rate, Lawless instituted a program of awarding scholarships to some entering students whose LSAT scores indicated that they were likely to be especially successful.

Lawless also proposed a significant curricular change. He wanted to emphasize legal writing in the curriculum. Thus, he urged that students take legal writing courses in both semesters of their first year and again in their second year. The two campuses implemented Lawless' recommendation and expanded the number of required legal writing courses.

Lawless also believed in the value of overseas study programs. In 1984, WSU established its first summer study abroad program, at Cambridge University, a program that would continue successfully until 1995, when the law school's application for ABA accreditation would mandate its discontinuance. In 1985, WSU established its second program, in Beijing, China.

Eleven students and Professor John Black pose in front of their dormitory during the first year of the China program.

The Second WASC Inspection

WASC accreditation rules require periodic evaluation of accredited institutions to determine whether the accreditation should be reaffirmed. As the 1981 WASC inspection approached, WSU anticipated criticism of its poor bar passage rates.

One administrator in a 1981 memorandum blamed WSU's poor bar passage rates on the founders' unwillingness to enforce the college's dismissal policies. He noted that every semester Boas had determined the maximum number of students that the college would be permitted to dismiss, resulting in the continuation of unqualified students. The same administrator acknowledged, however, that the new shareholders – Sherman, Siegel, Leavitt, and Toll – after the departure of Boas and Reis had insisted that the college's dismissal policies be enforced. The Orange County dean went further and questioned WSU's policies themselves. He attributed the low bar passage rates to grade inflation and lax dismissal policies that permitted "clearly unqualified" students to graduate. In its report, the WASC inspection team did note the declining bar passage rate, but then observed that WSU had formed a committee to identify the reasons.

The growth of the size of the full-time faculty appears to have raised the quality of instruction. Whereas the 1976 WASC inspection team had found the instruction merely "adequate," the 1981 team found that the quality of instruction ranged "from excellent to good" and commended the quality and dedication of the faculty. Students were well-prepared and actively engaged in classroom discussion. The team did find that faculty salaries were "seriously low" and called for the addition of more full-time faculty and better funding for the library. It expressed concern about the practice of dismissing students after one semester, believing that this gave the students insufficient time to demonstrate their ability. It also recommended the creation of a long range academic and financial planning process and the adoption of a formal budget. It applauded the shareholders' "expressed conviction" that their financial interests would be best served in the long run by enhancing the academic quality of the college.

Relocating the San Diego Campus

In 1983, the lease of the San Diego campus on the space in the Bank of California Building at 1333 Front Street expired and the bank wanted the space for its own operations. The San Diego law school thus was forced to relocate. The shareholders considered a wide variety of locations all over the county, including a facility used by Pacific Southwest Airlines as a flight simulator, the property occupied by the Alvarado Medical Center, and an office building located close to I-15. The shareholders wanted a building that would be adequate to meet ABA accreditation standards, in the event that they decided to apply for ABA approval.

Ross Lipsker found a three story, 45,000 square foot office building at 2121 San Diego Avenue in the Old Town section of San Diego. The building, which was still under construction, sat on a hill just above Interstate 5, with spectacular, unobstructed views of the downtown skyline, the harbor, the San Diego-Coronado Bridge, Point Loma and the Pacific Ocean. WSU chose that site, signed a ten year lease with an option to purchase and a right of first refusal, and relocated to the new campus during the Labor Day 1983 weekend. Its former campus at 1333 Front Street today houses the local offices of the Social Security Administration.

In 1983, the law school moved to a new campus in Old Town.

The college hired Neptune & Co., an architectural firm responsible for designing the campus of the Pepperdine University School of Law, to redesign the building, which originally had been designed as an office building. Ross Lipsker and Roy Mersky, the law librarian at the University of Texas, worked with the architectural firm to create the layout of the new campus, which necessitated structural changes to support the weight of the library books. The first floor housed the library, the bookstore and administrative and faculty offices. The second floor comprised several classrooms and a student lounge. The college would add a deli in 1986. The third floor was rented to a variety of tenants.

Members of the college community were pleased about two aspects of the move in particular. First, free parking was available on campus and on the street. Second, safety concerns that had surrounded the downtown campus were now significantly reduced.

Celebrating Twenty Years

As 1986 began, Lawless took a moment to note the twentieth anniversary of the college's founding. He tried to imagine the college twenty years later, in 2006. As he wrote,

> The Orange County campus will spread across land now occupied by Troy High School (to the west) and La Vista High School and the Endeavor School (to the south). It will have a complete campus with dormitories, a student center, even athletic facilities. Tunnels under State College Boulevard will connect Cal State Fullerton with Western State, for easy access. The ground will be beautifully landscaped, and there will be ample parking,
>
> The student body will be comprised of 1,600 law students, 400 MBA candidates, and 250 people enrolled in our undergraduate Legal Studies program, preparing for the day when they will enter law school.

Lawless then described his somewhat more modest vision for the San Diego campus:

> In addition to a gracious campus with comfortable housing in Orange County, we will have expanded our program in San Diego to take over the entire building at our present location in Old Town. We will have a patio deck on the roof so that our students may enjoy the warm sun of San Diego. (Perhaps a swimming pool will fit on the lot across the road!)

He also had a common vision for both campuses. In twenty years, the county bar association in both Orange County and San Diego County would be headed by WSU graduates, WSU graduates would be "keenly recruited" by major law firms throughout the United States and the college's "excellent bar pass rates will baffle even the Committee of Bar Examiners."

5

Unsuccessfully Seeking ABA Accreditation

Lawless urged the shareholders to submit an application for ABA approval. In March 1984, Jim White visited each campus for one day. He told the college administration that the law library in San Diego did not meet ABA standards, but that the library on the Orange County campus would meet ABA standards if modified.

Later in the spring, WSU held a retreat for the faculty of both campuses at Lake Arrowhead to discuss ABA accreditation. Jim White had urged the college to retain a consultant to advise it on other changes necessary to meet ABA standards. He recommended Dan Hoffman, the former dean of the University of Denver College of Law. Hoffman attended the retreat and offered his opinion that WSU would gain ABA approval if it applied.

Joel H. Goodman, while attending a law school recruitment event organized by an association of pre-law advisors, had met Jack Monks, the associate dean of Northeastern University School of Law. Jack's responsibilities at Northeastern included supervision of Northeastern's unique cooperative program of legal education. At Joel's suggestion, the college invited Jack to attend the retreat and to describe the Northeastern program, which Joel regarded as a model that WSU should adopt.

Preparing to Apply

Following the retreat, on May 10, 1984, WSU publicly announced its intention to apply for ABA approval. Fifteen years after the San Diego campus held its first class and eighteen years after WSU was founded, the college at last was prepared to apply for the ABA accreditation of which the founders had dreamed when they created the college and that Gary Woolverton had envisioned when he proposed the opening of the San Diego campus. The college had a president with national stature who was determined to lead the college to national accreditation.

Jim White had urged WSU not to apply for accreditation of both campuses at the same time. The shareholders, however, did not want to abandon the students and alumni of the San Diego campus. Accordingly, the shareholders decided that WSU would apply for ABA approval of both campuses.

As the college embarked on its most important bid for recognition, the basic tension between its desire to offer a respected academic program and its desire to offer admission to a broad range of students that had always underlain the college's mission was never more evident. In a letter sent to the students on the same day that the college made its announcement, Lawless noted that WSU "remains committed to the philosophy and tradition of providing quality education for both the full-time and part-time students." He went on to explain that WSU "may not file for ABA approval if it appears that to do so would compromise its mission or would otherwise not be in the best interests of the University or its students."

The students knew that an application would be in their best interests. On the day of the announcement, the students in Orange County published a special edition of their campus newspaper, *The Dictum,* reporting on the announcement. After a detailed explanation of the accreditation process, the article ended with the observation that "THE DICTUM staff congratulates and sincerely thanks the administration for their successful endeavors."

San Diego Dean Ross Lipsker, San Diego alumnus and Congressman Duncan Hunter, WSU President Bill Lawless, and Judge Earl Gilliam in the early 1980s.

Some of the student enthusiasm faded, however, when WSU announced a 20 percent increase in tuition. The fall 1984 edition of *The Restater* noted that the announcement of the decision to seek ABA approval had received a "lukewarm reception" because of the tuition increase and because of the college's indication that it might reverse its decision at any time. Some students believed that the announcement that the college would apply for ABA approval was made simply to justify a tuition increase and that the decision would later be reversed. The rumor that WSU ultimately would decline to apply for ABA approval would be revived in fall 1986 when the college twice missed its own announced internal deadlines for submitting its application.

The application process continued to entail significant tuition increases. During the 1983-84 academic year, the last academic year before the college decided to apply for ABA approval, tuition cost $156 per unit. By the 1986-87 academic year, when the application was filed, tuition cost $254 per unit. Tuition thus rose by $98 per unit, or 63 percent, over a period of three years. An article in the April 1986 edition of *The Restater* noted that annual tuition at WSU was only $270 per year (or about 3.8 percent) less than that at California Western, even though the latter was already ABA approved.

In fact, tuition had been rising steadily since the college opened. In the early years, the tuition was low and so a large percentage increase would have been small in dollar amount. Tuition was $30 per unit at the time the San Diego campus opened and over the course of a decade it rose by $68 per unit, to $98 per unit in 1980-81, an increase of 227 percent over a period of 11 years. Despite the significant percentage increase, the average dollar amount increase during this period was only about $6 per unit annually.

Over time, however, relatively constant percentage increases meant ever larger increases in dollar amounts. Between 1980-81 and

1983-84, tuition rose from $98 per unit to $156 per unit, an increase of $58, or 59 percent, over a period of three years. As already noted, the increase in the three years following the announcement of the decision to apply for ABA approval was 63 percent, almost the same percentage as during the prior three years. The dollar amount increase over those three years, however, was $98, compared with $58 during the prior three years. Students saw the larger dollar amounts and questioned the need for them.

In describing the application process in the *Western State University Magazine*, Lawless explained that the changes necessary in order to apply for ABA approval would be "few in number but great in importance." These changes involved, in particular, greater investment in people, the very strategy that he had been advocating since his arrival, although now he hoped that it would provide the path to ABA approval and not just the path to higher bar passage rates. He described only three changes that would occur. First, the faculty would be expanded, with as many as 15 new faculty members to be hired, including five in fall 1984. Second, the college's admissions standards would be tightened. Third, the college would expand the size of the library and its collection.

Changing Deans

As WSU began the process of preparing to apply for ABA approval, Ross Lipsker resigned as dean and returned to the faculty. Associate Dean Hadley Batchelder was named acting dean effective January 1, 1985. Hadley was prepared to lead the San Diego campus through the greatest challenge since its founding, the application for ABA approval. Named as an acting dean, he became a candidate for appointment as permanent dean.

Hadley had taught at the college since 1969, its first year of operation. While teaching as an adjunct, he had served as a city prosecutor and a criminal defense attorney. He had been appointed to a full-time teaching position in 1977 and had become assistant dean in 1980 and then associate dean in 1983, maintaining his private practice while also serving as a full-time member of the faculty and then as an administrator.

Hadley Batchelder served as dean of the San Diego campus from 1985 to 1988.

With Hadley's appointment as dean, George Kraft was appointed assistant dean for the 1985-86 academic year. George had already served as assistant dean from 1980 to 1983. At the end of the 1985-86 academic year, Thom Golden would succeed George Kraft as assistant dean.

To find a permanent dean, the college formed a 12 person search committee that included three members of the faculty (Professors

Moise Berger, Thom Golden, and Jim Wade); three members of the bench (U.S. District Court Judge Earl Gilliam, California Court of Appeal Judge Gerald J. Lewis, and Superior Court Judge Norbert Ehrenfreund); two alumni (Mary C. Avery and Bonnie Dumanis, who later would serve as superior court judge and district attorney); two students (SBA President Ben Hoff and Black Law Students Association President Kirk Harris); San Diego County Bar President Craig Higgs; and the college's ABA consultant, Dan Hoffman.

The team conducted a nationwide search for a successor and received 94 expressions of interest in the vacancy, including from five deans or associate deans at ABA accredited law schools. The committee narrowed the search to a few candidates, one of whom was Hadley. The faculty interviewed the candidates and recommended that Hadley be appointed. Lawless concurred and the shareholders appointed him.

Hadley's appointment caused some discontent among the outside members of the search committee, who had devoted a great deal of time to screening candidates from around the country, only to have the position filled by the incumbent. From the perspective of the shareholders, however, Hadley was knowledgeable about the college, he was well known to the shareholders, and he had already demonstrated his capabilities in the position. Further, appointing any candidate other than Hadley would have required increasing the budget to include a full salary for a new dean, rather than simply giving a modest raise to an existing employee. At a time when the college's enrollment and hence its revenue were declining and the college was incurring large costs in order to meet ABA standards, the opportunity to appoint a familiar candidate at little additional cost was surely attractive. Moreover, in the event that the application for ABA approval was never submitted or was unsuccessful, the college would not be saddled with a highly paid dean who was no longer needed to steer the college through the accreditation process.

In a very cruel twist of fate, on the very day that Hadley was appointed permanent dean, his wife Maria was diagnosed with cancer. Hadley would lead the ABA accreditation application of the San Diego campus while also dealing with a tragedy in his personal life.

Experiencing Doubts

On February 28, 1986, Lawless reported to the students, faculty and staff on the college's progress toward ABA accreditation. He noted that the quality of the faculty was "beyond question," but that admissions policies must be tightened in order to improve the academic program and bar exam results. Lawless would tell the San Diego students at an open forum held in fall 1986 that two-thirds of the students at WSU would not be eligible for admission to an ABA approved law school and that WSU's poor performance on the bar exam was attributable to its admissions standards. He would also tell the students that the library must be expanded.

Admissions standards were tightened considerably as a prelude to the college's submission of its application. As a result, the fall entering class in San Diego fell in size from 150 students in fall 1984 to 128 students in fall 1985 and then plummeted to 43 students in fall 1986. By then, total enrollment in San Diego had dropped to 416 students, less than a third of what it was at its peak in 1977.

The full-time faculty in San Diego numbered 11. Hoping to promote scholarly publication by the faculty and thereby increase the probability of receiving ABA approval, the San Diego campus in 1985 hired the first faculty secretary in its history, to support those faculty members who were seeking to publish. The college also adopted a tenure plan, but the plan would take effect only if the college received ABA approval.

Despite these changes with respect to admissions and the faculty, as the date of WSU's application for provisional approval approached, some within WSU questioned whether the college was ready to make a successful application. On June 10, 1986, the Orange County dean, James Brower, wrote a memorandum to Lawless opining that the likelihood of obtaining provisional approval was "minimal at best." He noted that "[w]hile it may be possible to fall short on some of the ABA standards, to be below most of them presents a somewhat dismal prospect." He called for increases in faculty salaries and the size of the library and an acceleration of plans for a new building in Orange County to lend credibility to WSU's promise to construct a new building following receipt of provisional approval. He noted that the admission of an additional 20-25 students would provide revenue sufficient to cover all of the expenditures he proposed.

Students were also anxious about the application process. The October 1986 edition of *The Restater* reported "continuing campus unrest over the status of WSU's proposed application for provisional approval." The article observed that it was "common knowledge that many students are personally concerned about the success of the pending ABA application, and many of those students have contacted the A.B.A. or their representatives regarding both the status of the University as a whole, the status of this particular campus, or their own personal status." The SBA called a meeting of students on Monday, September 8, in an effort to prepare questions for Lawless, who had scheduled an open forum with students later in the week. About 70 people attended the SBA meeting, including Hadley Batchelder.

The meeting with Lawless was held on Wednesday, September 10, at 5 p.m. in Room 200, which seated about 100 people and was filled to capacity, with many people standing in the aisles. The students at the Monday meeting had prepared charts showing the estimated new revenue earned by WSU from the tuition increases announced in connection with the application for ABA approval. They placed the information on the blackboard at the front of the room. Lawless began the meeting by remarking that he would not present his case "in a rigged courtroom" and then he erased all of the figures from the board. Perhaps in an effort to consume the available time before students had to leave for 6 p.m. classes and thereby to limit questions, Lawless delivered an incredibly detailed description of the history of WSU and the requirements of the various regulatory agencies that supervise legal education. He also described the process by which the college had reached the decision to apply for ABA approval and told the students. "If I had to sum it up in one sentence, it is – we are pressing for higher quality at this law school." He suggested that the students "not throw poison darts and rhubarbs" and help the administration instead. With only ten minutes remaining before the start of 6 p.m. classes, Lawless opened the floor for questions.

Most of the students' questions concerned their fears that the college did not meet ABA standards. They asked about the college's lack of title to the San Diego campus, the college's proprietary status, the high student-faculty ratio, the low faculty salaries, and the admission of students without undergraduate degrees.

Several questions concerned the recent tuition increases, which obviously angered students. One student asked whether the college would give the students an accounting of the college's expenditures since 1984. Lawless said that it would not. Another student noted that a recent edition of the *Western State University Magazine* had quoted Lawless as saying that the application for ABA approval would costs $3 to $5 million, but that the tuition increase had generated $12 million. The student then asked where the remaining money was. Lawless responded, "That's not a pertinent question. I'll take another." Invited to pose another question, the student returned to the theme of the low faculty salaries, asking, "If, as you say, our faculty is among the top 15% in the nation, why aren't we paying them what they deserve?" Lawless responded, "We will." The student retorted, "In the next century?" Lawless responded, "I'll take another question."

Applying for ABA Approval

On October 2, 1986, WSU formally applied for provisional ABA approval. With the application process having begun, Hadley Batchelder sought to answer some of the questions students had been asking about the process by publishing a message in the November edition of *The Restater.* Hadley said in his message that he was "cautiously optimistic" about the college's probability of success. He observed that the college questioned whether the ABA was ready to accredit a proprietary law school. He was also concerned that the ABA would refuse to accredit WSU on the ground that, in light of declining applications for law school nationwide, the market could not absorb another law school. Addressing a common worry that the ABA would approve the Orange County campus but not the San Diego campus, Hadley said that, in such an event, the San Diego campus would continue to operate as a state accredited and WASC accredited law school. He also said that, in that event, students of the San Diego campus could transfer to the Orange County campus.

Student anxiety was palpable. A front page article in the December edition of *The Restater* observed that WSU "has come to the crossroads" and that the ABA inspection team "holds our futures in their hands." If WSU was approved, the author wrote, the benefits to the students would be "innumerable." He noted, "Some of us came here in a crapshoot praying that this would someday happen." He added, "Just to dream that the possibility exists that we now might someday be able to practice law anywhere in the country is extremely exciting." He worried that student resentments toward the college would undermine the accreditation application. He urged students to "take a positive approach" during the inspection. He noted that "critics will always be present." He wanted these critics to ask themselves what they would gain "from disseminating inaccurate information, raising harmful innuendo and displaying an arrogant disparaging attitude." The fear was that some students were insulted that ABA accreditation requirements discouraged the admission of students such as themselves and, not needing a degree from an ABA approved law school for their own careers, might disparage the ABA or the college in ways that would undermine the application.

An ABA site evaluation team inspected WSU on January 18-23, 1987. The team consisted of Dean William L. Wilks of the Dickinson School of Law, Assistant Dean Joyce P. Curll of New York University, Dean James F. Hogg of the William Mitchell College of Law, Professor Robin K. Mills of Emory University, Dean Carl C. Monk of Washburn University, and Dean David G. Trager of the Brooklyn Law School.

Dean William L. Wilks, the chair of the 1987 ABA site evaluation team, answers questions during the site evaluation. Seated, from right to left, are Dean Joyce P. Curll, Professor Robin K. Mills, and Dean James F. Hogg. Note the narrow tables and plastic shell chairs in use since 1969 and the cramped classroom seating.

The team noted that the shareholders took pride in the perception that WSU was the best of the state accredited law schools and professed "a sincere desire" to obtain ABA accreditation. The shareholders also expressed "a willingness to do what must be done to insure that a quality product is produced by these law schools and [foresaw] continued profitability with a new improved status."

Following the inspection, Lawless was optimistic. On January 23, 1987, he sent a memo to the students, faculty and staff. He said that the team had found the faculty, students, staff and curriculum to be "generally consistent" with ABA standards, although the size of the library was not adequate. Lawless believed that the college was "very much 'on course.'" In an interview with the *Orange County Register* published on February 17, Lawless said that WSU also would need to raise faculty salaries.

Hadley Batchelder, in a message published in the February 1987 edition of *The Restater,* said that he was "guardedly optimistic." The team had praised the faculty and the quality of the instruction. The one "disquieting note" that Hadley had heard was a concern that the San Diego campus simply would not be able to attract enough students to survive financially, even if it received provisional approval.

An analysis by a student, Georges N. Smetana, sounded some alarms. He noted that the librarian on the evaluation team had referred to the library on the San Diego campus as "a cute little library." Asked by students for more specifics about the library, she was "vague" in her responses. After reviewing other concerns noted by the site evaluation team, such as low faculty salaries, Smetana observed that all of the problems could be solved by further investments by the shareholders. Unfortunately, the team had questioned whether the college had the resources and could attract a sufficient number of students to finance the necessary investments. Smetana concluded that whether the college would receive ABA approval was "an even bet."

The Third WASC Inspection

Meanwhile, in February 1987, as WSU awaited the results of the ABA inspection, WASC conducted its regularly scheduled site inspection. The WASC team concluded that, as a result of its application for ABA approval, WSU was the strongest academically that it had ever been.

The improvements in the quality of the academic program that had appeared with the appointment of a full-time faculty in the mid

1970s were still evident. The WASC team observed that the quality and dedication of the faculty at both campuses were "outstanding." It found a "high level of teaching effectiveness," with teaching on the San Diego campus ranging from "good to excellent." The faculty had ceased using readers to grade the students' exams and had assumed responsibility for grading exams in exchange for not being required to teach during the summers. The team also noted increased autonomy at the San Diego campus since the last inspection. In particular, the San Diego campus was allowed to adopt curricular requirements that were different from those in effect on the Orange County campus.

The continued growth of the full-time faculty, however, had done little to promote scholarship. The team found "little evidence" that the senior faculty were engaged in scholarly research. Most faculty members had published nothing at all or something brief, such as a book review.

The WASC team expressed a concern that, if the ABA denied approval, the college would abandon recent improvements in the academic program. More specifically, it might reduce the size of the full-time faculty and increase the size of the student body by lowering admissions standards.

In expressing its concern about the consequences of a denial of ABA approval, the WASC team remarked on the impact that lower admissions standards would have on the college's bar passage rate. For example, it examined the results on the July 1986 bar exam of 40 Orange County graduates with LSAT scores of 19 or below (on a scale of 10 to 48). A score of 19 was approximately the 8th percentile and was roughly equivalent to a score of 137 on the current scale. Of these 40 students, only two had passed, a passage rate of 5%. The team further noted that the passage rate for those taking the bar exam multiple times declined with each subsequent attempt. Thus, the team believed that it was unlikely that these graduates would ever succeed. It observed that retaining students with less than a 10 percent chance of passing the bar exam was "difficult to justify." The San Diego campus acknowledged the strong correlation between LSAT scores and bar passage rates and responded to the WASC criticism by promising never again to admit a student with an LSAT score below 20. A score of 20 represented approximately the 10th percentile and is roughly equivalent to a score of 138 on the current scale. At that time, approximately 13 percent of the students admitted on the San Diego campus had a score below 20.

The WASC team also found that the uncertainties surrounding the ABA approval process were affecting faculty morale. It noted that "many" of the full-time faculty had "expressed their determination" to leave WSU if the ABA denied approval. Morale problems were especially severe in San Diego, where the team found "widespread paranoia" that ABA accreditation would be granted only to the Orange County campus, casting the San Diego campus "adrift." Even the San Diego students would speculate in the April 1987 edition of *The Restater* that the ABA might accredit the Orange County campus, but not the San Diego campus. They did not even consider the possibility that the reverse might happen.

The WASC team ruminated on the nature of a for-profit institution. It noted the "inherent tension" between increased academic quality and increased profitability, suggesting that quality would be pursued only if it were also profitable. The team's report observed that even the bid for ABA accreditation was based on the assumption that an accredited law school would be more profitable in the long run.

The 1987 WASC team, as had other teams before it, criticized the name of the institution. It noted that the Orange County campus was located on North State College Boulevard, across the street from California State University at Fullerton. The team was concerned that WSU's name, its proximity to CSU, and its address could combine to create the misimpression that Western State University was a state university.

ABA Accreditation Denied

Meanwhile, the ABA Accreditation Committee considered the ABA site evaluation team's report at its meeting in Indianapolis on Friday, April 24. WSU was represented at the meeting by Lawless, the four shareholders, and Dan Hoffman. Following the meeting, Lawless sent a memorandum to the students, faculty and staff stating that he believed the hearing to have been "full, fair, and extensive."

The Accreditation Committee found numerous violations of ABA standards, with virtually all violations occurring at both campuses. The committee recommended that WSU's application for provisional approval be denied.

The committee did find, based on the report of the site evaluation team, that the quality of teaching was "good." Further, in recent years, potential for scholarship had been a "serious criterion" for hiring and a few of the recently appointed faculty members had published. At the same time, however, WSU had no sabbatical leave or summer stipend program to encourage scholarship and no current plans to establish either. Thus, the Accreditation Committee found that WSU was providing insufficient institutional support for research and that this failure violated the accreditation standards.

A related concern was that faculty salaries were "substantially below" those of ABA approved law schools in California. The shareholders had agreed to raise salaries over a number of years until the median for other ABA approved law schools in California was reached, but only if the college received provisional approval. The Accreditation Committee concluded that faculty salaries were "inadequate to attract and retain a competent faculty" and therefore WSU was in violation of the accreditation standards in that regard as well.

Further, the Accreditation Committee found "no tradition with respect to the faculty's role in governance." Members of the faculty still were not allowed to choose their own course materials, although the shareholders had promised that this would be allowed in the future. The lack of faculty governance also violated ABA standards.

As already noted, WSU did not own its campus in San Diego. The San Diego campus had no moot courtroom and its library occupied only about 7050 square feet. In Orange County, the building was inadequate for the size of the student body. WSU intended to construct a new library in Orange County in order to relieve the space demands, but only if the college received provisional approval. The Accreditation Committee found that the physical facilities on both campuses violated the standards

The library collection in San Diego contained only 44,000 volumes, far smaller than that at any ABA approved law school in the country. The Orange County campus had a larger collection, but both were too small and thus the size of the two collections violated ABA standards.

Finally, the committee found a violation with respect to the adequacy of financial resources, resting on several considerations taken together. WSU had no endowment and was completely dependent on tuition. Yet, it was accepting marginally qualified applicants, its applicant pool was declining, and its graduates had a low bar passage rate.

For example, the median LSAT score on the San Diego campus was 26, which was approximately the 25th percentile (and the equivalent of about a 144 on the current scale). Some students, however, were admitted without an LSAT score and so the actual median may have been lower. The median undergraduate grade point average was 2.52. The attrition rate for recent classes had been above 50 percent, including both the students who were dismissed and those who withdrew. Bar passage rates for the San Diego campus over the prior four years generally ranged from about 23 percent to 35 percent, although on one administration the rate had risen to 38 percent. The committee observed that WSU's low admissions standards combined with its low bar passage rate separately raised questions of compliance with the standards.

On May 27, 1987, WSU submitted to the committee a request for reconsideration of its decision. The shareholders executed $2 million in promissory notes and pledged to exercise their option to purchase the building in San Diego and to construct a moot courtroom, if the college received provisional approval. WSU also adopted a statement on faculty governance and set up a program to promote faculty scholarship. At a meeting in Sacramento in June, however, the committee denied WSU's request for reconsideration.

The Council of the Section on Legal Education, at its meeting in San Francisco on August 10 to 12, concurred with the Accreditation Committee. In publicly announcing the council's decision, WSU explained that the "principal ground for denial was the school's unwillingness to construct and occupy the planned new library building in Fullerton before receiving provisional approval." According to WSU, at least $4 million would have been necessary to construct the new building. WSU also explained that, contrary to WSU's understanding, the ABA determined that the San Diego campus could not be considered a branch campus, thus necessitating that the San Diego campus independently meet each of the accreditation standards. In an interview with *The Restater,* Art Toll complained that the ABA standards were "subjective." Orange County Dean James Brower criticized the standards as "vague" and "subject to abuse." He blamed the denial of accreditation on WSU's proprietary status.

Aftermath of the Denial

Lawless had been appointed president under a five year contract, which expired in 1987. In May of that year, as WSU's request for reconsideration lay before the ABA Accreditation Committee, Lawless left WSU. On September 1, Lawless would become dean of the National Judicial College in Reno, Nevada, a position he would hold until 1990. He would pass away in 2007, at the age of 84. Meanwhile, the shareholders named James Brower, then dean of the Orange County campus, as the acting chief operating officer, pending the appointment of a new president.

In attempting to determine why the ABA application failed, the students appear to have concluded that the ABA had treated WSU unfairly because it was a proprietary law school. Student Georges N. Smetana, writing in the September 1987 edition of *The Restater,* alleged that WSU was led "down the garden path" by the ABA, which had "lulled W.S.U. into a false sense of security." The ABA had expected the college to spend millions on a new library, with no promise of accreditation. He cited the college's position that further expenditures were financially impractical without a guarantee of provisional approval, a position that Smetana thought made "a lot of sense." He asked the question posed by every dean who seeks to take a law school through the accreditation process: how does a law school attract students who are strong enough academically to meet ABA standards when that law school cannot guarantee them an ABA accredited legal education?

An editorial in the same edition observed that "in what was the first proprietary application in A.B.A. history, the Accreditation Committee saw fit to railroad W.S.U.'s application into oblivion." The editorial criticized the ABA for giving "undue" weight to the college's proprietary status, rather than considering the quality of the education that it provided. The editorial, however, did also wonder how the additional revenue generated by recent tuition increases had been spent. No "radical" changes at the San Diego campus had occurred. The editorial asked whether the shareholders had taken "disproportionate profits" or whether there was "an A.B.A. war chest sitting somewhere in an Orange County bank account." The editorial noted that it had requested an interview with the shareholders, but had received no response.

The following month, however, the October edition of *The Restater* featured the interview that the newspaper had requested. Art Toll told *The Restater* that "the necessary monies will be made available if we can get the accreditation." He explained that the college had not purchased the San Diego building because it already had a long term lease with an option to purchase and so stability was not a problem. Money spent to purchase the building could be better used to meet other needs. He also denied that the shareholders had ever considered dropping the San Diego campus from the application. He concluded the interview with a "passionate" statement that the goal of the shareholders was to provide "the highest quality legal education possible so that the students can truly be proud of the degree they receive at Western State University."

Meanwhile, in 1987, the owner of the Old Town building experienced financial difficulties, as a result of which the San Diego campus went into foreclosure. To ensure that the college could remain in that location, WSU purchased the building from Great Western Bank for $6.4 million on September 29, 1987, thereby curing in San Diego one of the many violations of the ABA standards.

The front entrance to the law school campus in Old Town, which the college purchased out of foreclosure in 1987, four years after occupying the building.

WSU appealed the council's recommendation to the House of Delegates at its mid-year meeting held in February 1988 in Philadelphia, but lost the appeal. At that point, WSU abandoned its application for ABA approval and publicly stated that it would not pursue ABA accreditation in the future. Two other law schools were denied provisional approval contemporaneously with WSU. One of them, St. Thomas University in Florida, reapplied and subsequently received provisional approval. The other, Old College Nevada School of Law, ceased operations following the denial of its application.

The ABA's denial of approval alarmed WASC, which believed that WSU had not engaged in sufficient planning for that possibility. At its June 1987 meeting, the commission questioned WSU's acting chief operating officer, James Brower, closely concerning the status of the application for provisional approval. On July 1, the commission sent WSU a letter requesting information on a variety of matters, including the college's concept of its mission in the wake of the accreditation denial, its governance, its finances and the anticipated size of the faculty in the future. Brower responded by informing the commission that the college was rededicating itself to its original mission and reaffirming its 1981 mission statement. He also reported that the college already was searching for a new president to replace Lawless. Finally, he told WASC that the shareholders intended to maintain a student-faculty ratio of 40:1. WASC reaffirmed the accreditation of both campuses, but with a warning.

The college had hoped that its pursuit of ABA accreditation would increase its enrollment and raise its bar passage rates. The failed application, however, devastated the college, leaving it weaker than it was before. Enrollments were dangerously low and its WASC accreditation was in jeopardy. So concerned was the college that faculty members were sent a memorandum advising them that any faculty member who disclosed to students the warning letter from WASC would be terminated immediately.

The denial of ABA accreditation had severe repercussions for the San Diego campus in particular. In an effort to obtain ABA approval, WSU had raised admissions standards, which had reduced enrollment. By spring 1988, the enrollment at the San Diego campus had fallen to 319 students. The drop in enrollment was so precipitous that during the ABA site evaluation members of the team had expressed the concern that the San Diego campus might not be financially viable, even if it received ABA approval.

The college could not cover its expenses at that level of enrollment and, for the first time in its history, WSU suffered an operating loss. The loss exceeded $200,000 in fiscal year 1988 and $400,000 in fiscal year 1989. The shareholders met with the San Diego faculty and told them that the San Diego campus would be closed if enrollment did not increase.

Because of the diminished enrollment, the shareholders also considered reducing the size of the San Diego faculty. Two members of the faculty had resigned during the unsuccessful application for ABA approval. In fall 1987, Hadley informed the faculty that, if three more members of the faculty did not resign, then three members of the faculty would be terminated. On December 2, 1987, the faculty sent a letter to WASC expressing concern about the threatened dismissal of three members of the faculty. Dick Leavitt and Art Toll met with the faculty on December 17 and assured them that the future size of the faculty would be based on enrollment, that for this purpose the enrollment would not be assessed until fall 1989, and that until that time the size of the faculty would not be reduced except by voluntary attrition or agreement. The faculty subsequently sent WASC a second letter reporting on the meeting with the shareholders and stating that the faculty preferred to handle the issue internally.

The controversy over faculty dismissals gave Ross Lipsker an opportunity to try to reclaim his deanship. Several faculty members, including Lipsker, argued that Hadley was not fighting vigorously enough for the interests of the faculty, particularly in resisting the possible elimination of faculty positions, and urged his termination as dean. Tragically, as Hadley confronted the group of faculty seeking his ouster, his wife Maria was dying of cancer. Hadley resigned as dean effective June 1, 1988, and returned to the full-time faculty. His wife passed away in December of that same year.

As the effective date of Hadley's resignation approached, the faculty was unable to agree on his successor. While some members of the faculty urged that Ross Lipsker be reappointed, others opposed his reappointment. As a compromise, George Kraft was appointed acting dean, effective June 1, 1988, to serve until a permanent dean was appointed. A year and a half later, Lipsker would resign from the faculty, severing his ties with the law school. Thom Golden, whom Hadley had appointed assistant dean in 1986, also resigned from his administrative position effective June 1, 1988, on the same day that Hadley's resignation became effective, and returned to the faculty.

George Kraft served as acting dean of the San Diego campus from 1988 until 1990.

One favorable consequence of the failed application for ABA approval was, for a brief time, higher bar passage rates. On the July 1989 bar exam, the San Diego campus achieved a 67.4 percent first time pass rate, which was only about 12 percentage points below the pass rate for all California ABA approved law schools. By comparison, the year before, the pass rate for the San Diego campus was more than 30 percentage points below the pass rate for all California ABA approved law schools. On the very next bar exam, the February 1990 bar exam, the San Diego campus achieved a first time pass rate of 75.9 percent, which was about 11 percentage points above the pass rate for all California ABA approved law schools. This was an improvement of more than 20 percentage points compared with the pass rate on the February bar exam of the year before.

The improvements were as short-lived as they were dramatic. The year after the San Diego campus received its 67.4 percent pass rate on the July 1989 bar exam, its pass rate plunged by 30 percentage points. Similarly, its 75.9 percent pass rate on the February 1990 bar exam was followed the next February by a drop of 20 percentage points. WSU's brief experiment with higher admissions standards had produced some excellent bar exam results, but the experiment was over.

6

Making a Comeback

The failed ABA accreditation application resulted in a transfer of the leadership of both the college as a whole and of the San Diego campus to a new generation. With the departure of Lawless and Hadley's resignation, the college and the San Diego campus soon would be led by people who had no affiliation with the college prior to the 1986 application. The new generation would lead the San Diego campus in a comeback that would enable it within a decade to apply successfully for ABA accreditation.

The shareholders had been impressed by Jack Monks' presentation at Lake Arrowhead in 1984 and decided to offer him the presidency. Jack had worked for 15 years as a marketing executive in New York City, at one time serving as vice-president of Ted Bates & Co., and then had attended law school at Fordham University. He initially declined the offer of the presidency, but the shareholders persisted and Jack finally accepted their offer. On June 1, 1988, a year after Lawless' departure, Jack Monks became the second president of Western State University College of Law.

Jack set out to rebuild the morale at WSU following the denial of ABA accreditation. He embraced the view that WSU would be financially successful only by offering a strong academic program and urged the faculty and staff to take pride in performing well the mission of serving a predominantly southern California population of mature, working adults. For Jack, the abandonment of the dream of ABA approval did not mean that the college should retreat with respect to any of the improvements that it had made in its academic program.

Jack understood that to improve its academic quality, the college would need to attract stronger students. To do so, he proposed to increase funding for scholarships. As already noted, Lawless had adopted a policy of awarding scholarships to some students with high LSAT scores. In spring 1989, Jack announced the creation of a new LSAT scholarship policy in which every student entering the college with an LSAT score of 31 or higher would receive a scholarship. A score of 31 at the time was approximately the national median and roughly equivalent to a score of 150 on the scale now in use. These scholarships would range in amount from 10 percent of tuition to 67 percent of tuition, depending on the score. The LSAT scholarships would apply to tuition for the first year. Recognizing that first year grades were a better predictor of success on the bar exam than LSAT scores, Jack further announced that the college would award second and third year students scholarships based on their law school grade point average, with every student with an average of 2.5 or higher receiving a partial scholarship ranging from 5 percent to 67 percent of tuition. In 1992, in response to student suspicions that grades were kept low to avoid paying scholarships to students, the college would begin to award the scholarships based on class rank rather than grade point average.

Jack Monks served as president of WSU from 1988 to 1996 and led the college through its recovery from the failed application for ABA accreditation.

Jack's scholarship policy made an important contribution to the future success of the law school. When the better students attracted by the LSAT scholarships began to graduate, they passed the bar exam at higher rates than WSU students typically enjoyed, although not as high as the rates earned by the small classes admitted in connection with the 1986 application for ABA approval. These higher bar pass rates generated by the LSAT scholarship program would enable the law school to obtain provisional ABA approval when it applied during the 1995-96 academic year. It was an important way in which Jack's commitment to academic quality yielded long term benefits for the college.

Jack believed that the San Diego campus could again become financially viable and persuaded the shareholders to cease their discussion of closing the campus. Early in his term as president, he came to the San Diego campus for a week and met with every employee on the campus. He wanted to know what everyone did, what they wanted to achieve and how he could help them.

Jack soon learned of a significant problem on the campus, although not initially from anyone on the campus. A female student transferred from the San Diego campus to the Orange County campus and informed Jack that a few members of the faculty in San Diego were making sexual advances toward students. An investigation identified other students with similar stories. Jack called a meeting of the San Diego faculty, revealed in general terms what he knew, and demanded an end to a situation that had become so notorious that word of it had reached Fullerton.

Present at the meeting was Mary Lynne Perry, who had joined the faculty in 1986, having practiced law at two major firms, O'Melveny & Myers and Gibson, Dunn & Crutcher. After the meeting, Mary Lynne, who was the most junior member of the faculty and who had been unaware of the problem, followed Jack into his office to discuss the revelations from the meeting. Thus began a candid conversation and a close working relationship.

Choosing a New Dean

Jack Monks believed that retaining George Kraft as an acting dean for a year would permit a certain amount of what he termed "healing" to take place. By April 1989, however, he saw no need for further delay in appointing a permanent dean. The college had new leadership and Jack wanted new leadership for the San Diego campus as well.

On April 24, Jack announced the appointment of a search committee consisting of four faculty members (Professors Karla

Castetter, Bill Slomanson and Mary Lynne Perry as well as Professor Frank Doti of the Orange County campus); one staff member (Jennifer Keller); three alumni (San Diego County Bar President Marc Adelman, Martin Kruming, who was editor of the *San Diego Daily Transcript,* and Helen Rowe, who was active in the San Diego County Bar Association); and a representative of the community (Justice Pat Benke of the California Court of Appeal). Members of the faculty sent Jack a memorandum four days later calling for increased faculty representation on the committee, but Jack declined to change the committee's membership.

Helen Rowe, a 1980 graduate of the law school, a very active member of the local legal community and a strong supporter of the law school, served on the 1989 dean's search committee.

In announcing the search, Jack described the qualities to be sought in the next dean. He wanted to find someone who was oriented to the needs of nontraditional students, able to enlist the support of the faculty, supportive of legal scholarship, a recognized and respected member of the San Diego legal community and a dynamic leader. Jack explained that he thought that the future of the San Diego campus was "promising" and that he wanted someone with energy and enthusiasm who would make the most of the opportunities available to that campus.

The committee interviewed a number of candidates, but Jack was not satisfied with the applicant pool. Eventually, he asked Mary Lynne whether she would be willing to serve as interim dean. Largely because of her faith that Jack represented a force for change at WSU, Mary Lynne agreed to his request. In January 1990, Jack announced her appointment. Mary Lynne asked Karla Castetter, the library director, to serve as assistant dean.

Meanwhile, during the search for a new dean, the college had decided to terminate the China program as a result of the 1989 Tiananmen Square massacre. Moise Berger and a group of about a dozen students were in Beijing when violence erupted. Although some students regarded themselves as witnesses to history in the making and wanted to remain in China, to ensure the safety of the students, WSU terminated the program immediately and Mary Lynne, who was the director of the college's summer abroad programs, arranged for the students' travel back to the United States. The WSU contingent traveled to the airport in Beijing as gunfire sounded in the distance.

Television crews interview Moise Berger as he and his students return from the WSU China program following the Tiananmen Square massacre.

At the time he appointed Mary Lynne as interim dean, Jack hoped that she eventually would accept an appointment as permanent dean. In the spring of 1991, Jack asked Mary Lynne whether she would agree to accept a permanent appointment. To ascertain whether the faculty would support such an appointment, Mary Lynne asked the faculty to make a recommendation to Jack concerning her proposed appointment, either for or against. On May 6, 1991, the faculty held a special meeting in Mary Lynne's absence to discuss her deanship. After a 90 minute discussion, the faculty adopted a motion endorsing her for the permanent deanship.

At about the same time, Jack asked Pat Benke if she would chair the search for a permanent dean, if one were needed. Pat was still a justice of the California Court of Appeal, but she had also been appointed to the faculty the year before, although on a less than full-time basis.[2] The search committee was to be the same committee that had conducted the unsuccessful search in 1989, except that Frank Doti, the faculty member from the Orange County campus, and Mary Lynne, who was now interim dean, were no longer on the committee. During the summer, in anticipation of the first meeting of the committee, Pat met individually with members of the faculty to gather their opinions about the search. At its first meeting, on August 28, the committee heard Pat's report on her conversations with the faculty and then voted overwhelmingly to recommend that no search occur and that Mary Lynne be appointed the permanent dean. Despite the faculty's May 8 endorsement of Mary Lynne's permanent appointment, the committee made its recommendation subject to formal faculty approval. To obtain that approval, the committee called a special meeting of the faculty to be held on Friday, September 6. At the special faculty meeting, Pat explained the committee's recommendation and received the endorsement of the faculty. On October 8, Jack announced Mary Lynne's appointment as permanent dean.

---

2   Pat changed to adjunct status in 1995 in order to devote more time to a blossoming career as a novelist. Pat published *Guilty By Choice* in 1995, followed by *False Witness* in 1996, *Above the Law* in 1997 and *Cruel Justice* in 1999.

Mary Lynne Perry served as dean of the San Diego campus from 1990 to 1994 and led the renaissance on that campus in the aftermath of the failed 1986 application for ABA accreditation.

At the time of her appointment as interim dean, Mary Lynne and her husband had recently opened a winery in Oregon and supervision of the winery required a great deal of her time. Accordingly, one of the conditions that Mary Lynne placed on her acceptance of the deanship was that she not be required to serve during the months of June and July, so that she could devote the time to her winery. This meant that the assistant dean would serve as acting dean during June and July of each year. Jack very much wanted Mary Lynne in the dean's office and accepted the condition. During the summers, Karla would serve as acting dean, assistant dean and library director.

Mary Lynne approached the deanship with the idea that she wanted to change the very nature of the position. The 1987 ABA site evaluation team had observed that, while Lawless carried the title of president, his managerial responsibilities were similar to those of the dean of a university-based law school. Further, while each of the two campuses had a dean, these two individuals had responsibilities similar to those of the associate dean at most law schools.

Mary Lynne perceived that the dean in San Diego in the past had operated largely in reaction to events. The dean's principal function, in her mind, had been to await complaints from the faculty, staff or students or orders from the central administration and then to respond. She believed that the dean should become an active force for change on the campus, with an affirmative agenda.

Thom Golden served as assistant dean under Hadley Batchelder, while Karla Castetter served as assistant dean under Mary Lynne Perry. Karla also served as library director during her entire career at the law school, including the critical years when the law school acquired ABA approval, an accomplishment in which her excellent management of the library played a critical role. They are pictured here at a 1988 WSU holiday party in Orange County.

Mary Lynne thought that an active dean was especially necessary in San Diego, if it was ever to gain autonomy from the Orange County campus. The fact that Ross Lipsker had been sent to San Diego to serve as assistant dean in 1974 merely to assuage the CBE reflected the fact that the central administration in Orange County had never really intended for the San Diego campus to have much autonomy. Mary Lynne hoped that a more active dean could loosen the control that the Orange County campus exercised over policy in San Diego.

Mary Lynne also believed that perhaps the most pressing need in San Diego was to create ties between the San Diego campus and the local community. WSU's unconventional nature as a proprietary, state accredited law school, in her mind, had served as an excuse to avoid interaction with the legal community and the adoption of new programs and policies. The insularity of the San Diego campus had also disadvantaged its graduates when they entered the job market. Mary Lynne wanted to bring the San Diego campus into the mainstream of the community, both to open the campus to new ideas and to build the reputation of the college. She spent much of her first months in the dean's office meeting with the deans of the two ABA approved law schools in San Diego as well as with various leaders of the local bench and bar.

The Fourth WASC Inspection

To assess the long term impact of the denial of ABA approval, WASC scheduled a special visit to WSU in 1990. The team found that Jack Monks had created a sense of trust among the faculty and that morale had improved. The shareholders were no longer involved in the day-to-day administration of the school. WSU had also embraced an increased commitment to academic quality. Under Jack's leadership, funding for student scholarships had doubled, faculty salaries had increased, and, for the first time, faculty members were provided with funds to support their professional development. WSU became a fee-paid member of the AALS, which gave the faculty access to many AALS services and programs. The board of directors had added "public members," individuals with no financial interest in the company who, in theory, would be advocates for academic quality.[3] The college had suffered two years of operating losses, but was again profitable. WASC removed its warning and scheduled its next regular visit for 1993.

Although the 1990 WASC report generally found that conditions at the college had much improved since Jack Monks' appointment, it did offer one important criticism. The team found that the college's B.S.L. degree was out of compliance with WASC standards, essentially because of the extent of double-counting of units. Students were earning an undergraduate and a professional degree by counting the same courses toward both degrees. As a result of that report, WSU discontinued its B.S.L. program effective with the spring 1993 entering class.

A First Encounter with WSU

In the spring of 1990, shortly after Mary Lynne's appointment as interim dean, I received a telephone call from Bill Slomanson. At that time, I

---

3   None of the public members was otherwise involved in legal education. One was a financial planner, one was a businesswoman who specialized in U.S.-Mexico business development, and one was a real estate developer. All were compensated by WSU for their work on the governing board. In my limited contact with them, they seemed to regard their primary role as providing useful advice to the shareholders.

was ending my first year as a visiting professor at Whittier Law School, then located in Los Angeles. Because my appointment was as a visitor, my wife, Lidia, and I had decided to keep our home in San Diego and I was commuting from San Diego to downtown Los Angeles. Bill had heard about my epic commute from a mutual acquaintance at California Western and asked whether I would like to join the WSU faculty and end the commute.

All that I knew about WSU at the time was that it had been denied ABA approval, a fact that had been prominently reported in the local newspaper. Intrigued, I accepted the invitation to interview with the faculty and received an offer. The school's lack of accreditation and its proprietary status, however, deeply troubled me because of the limitations that these circumstances imposed on the quality of the college's academic program. I did not want to join the faculty unless the college had a realistic prospect of obtaining ABA approval in the near future and perhaps converting to a nonprofit someday in the more distant future. I spoke candidly to Mary Lynne about my reservations and she suggested that I teach at WSU as an adjunct for year, while continuing to teach full-time at Whittier. After a year, I could decide whether I wanted to accept WSU's offer. I took her suggestion.

As part of my year-long trial run at WSU, Mary Lynne invited me to attend monthly faculty meetings. Those meetings revealed that a very small number of the faculty wanted to reapply for ABA accreditation, but a solid majority was opposed. Many of those who joined the faculty in the 1970s were still at the college and at least some of them opposed an application for ABA approval because it would entail changes in expectations about faculty performance. Further, the failed 1986 application had nearly destroyed the San Diego campus and no one wanted to relive that experience.

The first step toward a new application thus was to attract more faculty members who wanted to apply and whose presence on the faculty would increase the likelihood of a successful application. In other words, to transform the college, we needed first to transform the faculty. That became the most important project of the next several years.

Faculty candidates were screened by a committee then known as the Faculty Personnel Committee, but now known as the Faculty Appointments Committee. The Faculty Personnel Committee was appointed by the Faculty Executive Committee, which was elected by the faculty. The Faculty Executive Committee consisted of a faculty chair, a faculty vice-chair, and a faculty secretary. No one wanted to be the faculty secretary because the secretary was responsible for taking notes at monthly faculty meetings, which at that time were held on Fridays, when no classes were in session, and nearly always lasted for three to five hours, and then composing minutes of the lengthy meetings.

The etiquette was that one was supposed to be nominated for a position on the Faculty Executive Committee by others, but, when the election was held in spring 1991, I circulated a memorandum announcing that I was a candidate, even though I was not yet on the full-time faculty and was still teaching only as an adjunct. The relief that someone actually wanted the job of faculty secretary apparently outweighed any disapproval of my gauche self-promotion or my adjunct status and I was elected without opposition. At the first meeting of the Faculty Executive Committee, I asked to be appointed to the Faculty Personnel Committee and the other two members of the committee acceded to my request. I would continue to serve as faculty secretary until I became dean in 1994 and consequently I was able to retain my seat on the Faculty Personnel Committee. As a member of that committee, I tried to ensure that it would interview only candidates whose presence on the faculty would advance the goal of ABA accreditation.

Meanwhile, during my year as an adjunct, I received a letter from a close friend from law school, Marybeth Herald, who for the past decade had been practicing law on the Pacific island of Saipan. Marybeth told me that she was interested in moving back to the continental United States and was looking for an appointment to a law faculty. I told her about my situation at WSU and urged her to apply for a position on the faculty. She did so and received an offer.

Now we both had offers of full-time positions at a state accredited, for-profit law school that less than three years before was on the verge of closing. By this time, Whittier had granted me a permanent appointment and so I had a tenure track appointment at a fully accredited, nonprofit, college affiliated law school. Marybeth was operating a very successful law practice on a tropical island. Because of the stigma attached to teaching at a state accredited law school, to say nothing of a proprietary law school, teaching at WSU even briefly might doom our chances of ever teaching anywhere else. By accepting the offers, we could be destroying our academic careers at their inception. The risk seemed enormous, but so did the opportunity to build an outstanding law school. We scheduled a transoceanic phone call and discussed the situation. In what could have been a kind of professional suicide pact, we finally agreed that each of us would accept the offer if the other one did. Within a few days, we both accepted our offers.

A Renaissance in San Diego

The appointment of Jack as president and Mary Lynne as dean marked the beginning of a renaissance in San Diego. When Jack accepted his appointment in 1988, the San Diego campus was the weaker of the two campuses – so weak that many had thought that it would or should be omitted from the ABA application process and, after the application failed, the shareholders had considered closing it. By 1994, when Mary Lynne resigned as dean, the San Diego campus was unquestionably the strongest of the three WSU campuses that by then were in operation.

The renaissance occurred in part because both Jack and Mary Lynne were committed to building the academic strength of the college and, in the case of Mary Lynne, the San Diego campus in particular. The renaissance was also attributable in part to two fortuitous circumstances that facilitated their efforts to strengthen the academic program in San Diego.

First, during the early 1990s, the San Diego campus witnessed the departure of many of the full-time faculty hired in the 1970s. Moise Berger, Steve Finz, Joel D. Goodman, George Kraft, Ross Lipsker, and Harvey Nieman all left the faculty in those years. These were not the first departures from the full-time faculty. Abbe Wolfsheimer had resigned in 1985, when she was elected to the San Diego City Council. Two other members of the faculty had left during the first application for ABA approval. Art Schaffer had retired in spring 1986 and Judy DiGenarro had returned to private practice in spring 1987. These three departures in the mid 1980s, combined with the numerous departures of the early 1990s, resulted in the loss of the entire full-time faculty from the 1970s, except for Hadley Batchelder. The first generation of full-time faculty on the San Diego campus essentially was gone.

Abbe Wolfsheimer, the second woman to serve on the full-time faculty, resigned in 1985 when she was elected to the San Diego City Council, where she would serve two terms and earn a well deserved reputation for exercising independent judgment. Her decision not to seek a third term was a great loss for the city. Although many of the faculty of her generation did not engage in legal scholarship, she wrote a property casebook while on the faculty.

The members of the faculty hired in the 1970s in most cases did not aspire to careers as traditional law professors. Most devoted little or no time to scholarly research and writing. Rather, they were former practitioners who enjoyed teaching and, in some cases, they maintained law practices while teaching on the full-time faculty. Their career ambitions were fully consistent with the law school's policies at that time and the 1981 WASC accreditation report praised the dedication and competence of the faculty. The application for ABA approval in the mid 1980s had signaled that the college was moving toward a more traditional model, at least with respect to expectations that the full-time faculty would truly work full-time and would engage in research. Although the application failed, Jack Monks made clear that the college did not plan to retreat in any way from its pursuit of academic quality. Mary Lynne pushed aggressively to encourage faculty scholarship. She successfully proposed a merit pay plan in which scholarly publication was weighted equally with teaching in the evaluation of faculty, a remarkable feat at a time when almost none of the full-time faculty published at all. Mary Lynne also announced a change in the manner of recruiting new faculty. Rather than hiring local practitioners who enjoyed teaching, as had been the practice in the past, Mary Lynne (at my urging) decided that we would conduct a nationwide search for faculty by interviewing candidates at the AALS Faculty Recruitment Conference, the forum in which ABA approved law schools typically recruited most of their faculty. These changes and others indicated that expectations were rising and they altered traditional ways of operating, with the result that the college was no longer the right environment for some longtime members of the faculty. The job for which they had been hired was no longer the job that they were expected to perform. One by one, for these reasons and for other reasons particular to their individual circumstances, nearly all of them left.

Second, applications to attend law school began to rise rapidly in the late 1980s, which facilitated the process of rebuilding enrollment after the disastrous application for ABA accreditation. The number of applications to attend law school rose nationwide from 231,952 in 1985 to 426,173 in 1992, a dramatic increase of 84 percent in just seven years. As a result of the higher admissions standards adopted during the application for ABA approval, enrollment in San Diego, as already noted, had plunged to 319 students in spring 1988. In a mere four years, however, enrollment more than doubled, soaring to 698 students in the spring of 1992. Enrollment also increased in Orange County. In 1990, with the Fullerton campus already enrolling some 1300 students, WSU opened a third campus, located in Irvine, which soon would surpass the San Diego campus in size. The college had told WASC in 1988 that it would maintain a 40:1 student-faculty ratio. Accordingly, just as it was ready to terminate faculty when enrollment fell, the college was prepared to hire more faculty when enrollment rebounded, in order to maintain its 40:1 student-faculty ratio.

With the departure of the first generation of the full-time faculty and a growth in enrollment that justified a larger faculty, Mary Lynne would have the opportunity to remake the faculty. Our receipt of ABA approval in 1996 would give me the opportunity to continue that process. In 1990, the San Diego campus began to hire faculty at the rate of two or three persons a year, a trend that would continue for well over a decade. During Mary Lynne's four years as dean, the San Diego campus would add ten new full-time faculty members. As dean, I would hire more than 30 new full-time faculty members. Some of these new faculty members replaced senior faculty members who had departed, which only enhanced the impact of the new appointments. The addition of these new faculty members would revolutionize the San Diego campus. The ten new faculty members hired by Mary Lynne more than any other single factor accounted for the emergence of the San Diego campus as the strongest of the three WSU campuses by 1994.

Change did not always occur easily. One senior member of the faculty began to make threatening phone calls to Mary Lynne. After she reported the threats to the police, officers placed a wiretap on her telephone in order to gather evidence. The tension reached such a point that another member of the faculty for a time came to campus armed with a pistol for self-defense, although that unquestionably was an overreaction. Jack and Mary Lynne stood firm, however, and gradually, as the faculty who had come to WSU with one vision of the college left and were replaced by a faculty with a different vision, the campus culture changed.

The process of transforming the faculty necessitated that we find prospective faculty members who shared our vision of what could be achieved at the law school. At the annual AALS Faculty Recruitment Conference, we were competing for candidates against ABA approved, nonprofit law schools that paid their faculty significantly more than we did for teaching loads that typically involved teaching four courses a year, rather than the six that we assigned.

The college would approve funds to send only two interviewers and so the dean always traveled with one other member of the Appointments Committee. In the years that Mary Lynne was the dean, that other member was always me. She and I agreed that our goal was to appoint new faculty who were stronger than any of us already on the faculty.

Although most law schools scheduled 30 minute interviews with candidates beginning at 9 a.m. and ending at 5 p.m., our need to find the special individuals who could thrive in the challenging environment that we offered required us to interview a very large number of candidates. We began our interviews as early as 8 in the morning and often continued until about 7. We scheduled the interviews at 20 minute intervals and often we conducted two at the same time. When we conducted two interviews at once, each of us would begin an interview with a different candidate in adjacent rooms. After 10 minutes, we would switch rooms so that both interviewers met, and could compare, all of the candidates. We continued this procedure for both days of the conference. It became the practice that we followed for many years thereafter.

The unconventional nature of WSU required that we spend the first half of a 20 minute interview attempting to address concerns about our lack of ABA approval, our proprietary nature, and our heavier teaching loads. Then we tried to persuade candidates that our law school presented an opportunity for adventure, growth and entrepreneurship. New faculty members could immediately become significant players in the institution. Because we were not part of a university, obtaining approval for new courses or programs required very little bureaucratic maneuvering.

Not every candidate wanted the opportunity that we offered. Some were looking for a secure environment, where they could learn from more senior colleagues and fit themselves into a well-established structure. Others were looking for traditional indicia of prestige. We could offer these kinds of candidates nothing.

The process was incredibly arduous. We typically interviewed as many as 75 candidates in two days. We studied their resumes, read all their published writings, and then struggled to remember our brief time with each candidate long after the interviews ended. It was also a great deal of fun. We were unconventional and, to some extent, we reveled in our unconventionality. Our interviews were lively, fast-paced, and usually filled with laughter as we sought to convey the dynamism, collegiality, and shared quest for excellence that characterized our rapidly growing faculty.

Through this process, we found some superb candidates who came prepared to build a law school. The result of hiring a large number of faculty members over a relatively short period of time was that we soon had built a faculty with a strong collective sense of mission. Although the newer faculty members would have some sharp disagreements with some of the more senior faculty over changes related to our preparation to apply for ABA approval, once we were past those disagreements we became a very cohesive faculty the members of which have always worked well together and enjoy each other's company. As we have continued to expand our faculty, we have looked for candidates who would fit within the personality of our institution and thus the atmosphere that we built in the early 1990s has remained.

The generational shift in the faculty that began in the late 1980s accompanied a broader shift in gender roles in the legal profession. In the 1970s and early 1980s, the San Diego campus, like the legal profession, was largely a male preserve. No woman had ever been dean, associate dean or assistant dean. Throughout the 1970s, only two women – Judy DiGennaro and Abbe Wolfsheimer – served on the full-time faculty. Joy Delman would join the faculty in 1983 followed by Karla Castetter in 1984 and Mary Lynne Perry in 1986, but the departure of DiGennaro and Wolfsheimer in the middle of that same decade meant that by the end of the 1980s only three women would be on the full-time faculty: Joy, Karla and Mary Lynne.

Abbe Wolfsheimer, left, the second woman to join the full-time faculty, is pictured here at the law school's 25th anniversary celebration with Joy Delman, the third woman to join the full-time faculty. By the end of the 1990s, Thomas Jefferson would be ranked second in the nation for the percentage of women on the full-time faculty.

The college at that time was, in many ways, a boys' club. One illustration of this was an article published on the first page of the October 1987 edition of the *The Restater* in which a male student, writing about his conversation with a female professor, added as an aside that the professor "incidentally, looks great in a tight sweater." The atmosphere for female students and even female faculty could be challenging and, as Jack Monks had discovered, occasionally even treacherous.

The appointment in 1990 of Mary Lynne as dean and Karla as assistant dean ushered in profound changes in the role of women on the San Diego campus. Before the end of the decade, Thomas Jefferson would rank second in the nation for the percentage of women on the faculty and a woman would serve as either dean or associate dean, or both, every year but one from 1990 to 2005.

7

Reforming the Academic Program

As soon as Marybeth arrived from Saipan, we began to discuss the changes to the academic program that were necessary to prepare the San Diego campus to apply for approval from the ABA. Accreditation by the ABA would commit the law school (and its shareholders) to offering a stronger academic program, would attract more talented students and faculty, who by their presence would further strengthen our program, would raise the prestige of the law school thereby increasing employment opportunities for our graduates, and would permit our graduates to seek admission to practice law anywhere in the country. With Mary Lynne, we formed a working group to help us compile the information needed to evaluate the law school's readiness. Mary Lynne was strongly supportive because she shared our goal and this was just the kind of affirmative agenda that she wanted.

We knew that the library would be critical to a successful application and so we asked the librarian, Karla Castetter, who also shared our goal, to join us. We included as well Shari O'Brien, the assistant dean for administration, who had a command of the details of the law school's operation and who also supported another application for ABA approval. Because of the controversial nature of our project, we decided to meet off campus. Over a period of a few months, the five of us met periodically at the Coyote Café in Old Town to review the ABA accreditation standards and to exchange information on what would be necessary to comply with them.

On May 22, 1992, the five of us sent Jack a 41 page memorandum that I wrote with numerous suggestions from Marybeth proposing that the San Diego campus apply for ABA approval. It argued that, as an accredited law school, the San Diego campus would provide a better legal education and a more marketable degree for students, while generating a larger and more stable income for the shareholders. It discussed the steps required to bring us into compliance with the standards and estimated the cost of those steps. Jack traveled down to San Diego to meet with us. He congratulated us on our initiative, but cautioned that it simply was too soon to talk about ABA accreditation. The shareholders were unwilling to consider the idea.

One of the impediments to obtaining ABA approval if WSU filed an application, Marybeth and I believed, was the academic atmosphere at WSU. The college, in some intangible way, did not *feel* like an ABA accredited law school. Rather, it felt more like a three or four year long bar review course. For example, of the 88 units required for graduation, 72 were in required courses. The required courses were those subjects tested on the California bar exam or foundational legal skills courses, such as legal analysis or legal research. To emphasize the relative importance of bar related courses, the college graded all elective courses on a credit/no credit basis, meaning that students paid little attention to their electives. If they failed an elective, they could just take another one or the same one again, without any impact on their grade point average. If they excelled in an elective, nothing on their transcript would reflect their accomplishment.

As had been the case since the college's founding, all faculty members who taught a particular required course were in a department organized around that course. Thus, for example, the college had a Civil Procedure Department and a Constitutional Law Department. Each department had a chair, who was the senior person teaching the course. The chair selected the casebook to be used by all members of the department and prepared the syllabus, which all members of the department were required to follow. The chair also drafted the final exam for use in all course sections, drawing on questions submitted by members of the department, which the chair could modify. After exams were administered, students were permitted a single day on which they could go to a room where their exams were stored and review their exam answers. If they wished to discuss the exam with their instructor, they were required to photocopy the exam, because the original could not leave the room. Many students were precluded by their work schedules from reviewing their exams on the appointed day and long lines at the photocopy machine effectively prevented them in many cases from making a copy of the exam, which eliminated any possibility of discussing their answers with their instructors.

Students were allowed to petition to have grades changed. The petitions were reviewed by a committee and were sometimes granted. In a typical situation, a student would approach his instructor and explain that, because of the low grade he received in the instructor's class, he was about to be academically dismissed, lose his scholarship, or suffer some other serious adverse consequence. Often, only a very slight change in the grade would raise his average enough to avert the problem. The student would implore the instructor to reread the exam and to consider how certain she was that the exam merited the original grade and not a slightly higher grade. When they met with members of the faculty to discuss their past exams, students would focus not on trying to improve their performance but on trying to gain support for their grade appeal. In many cases, the instructor, whether acting out of sympathy or genuine conviction that the original grade had been perhaps a little too harsh, would support the student's appeal. Because grades could be changed after the instructor learned the identity of the author of the exam, the system provided a means of circumventing anonymous grading. The integrity of the entire grading process thus was threatened on a regular basis.

No policy existed regarding the grade distribution in a class. In years past, the dean had reviewed all grades before they became final and could adjust them, if he thought that they were inappropriate. Mary Lynne, however, believed that for the dean to change the grades violated the instructors' academic freedom and that, in any event, a dean should not revise the grades given to exams that she had not read. So, Mary Lynne discontinued the process.

Marybeth and I conducted a study one semester that showed the incredible variation in grading practice. We found that that in one upper level class the *average* grade was a 3.1 while in another upper level class the *average* grade was a 1.9. Grades in different sections of the same course could vary widely. Student grades sometimes depended more on their choice of instructor than on their exam performance. Many law schools used a mandatory grading curve to ensure consistency across sections and we decided that the San Diego campus needed to adopt that practice. We collected data showing all of the grades awarded to students over the prior several years and designed a curve that, in effect, would force every instructor to award grades consistent with the typical grades awarded by the faculty as a whole. The goal was not to raise or lower grades, but to create consistency across instructors.

To protect its bar passage rate, the college had adopted strict dismissal rules. One such rule permitted students to be dismissed on the basis of a poor semester average, regardless of their cumulative grade point average, a rule that had caused many students to be dismissed in their final year or even their final semester, even though they had earned 88 units with a cumulative grade point average of 2.0 or higher, which were the requirements for graduation. Because electives were graded on a credit/no credit basis, a grade below a C in a single required course could dictate a student's semester average and end that student's law school career. Given that the average grade in Remedies, a year-long required course offered in the final year, was sometimes below 2.0, more than a few students were dismissed under this rule in their final semester.

Students chafed under the highly regimented program. In April 1991, Mary Lynne participated in a question and answer session that was reported in *The Restater.* The first question asked was whether WSU would apply for ABA approval. She answered "No." After that, most of the questions dealt with problems involving the grading and bluebook review policies.

Marybeth and I formulated a long series of proposals to address all of these issues and others. Over a period from 1991 to 1994, we were able to cobble together majorities to change academic policies that in some cases dated to the founding of the college. For support, we generally could rely on those members of the faculty who were most enthusiastic about the goal of ABA approval, including not only Mary Lynne, but also Bill Slomanson and Karla Castetter. Julie Greenberg was appointed to the full-time faculty at the same time that Marybeth and I were appointed and she soon joined in the reform effort, bringing her own ideas. In my first year on the Faculty Personnel Committee, Mary Lynne and I recruited Ellen Waldman and, after her arrival in fall 1992, she too became a relentless voice for reform. As dean, Mary Lynne provided invaluable support for the reforms by ensuring that we had access to the information that we needed to formulate sound proposals. By 1992, we had a core of seven faculty members committed to seeking ABA approval on a faculty of only about 15, which meant that we needed to pick up only one or two votes for any proposal to pass. In some cases, our proposals were defeated the first time that they were presented, but we would wait a few months and present them again. The faculty was small and collegial and so our more senior colleagues, even when they disagreed with us, tolerated our efforts to keep certain ideas alive.

As a result of these reforms, the departmental system was abolished and every faculty member gained the prerogative to select his or her casebook and prepare his or her own syllabus and exam. Students were allowed to obtain their past exams and review them with their instructors at any time. The proposed grading curve was adopted. Grade changes were prohibited except for cases of clerical errors. We ceased dismissing students on the basis solely of their semester average. The number of required courses was reduced to give students the opportunity to take electives related to their professional interests and electives became graded courses. Gradually, our academic program began to resemble those at ABA approved law schools and to look less like an extended bar review course.

None of these changes could be advocated as a prelude to applying for ABA approval, however, because most (though certainly not all) of those who joined the faculty prior to 1990 were opposed to another application. To attract swing votes, each proposal had to be justified on its own merits as sound academic policy.

Challenging the Admissions Policy

We also knew that we needed to raise admissions standards, if we were to have any hope of a successful application for ABA approval. The Faculty Executive Committee appointed Marybeth to the Admissions Committee in 1991, her first year on the faculty. She would remain on the committee continuously until 2008, setting a record for continuous service on that committee that surely will never be matched. Other members of the committee came and went, but Marybeth remained because she understood that improving the strength of the entering class, along with improving the strength of the faculty, was the most important task that we faced.

The Admissions Committee at that time was by far the busiest committee on campus. It met weekly during much of the year and the members painstakingly reviewed hundreds of files of individual applicants. The committee was also responsible for hearing the petitions of students who were dismissed for academic reasons, requiring additional meetings to decide on the fate of dozens of students each semester. By remaining on the committee for so long and having the opportunity to follow over an extended period of time the progress of individual students from their application to law school through the receipt of their results on the bar exam, Marybeth became the faculty's institutional memory with respect to admissions. As new members of the committee were appointed each year, they quickly recognized her accumulated expertise and she gained considerable influence on the committee. She was able to use that influence to steer the committee toward the admission of progressively stronger entering classes.

In 1991, the college was accepting some students with LSAT scores that placed them in the bottom five percent of all law school applicants in the nation, despite the promise to the contrary made to WASC in 1987. The college's "whole person" admissions policy authorized the Admissions Committee to give considerable weight to factors other than LSAT scores and undergraduate grade point averages. College policy required that applicants be interviewed by one of the admissions counselors, who would often write glowing reports about the maturity and commitment of the applicants that they interviewed. One of the counselors would sometimes attend meetings of the committee and advocate the admission of those whom she had interviewed.

Marybeth and I found, however, that students with very low LSAT scores only rarely succeeded, no matter how much they impressed the admissions counselors. For example, in January 1995, I conducted a study of every student admitted since 1990 with an LSAT score below 140, a total of 141 students. Of these 122, or 87 percent, either had been dismissed, had withdrawn, or would be dismissed at the end of the semester. Only seventeen, or 12 percent, were still enrolled. Two had graduated, but neither had been able to pass the bar exam. In short, these students had perhaps a 1 in 10 chance of graduating from law school, but it was not clear that any of them would pass the bar exam.

From her position on the Admissions Committee, Marybeth led an effort that continued for a decade and a half to raise gradually the scores of students in the bottom of the entering class. The struggle to attach greater significance to statistical predictors was especially difficult in the beginning because it directly challenged the "whole person" admissions policy that the college had espoused since its founding. Of course, the massive attrition rates and low bar passage rates that had characterized the college throughout its history amply refuted the claim that college somehow could identify which applicants with low LSAT scores and undergraduate grade point averages nevertheless would succeed in law school. As WASC had observed as early as 1976, the policy in practice had functioned merely as a pretext for ignoring predictors of failure and allowing the admission of applicants with little probability of success.

The combination of Jack Monks' scholarships, which attracted stronger students at the top of the class, and the efforts of Marybeth and the other members of the Admissions Committee to raise standards at the bottom of the class, fueled a long, slow process of gradually building the strength of the student body, a process that would be accelerated by our receipt of provisional ABA approval in 1996 and then full ABA approval in 2001. As experience would show, only when the college began to place greater emphasis on traditional predictors of success such as LSAT scores and undergraduate grade point average did its attrition rates fall and its bar passage rates rise.

Division within the Faculty

Over time, the faculty began to divide into two factions. One faction was composed of many, but not all, of the faculty hired prior to 1990. Some of these faculty members had never been enthusiastic about ABA approval because they were satisfied with the status quo, one in which faculty members were expected to do little more than teach eight or nine hours per week, meet with students during brief office hours, serve on a couple of committees, and attend occasional school events, for which they earned a full-time salary. Engaging in serious scholarly research would have more than doubled their workload during the school year and would have turned summers into times for intensive research and writing rather than three month vacations. Further, all of the faculty hired prior to 1990 had lived through the disastrous 1986 application and many feared that another application, even if desirable in principle, would fail as well and would place the law school at extreme risk. The other faction was composed of faculty members who favored the improvements in the quality of the academic program associated with ABA approval and believed that the law school could obtain ABA approval if it pursued the goal in the right way.

Faculty hiring became contentious as everyone gradually recognized that the new faculty that we were appointing wanted to pursue ABA approval, something that many of the senior faculty regarded as institutional suicide. One senior member of the faculty complained that we were hiring too many Harvard graduates, a pointed criticism given that, at that time, Marybeth and I were the only Harvard graduates on the faculty. Another faculty member argued that, for every candidate from the AALS Faculty Recruitment Forum who was interviewed on campus, the law school should interview a candidate from the local legal community. Local candidates, generally practitioners with no record of scholarly publication, were viewed as less likely to support another accreditation effort. Hiring local candidates, in effect, would have perpetuated the type of faculty appointed in the 1970s.

Meanwhile, in the spring of 1992, Mary Lynne asked me to serve as associate dean for the upcoming year, taking the place of Karla Castetter, who was serving heroically as both library director and associate dean (although her title technically was assistant dean). I had no interest in law school administration and so I declined and urged Mary Lynne to offer the position to Maureen Markey, who, as it turned out, had already refused it. Mary Lynne persisted, arguing that I could not very well harangue her about the need to reform the law school and then refuse to help her by accepting the appointment. Finally, I reluctantly agreed to accept the appointment for the 1992-93 academic year, on the condition that I be allowed to continue to carry the regular faculty teaching load so that I would not lose contact with the students. At the end of the year, I realized that I had spent much of the year learning the law school's policies and that for me to remain associate dean for one more year, now that I better understood the requirements of the position, made sense.

In those days, the primary responsibility of the associate dean was dealing with student petitions. The law school's academic program was heavily regulated, but students could petition for a waiver of many of the rules. Dealing with hundreds of petitions gave me an intimate understanding of the law school's academic policies and of the ways that those policies affected students as a practical matter. The problems that I saw in my role as associate dean became the basis for some of the reform proposals that we were continually bringing before the faculty from 1991 through 1994.

Welcoming the National University Students

Despite the mass exodus of its students to the San Diego campus of Western State University in 1969, Cabrillo Pacific University College of Law had continued to operate. A decade after the exodus, however, Cabrillo Pacific was acquired by National University, which eventually relocated the law school to a building on Miramar Road, across from the Miramar Naval Air Station.

One evening in early August 1993, Mary Lynne called me at home to tell me that she had just been notified that the National University School of Law was closing. For the second time in history, the paths of WSU and Cabrillo Pacific/National would cross, with fateful results for both of them. Their paths had crossed at the birth of WSU's San Diego campus. Now they would cross again, at the death of National's law school.

National, like WSU, was accredited by the CBE, but not the ABA. In recent years, National had been very publicly touting its intention to apply for ABA approval. National's law school building displayed a large banner that read "On Our Way to ABA!" National's first time bar passage rate during the prior two years, however, had been only 25 percent. WASC had criticized its admissions standards, which were responsible for its poor bar results, and the quality of the school was not a source of pride to the university. Further, the law school was operating at a deficit if indirect costs were taken into account. The university apparently had decided that obtaining ABA approval would require more resources than it could afford and that these resources could be better spent bolstering other programs. By summer 1993, National was seriously contemplating the closing of its law school.

One problem with closing the law school was that such a decision would leave hundreds of students without a means of completing their degrees. Because National was not ABA accredited, units earned at National could not be transferred to an ABA accredited law school. WSU, however, could accept those units, if it chose to do so.

During the course of evaluating whether to close the law school, the National administration approached the WSU administration about the possibility of admitting the National students to WSU. On August 9, 1993, just sixteen days before the start of fall classes at WSU, National and WSU concluded a formal agreement under which WSU would accept as transfer students the entire National student body. WSU would accept all units earned by National students at National and would award them a WSU degree once they met WSU's degree requirements. National students thus could receive a WSU degree even if they had earned only a single unit at WSU. The National students learned that their law school was closing on August 10, the day after National and WSU reached their formal agreement, when the arrangement was announced publicly.

National had expanded its law library in preparation for its application for ABA approval and the deal between National and WSU allowed WSU to purchase that entire library for about $400,000. The National library largely duplicated the library at the San Diego campus of WSU, but the shareholders believed that the National law library would be useful in the event that they opened another campus someday. The library staff of the San Diego campus added to the San Diego collection any titles in the National collection that did not duplicate those on the San Diego campus and then stored the rest of the National collection at a facility in Mira Mesa, where it could be accessed if needed. Because the books were accessible, we could include them in our volume count for accreditation purposes.

The WSU central administration in Orange County had negotiated the agreement between National and WSU without the knowledge of anyone on the San Diego campus. By the time Mary Lynne was notified, we had just over two weeks to incorporate the National student body into our fall classes. We scurried around trying to identify the curricular needs of our many new students, to create new sections or expand existing sections to accommodate them, and to register and orient them before classes began.

As we began to examine the files of these students, we discovered that a significant portion of the National students were former WSU students who had been dismissed academically from WSU and then admitted to National. Now they were returning to WSU, often with only a few courses left to take. While many of the National students were a genuine asset to WSU, we feared greatly that the National students, as a group, would pull down our bar passage rate and doom any attempt to obtain ABA approval, at least for the next few years.

Mary Lynne was able to use the large infusion of National students as justification for expanding the law school campus to include the entire third floor of our building. In 1991, she had been able to move a few administrative offices to the third floor, but the rest of the floor was rented to tenants. The shareholders agreed to the expansion on the condition that we use the third floor space in its existing condition, without any significant modifications. By the end of 1993, the last of the tenants had vacated the third floor and the entire faculty and the remaining administrative staff moved in, adapting the existing office configurations to our needs, with minor changes made by our facilities staff.

One of the great benefits of relocating our administrative offices to the third floor was that it improved their accessibility to students. Previously, the administrative staff worked in a locked suite on the first floor that students could access only with an escort. Moving the faculty and staff offices to the third floor also permitted us to expand the library to fill the entire first floor, which doubled the size of the library. We created our first moot courtroom, on the second floor. On November 17, 1995, we would formally dedicate the moot courtroom to Judge Gilliam.

The Fifth WASC Inspection

In February 1994, WASC conducted its regular inspection in conjunction with the reaffirmation of our accreditation. The team found that the institution as a general matter was "operating soundly," but it voiced a number of concerns.

Perhaps chief among its concerns was our high attrition rate. Approximately 50 percent of each entering class was either dismissed or withdrew prior to graduation. To the inspection team, this statistic indicated that our admissions standards were too low or that we were not providing adequate remedial education for the students that we admitted. The team urged the college to raise its admissions standards and to provide more extensive academic support programs.

Of special concern was that about 20 percent of each class was admitted to the law school without a bachelor's degree. WASC considered the Juris Doctor degree to be a graduate-level degree that should be awarded only to students who had completed their undergraduate education.

The WASC inspection team also found that the faculty was badly divided over the issue of ABA accreditation and that every question that came before the faculty was seen as a proxy for the issue of whether to pursue ABA approval. The team expressed concern that an atmosphere did not exist in which members of the faculty felt comfortable discussing the accreditation issue openly. The team suggested that adoption of a tenure plan would be one way to address this problem because it would limit the grounds on which members of the faculty could be terminated.

Finally, WASC expressed concern that the college had "not fully succeeded in attracting lower income students or significant numbers of students from underrepresented groups." It also called on the college to increase faculty diversity, an unsurprising recommendation given that no person of color ever had been appointed to the full-time faculty. After receiving the report of the team, the WASC Commission voted to reaffirm our accreditation. It scheduled our next accreditation visit for spring 2002, with an interim inspection scheduled for spring 1998.

8

Changing Deans

In March 1994, as I was nearing the end of my second and final year as associate dean, Mary Lynne stunned me with the news that, after four years as dean, she had decided to resign. Her last day in the office would be May 31. Her winery in Oregon was demanding increasing amounts of her time and she could no longer manage that business while also serving as dean of the law school.

Mary Lynne asked me whether I would be willing to serve for a year as acting dean, pending a search for a new dean. I reminded her that I had never wanted to be the associate dean and told her that I definitely did not wish to be the dean, but that I would be willing to serve in an acting capacity for a year. I called Marybeth immediately, told her of my impending appointment as acting dean, and asked her whether she would accept an appointment as associate dean.

At our April 4 faculty meeting, Mary Lynne informed the faculty of her resignation. Jack Monks attended the meeting and, following Mary Lynne's announcement, he told the faculty that he was appointed me acting dean, effective upon Mary Lynne's departure. On April 6, I announced that Marybeth would serve as associate dean.

This photograph of me was taken just prior to my appointment as acting dean in 1994.

As associate dean, Marybeth could reduce her teaching load from three courses per semester to two. Two courses per semester, of course, was the normal teaching load for a full-time faculty member at all or virtually all other ABA approved law schools. She would carry that load while also performing her administrative responsibilities.

Mary Lynne's chief legacy was to create an environment in which the San Diego campus could prepare for an application for ABA accreditation, including not only the reform of the academic program, but most importantly the transformation of the faculty. By the time that she resigned, Mary Lynne had hired more than half of the full-time faculty on the San Diego campus.

Marybeth Herald served as associate dean for eight years, from 1994 to 2002, the years when we separated from WSU, obtained ABA accreditation, and converted to a nonprofit. Hers was the longest tenure of any associate dean in the law school's history. She also served on the Admissions Committee for 17 consecutive years, during which time the strength of the entering class improved dramatically.

One of her most important hires occurred in 1993, when Mary Lynne recruited Linda Berger to redesign our program for teaching legal reasoning, research and writing in the first year. Linda spent a year developing a new program that called for hiring three full-time legal writing instructors to teach a two semester Legal Writing course. In 1994, Mary Lynne gained budgetary approval for the new positions. That summer, Linda, Marybeth and Karla interviewed and hired our first three legal writing instructors, two of whom remain on the faculty. Ilene Durst still teaches Legal Writing, but also teaches Immigration Law, Refugee and Asylum Law, and Law and Literature.

Aaron Schwabach now teaches Property, Computer and Internet Law, and International Environmental Law.

Mary Lynne had other important accomplishments. As already noted, she oversaw the expansion of the law school campus from two to three floors. Working with Earl Gilliam and Pat Benke, Mary Lynne created our first judicial externship program. Further, at a time when alternative dispute resolution was in it infancy, Mary Lynne established a mediation clinic that gave students the opportunity to participate in mediations conducted by local attorneys.[4] She also hired our first director of career services, Jean Calvo, and our first director of communications, Lori Wulfemeyer. Apart from the expansion of the campus, all of these accomplishments reflected Mary Lynne's strong desire to integrate the college into the community.

Mary Lynne took a sabbatical leave and then returned to the faculty. She taught at the law school until July 2000, when she resigned to devote her full attention to her winery.

----

4   The clinic was operated by an outside organization that provided our students with opportunities to participate in mediations in exchange for the use of our facilities. By the end of Mary Lynne's tenure as dean, the organization no longer needed the space on our campus and the program ended. Ellen Waldman would later found a new mediation program that remains in operation.

Mary Lynne hired Lori Wulfemeyer, center, as our first director of communications and I would later promote her to assistant dean of administration. Mary Lynne also appointed Jean Calvo, right, as our first director of career services. I would later appoint her as our first director of alumni relations. Mary Lynne hired Jan Dauss, left, as the executive assistant to the dean, the position that she still holds. The three are pictured here at the 1994 Barristers' Ball.

Setting Goals for a Deanship

I told the law school community that, as acting dean, I would have two goals. The first was to continue the improvements in the academic program that had begun during Mary Lynne's tenure. I did not say this publicly, but in my mind the improvements in the academic program all were linked to an application for ABA approval. I knew that we could not gain accreditation in a year, but I hoped to use my year as acting dean to persuade the shareholders to allow an application, which would be pursued by the new dean.

My second goal was to create a more humane institution. The law school's proprietary nature and its policy of nearly open admissions followed by high attrition, I believed, had adverse consequences for the students, for the academic program and for institutional governance. About half of the entering class either was dismissed or withdrew and those who remained were subject to highly paternalistic and regimented academic policies. Students who complained about the regimentation often were told that they were fortunate to have been admitted and that they should not question policies designed to give them their only chance of success. The faculty and staff to a large extent merely followed orders from the central administration in Orange County, acting at the behest of the shareholders. I hoped to create an institution in which students, faculty and staff alike felt more valued.

This is not to suggest that faculty, staff and students were generally unhappy. Many students recognized that WSU had given them an opportunity that other law schools would not have given them and they were grateful for that opportunity. To this day, many of our most loyal and successful alumni are those who attended the law school during our years before we received ABA approval. While some students condemned the paternalistic policies, other students thought them appropriate in light of weaknesses that they saw in their colleagues and even in themselves. The more senior faculty and staff had come to the law school with a full understanding of its mission and were reconciled to policies of almost open admissions followed by massive attrition and severe regimentation. In their mind, the law school provided opportunity, but there was a heavy price to be paid for open admissions. Yet, when in my capacity as associate dean I dealt with specific students and saw the impact of that price on individual lives, I came to believe that the price was often too high. Given our attrition rates and bar passage rates, in a typical entering class, the great majority of students, as many as 5 out of 6, would not graduate and pass the bar exam. I believed that we could create an academically stronger, more humane institution, while still providing opportunities for students with a reasonable probability of success.

Building Communication and Participation

Creating a more humane institution would require opening channels of communication and broadening the sense of participation in institutional governance. I decided to begin with the relationship between the dean and the faculty. Over the summer, I met with each member of the faculty and asked three questions: First, what did you perceive to be the strengths and weaknesses of my predecessor as dean? Second, what are your own professional ambitions as a member of the faculty? Third, what can I do to promote those ambitions?

In these conversations, I was startled to learn that members of the faculty by then were virtually unanimous in wanting to seek ABA approval. Many of the faculty, when I spoke with them, also asked me about my vision for the law school. I declined to answer the question in my private discussions with them because I wanted in those sessions to listen and to learn from them. I also did not want to give them an opportunity simply to echo whatever I said.

In September, however, after my private conversations had ended, I circulated a memorandum that attempted to answer their question. I told them, candidly, that I wanted us to separate from Western State University and to submit an application for ABA approval at the earliest opportunity. ABA accreditation, I said, would raise the quality of our academic program, increase the value of the students' degrees, and strengthen the financial stability of the institution. Although we obviously could not apply until we had the support of the shareholders, in the meantime I believed that we should operate in accordance with all ABA standards, as if we were already accredited. I also sent Jack Monks a copy of my memorandum.

One of the impediments to candid and critical discussion between a dean and a faculty is the dean's authority over faculty salaries. In 1992, Mary Lynne, to her great credit, had created a system of merit pay raises for the faculty. Under the system adopted during her tenure, the dean annually evaluated every member of the faculty according to his or her performance with respect to teaching, scholarship and service. Members of the faculty would be given from zero to two points in each area. Each point would have a monetary value. The size of a faculty member's annual raise would be the multiple of the number of points received and the monetary value of each point. Later the college would modify the system to allow awarding three points in each area.

Although Mary Lynne deserved enormous credit for creating our first system of merit pay, some members of the faculty complained that they did not understand the criteria that she used to make her point determinations. At the end of each year, Mary Lynne had sent letters to members of the faculty notifying them of their merit pay award, but not explaining the basis of the point allocations. Some expressed to me privately their concern that, in the absence of any explanation of the basis of their merit pay awards, they could not be sure that opposition to the reforms supported by Mary Lynne had not resulted in the receipt of fewer merit pay points. Mary Lynne agonized over the merit pay awards, as did I when I became dean, and unquestionably she tried to base the awards solely on the merits. For example, Mary Lynne personally observed the teaching of every member of the faculty every year so that she could evaluate teaching. She read the faculty's publications and reviewed their service contributions. Nevertheless, the absence of any written explanation for the award certainly allowed disappointed recipients to wonder about the true basis of the award.

The best way to address this concern, it seemed to me, was to increase the transparency of the process. In November, I sent a lengthy memo to the faculty in which I described the criteria that I intended to use in making merit pay awards. I listed 10 criteria under teaching, seven under service, and one under scholarship (the production of scholarly publications). I urged the faculty to comment on the factors that I identified and to suggest other factors that should be considered.

I tried to become as knowledgeable as possible about the contributions made by each member of the faculty. In addition to reviewing each faculty member's annual self-evaluation, I observed at least one class taught by every member of the faculty each year and I read every course evaluation in every course every semester. I also read every article written by anyone on the faculty and samples of exam questions drafted by members of the faculty as well as the comments that they wrote on student exam answers. At the end of the year, I sent each faculty member a letter notifying him or her of the number of points awarded and explaining the basis of the award in each of the three areas.

These letters provided an opportunity to give the faculty specific information about the basis for their merit pay awards, to reassure them that I was very well aware of the work that they were doing in each area, and to congratulate them for their accomplishments. My hope was that members of the faculty would come to see that the awards were based solely on their performance. I also hoped that the annual merit pay letters could be an occasion for celebration as the college officially acknowledged the contributions of each member of the faculty. Later, especially in cases where a faculty member was struggling in some area, I began to use the letters as a means of goal setting for the next year.

I was so anxious to avoid concerns that merit pay would be based on any consideration other than teaching, scholarship and service that I essentially terminated my social life involving members of the faculty. After my appointment as dean I ceased inviting individual faculty members to my home and I avoided socializing with the faculty except in settings where the entire faculty could be present. This self-imposed isolation from my friends and colleagues pained me greatly and was one of the most difficult aspects of my tenure as dean.

I also sought to improve communication with, and participation by, the staff. During the summer, I announced that I would meet with every member of the administrative staff individually to learn about his or her work responsibilities, to hear about any persistent problems, and to solicit suggestions for improving the law school. At a staff meeting that I called on June 9, I announced the formation of a Staff Liaison Committee (SLC), comprising five members of the staff elected by the rest of the staff to promote communication between the staff and the dean. Members of the staff who might be afraid to speak candidly to the dean about a problem could channel their comments through the SLC. The SLC was a tremendous success. During the first election, seventeen out of our forty staff members competed for five slots. Thirty of our forty staff members cast ballots. Every SLC election for the rest of my deanship was contested by multiple candidates for each seat, testimony to the staff's belief that the SLC mattered. Over the years, the SLC was critical in bringing to my attention a wide variety of staff concerns, some quite serious, and in helping me to resolve those concerns.

At a more personal level, I tried to be as visible and as accessible as possible. Rarely did I ask any member of the staff or faculty to come to my office, although often they came to see me. If I wanted to meet with someone, I walked over to his or her office. I believed that members of the faculty and staff felt more appreciated and comfortable when meeting in their own offices and the practice of walking from office to office gave me an opportunity to see students, faculty and staff who had no special reason to come to my office and to be available to them for casual questions or conversation.

I also wanted students to feel that the institution cared about their needs and aspirations. Over the summer, I formed a commission of students, formally called the Student Planning and Review Commission (SPARC), but soon known by everyone as simply "the Dean's Commission." The commission consisted of five students, appointed by the Student Bar Association, who were responsible for reviewing every aspect of our administrative program from a student's perspective and for making recommendations for creating a more effective and humane administrative process.

I invited the president and vice-president of the SBA to meet with me once every week to discuss student concerns, an invitation that I extended to the SBA officers every year for the rest of my deanship. In December, I recommended to the faculty that students be invited to attend meetings of the Academic Policy Committee, the Curriculum Committee, and the Long Range Planning Committee, and the faculty concurred. The SBA appointed the student representatives that year, but did not always do so in succeeding years.

These kinds of measures would give us a student's perspective on our policies and practices, but would do little to open channels of communication with the student body in general. In an era before e-mail, we communicated with students through the U.S. mail, but our budget did not permit us to send students anything more than registration materials. I decided that we needed student mailboxes on campus so that we could communicate with them more easily. I asked Jack for funds to build them, arguing that we could use the mailboxes to deliver registration materials, saving enough money in postage to pay for the mailboxes in less than two years. Jack denied the request, saying that the college did not have the money to build them and that he would not allow them to be financed with speculative future savings.

I decided to finance the mailboxes by charging outside vendors for access to them. I contacted the student representatives of each of the four bar review courses then operating actively in San Diego and told the students to tell their companies that we were building the mailboxes, that any bar review course that contributed $950 to their construction would have unlimited access to the mailboxes for two years, and that they did not want to be the only bar review company that did not have access. All four companies sent checks immediately. A friend with carpentry skills helped me sketch out a design and through the classified ads I found a carpenter, an unemployed anthropologist who had lost his job when the Reagan administration closed down a major nationwide archeological project. The carpenter built approximately 700 mailboxes for $3800, including labor and materials. The next time that Jack was on campus, I found an excuse to walk him past the mailboxes and to mention casually how useful they were in fostering communication with the students. Shortly thereafter, Jack approved college funds to construct mailboxes on the Fullerton and Irvine campuses.

With a new mode of information delivery, we now needed an organized system for distributing information through that mode. I asked our director of student services, Jane Barnhart, to start a weekly newsletter that we called *The Advisor.* The newsletter would be distributed to everyone on campus via their mailbox and would include announcements of policy changes and other information useful to students as well as faculty and staff. The first issue was published in January 1995 and it became a very effective means for keeping the entire campus informed of the many changes that would be occurring over the next decade. We publish it still, although now only in electronic form.

Over the summer, I made several appointments intended to improve the climate for students. In June, I created the position of academic counselor, a member of the faculty who would be available to advise students on any aspect of their academic program and who would have the authority to issue any waivers or permissions allowed by school policies. Prior to the creation of this position, students sometimes needed to obtain as many as three different signatures in order to obtain waiver of a policy. I thought that the position should be filled by someone with a law degree who would fully understand the academic issues involved. Professor Steve Root agreed to serve as the first academic counselor, followed by Professor Aaron Schwabach. By 1999, I had appointed Lori Wulfemeyer, who had a law degree from the University of Hawaii, assistant dean of administration and I shifted the responsibilities to her on a permanent basis.

The law school in its 25 year history had never appointed any person of color to the full-time faculty, a situation that undermined our efforts to create a more humane environment for all students. To remedy this situation, I asked three members of the faculty to assume primary responsibility for recruiting minority faculty. Ellen Waldman assumed responsibility with respect to full-time faculty, Marjorie Cohn with respect to adjunct faculty, and Linda Berger with respect to legal writing faculty.

Over the next five years, the diversity of our full-time faculty began to improve. In that time, we appointed K. J. Greene, the first African-American to serve on our full-time faculty. We also appointed the first Asian-American and the first Latino ever to serve on our full-time faculty.

9

Deciding to Apply for ABA Accreditation

During the summer, Jack invited me to attend a meeting with the shareholders in September so that they could meet the new acting dean of their San Diego campus. Bill Siegel had sold his interest in the law school to the other shareholders in 1991 and so now there were just three principal shareholders: Dick Leavitt, Mel Sherman, and Art Toll. Other family members held very minor shares and one of them, David Sherman (Mel's son), was a member of the WSU board of directors, along with the three principal shareholders. David in effect had taken the place of Bill Siegel on the board. So invisible were the other family members, however, that for many years I did not know that other family members held shares. I also later learned that Jack Monks and Joel Goodman had acquired minor shares in the college. For all practical purposes, however, Art, Dick and Mel owned and controlled the college.

I told Jack that I wanted to use the occasion to propose that the San Diego campus be allowed to separate from WSU and to apply for ABA approval. Jack replied, "If you want to do that, you'd better talk quickly. They will give you maybe ten minutes out of courtesy, but then they will cut you off and move on to another topic. They have no interest in applying for ABA approval."

Making the Case for an ABA Application

I began writing an 84 page report intended to demonstrate to the shareholders that an application for ABA approval was in their financial interest and would be successful. The report noted that while the law school's enrollment had rebounded from the low levels reached during the failed application for ABA approval, the law school's enrollment was again declining because of a shrinking applicant pool. Specifically, the number of law school applications nationally had fallen from 450,900 during the peak 1991-92 academic year to 381,300 in the 1994-95 academic year, when I met with the shareholders. Within two years, the number would drop to 302,000. The decline in applications corresponded to a decline in the number of applicants. The number of applicants to ABA approved law schools fell from 97,720 during the 1991-92 academic year to 76,715 during the 1995-96 academic year. It would reach 71,720 in 1997-98. These changes were the result of changes in the national population. The number of 22 year-olds in the United States had peaked in 1991-92 and now was falling. Nothing that law schools did would change the size of the population.

Enrollment on the San Diego campus was following the national trend. Beginning in 1988, enrollment had rebounded from the failed 1986 application for ABA approval. After peaking at 698 in spring 1992, however, enrollment fell to 643 just one year later. Enrollment would have continued to fall rapidly, if not for the admission of the National University students in fall 1993, which pushed enrollment up to 734 in that semester. After the initial infusion of National students, enrollment again dropped. By the time I met with the shareholders in fall 1994, enrollment had fallen to 632, including the National students. I told the shareholders that enrollment would continue to fall, especially once the National students graduated, and that the only way to expand the applicant pool and to reverse the decline in enrollment was to obtain ABA approval, permitting us to recruit students nationally.

Chapman University had announced several months before my meeting with the shareholders that it was planning to open a law school in Orange County in fall 1995 and to seek ABA approval. By the time of my meeting, the shareholders also knew that Whittier Law School, which was already ABA approved, was planning to relocate to Orange County and would be offering classes in Orange County to entering students by fall 1996. I was certain that the shareholders would be concerned about the threat that Chapman and Whittier posed for their Orange County campuses. I argued in my report that the best way to preempt these threats was for WSU to announce that it was seeking ABA approval for both its Orange County and San Diego campuses and, in order to give the announcement credibility, to apply immediately for the San Diego campus. I asserted that the Orange County campuses were not yet ready to apply and so an application for the San Diego campus was the only way to demonstrate immediately that WSU was serious about obtaining ABA approval.

In preparation for my meeting with the shareholders, I also tried to speak to as many experts on ABA accreditation as I could find. I had known Steve Smith, then dean of Cleveland-Marshall Law School and very much involved in ABA accreditation matters, since my undergraduate days, when he was the acting dean of the law school at my undergraduate university. I contacted Steve and he gave me a list of names of people with whom I should speak. Ironically, only two years later, Steve would be appointed dean of California Western School of Law, a position that he would hold until 2012.

I contacted the people suggested by Steve and questioned them intensively about the reasons that WSU's application had failed in 1986 and about the steps that we must take if we tried again. In August, Tony Santoro, who had led the law school at Roger Williams University through the accreditation process, generously sent me a sample feasibility study, to use as a model for the study that we would need to prepare if we applied.

During my two years as associate dean, I had had numerous opportunities to discuss WSU policies with students. The desire for ABA accreditation among the students was strong and constant. For example, in March 1992, a group of students spontaneously conducted a survey to gauge student concern about the law school's lack of ABA approval. They surveyed 163 students and found that 93 percent supported an application for ABA approval. In spring 1992, *The Restater* published a front page article headlined "Why Not A.B.A.?" written by Robert Waller, who later would serve as president of the Alumni Association. Robert argued that WSU was founded to provide the best quality legal education available and that achieving that goal required obtaining ABA approval. During the 1992-93 academic year, *The Restater* published a series of articles attempting to explore the reasons that the college was not ABA approved and arguing that it should seek ABA approval. Jack Monks wrote a response to one of them and said "Western State does not plan to apply for ABA approval." He explained that an application for ABA approval would require that the law school abandon its mission of providing a legal education at a reasonable cost to nontraditional students.

Jack's response reflected an ambiguity that often characterized WSU's defense of its admissions policy. WSU's mission was to provide a broad range of students with access to legal education. When seeking to justify that policy, the college would frequently emphasize, as Jack did, that this permitted nontraditional students, typically older, second-career students, to attend law school. Yet, WSU's mission went beyond providing access to nontraditional students to include providing access for applicants with a low probability of success, applicants who often were traditional students with poor LSAT scores and undergraduate grade point averages. Our efforts to raise admissions standards were always directed at reducing the number of high risk applicants, not at reducing the number of nontraditional students. Indeed, nontraditional students were often among our most highly talented students.

As it happened, I was scheduled to be the faculty supervisor of WSU's summer abroad program at Cambridge University during summer 1994. Ko Sharif, who was one of the students in the program and who also happened to be vice-president of the Student Bar Association, asked me one day about the prospects for ABA accreditation and told me how much the students wanted it. Jack had told me that the shareholders believed that many students opposed ABA accreditation because it would increase their tuition and would require the law school to modify its traditional mission of providing access for the very kinds of students who were currently enrolled. These, of course, had been the concerns expressed by some students during the failed 1986 application. I wanted to be able to answer that objection at my meeting with the shareholders. I told Ko that a demonstration of student support for an application for ABA approval would be helpful. When we returned to campus in the fall, Ko organized a petition drive.

At the first faculty meeting of the fall, held on September 9, I spoke to the faculty about my conversations with individual faculty members over the summer. I said that I believed that we had now reached a consensus that an application for ABA approval was desirable, that I would have my first and perhaps only meeting with the shareholders later in the month, that I wanted to propose to them that we apply for accreditation, and that I wanted to do so with the support of the faculty. A special faculty meeting to discuss the matter was scheduled for September 19. At the special meeting, several faculty members spoke in favor of my proposal and momentum for the idea was building. Then one of the more senior members of the faculty took the floor and said, "We've discussed the benefits of ABA approval. Now let's discuss the possible downsides." Her comment was met with a long silence. She smiled good-naturedly and said, "All right, then." That moment signaled the permanent end of any opposition to an application. The faculty voted unanimously in favor of a motion to request the governing board to seek ABA accreditation for the San Diego campus.

Meeting the Shareholders

On September 27, I met with Jack Monks, the two WSU vice presidents, Joel Goodman and Ernie Hurguy, and two of the three principal shareholders, Dick Leavitt and Mel Sherman. Art Toll was unable to attend because of a sudden death in the family. Jack introduced me and told the shareholders that I wanted to offer a few comments. Recalling his advice about brevity, I started speaking as quickly as I could, going directly to my principal points. Dick and Mel began to ask questions. I answered the questions and kept talking. Suddenly, two hours had passed. The shareholders thanked me and told me that they had a lot to consider. Before I left, I gave them a copy of my 84 page report and a copy of the petition circulated by Ko, which some 360 students had signed. I also told them that they should not accept merely on my authority the claim that the San Diego campus would obtain accreditation on the first application. They should hire an expert consultant to evaluate our prospects for success.

The following month, the shareholders asked me to meet with them again. This time, Art Toll was also in attendance. Dick introduced me to Art and asked me to repeat for Art's benefit the things that I had said at the last meeting.

As in my first meeting with the shareholders, many of their questions revolved around three concerns. The first concern was that WSU had applied for ABA approval in 1986 and had been rejected, a decision that they attributed to the ABA's bias against proprietary law schools. They wanted to know why I believed that a different result would occur this time. I told them bluntly that they had been rejected the first time because they had followed the wrong strategy. In particular, rather than meeting all of the standards and thereby demonstrating their commitment to the standards as a matter of principle, they had asked the ABA to approve WSU on the strength of a promise to meet the standards after provisional approval was received.

Their second concern was that the appearance of two ABA approved law schools in Orange County would pose a serious threat to the financial viability of the Fullerton and Irvine campuses. They argued that, if they were going to apply for ABA approval of one of the WSU campuses, both of the Orange County campuses needed the approval far more than did the San Diego campus. My reply was that neither Orange County campus was ready to apply and that the best way to meet the threat from the other law schools was to begin the accreditation process immediately in San Diego, thereby giving credibility to WSU's claim that it would apply for ABA approval in Orange County in the near future.

Their third concern was that, during the first application for ABA approval, the college's efforts to meet ABA admissions standards had reduced the size of the student body to such an extent that the college had lost money. It had returned to profitability only when it abandoned its quest for ABA approval and its higher admissions standards. They wanted to know how the San Diego campus would survive financially during an accreditation application. I explained that we had been quietly raising admissions standards since 1991 and that the student body in San Diego already came very close to meeting ABA standards. Dramatic changes in our admissions standards would not be necessary to gain provisional ABA approval. Once we had obtained provisional approval, we would have far less difficulty recruiting students.

Engaging Accreditation Consultants

In November, Jack came to see me in San Diego. Over lunch, he told me that he had some news about my proposal and that he hoped that I would take some time to think about what he had to say. The shareholders had been persuaded by my presentation and they wanted to investigate a possible application for ABA approval. The application, however, would be on behalf of one of the Orange County campuses, probably the Irvine campus, not the San Diego campus. The Orange County campuses were threatened by the decisions to open two ABA approved law schools in Orange County and the shareholders wanted to address that threat. The San Diego campus had been able to succeed despite competition from the University of San Diego School of Law and California Western School of Law, both ABA accredited, but the shareholders did not believe that the Orange County campuses could survive against competition from two ABA accredited law schools.

The shareholders also believed that the Fullerton campus was more likely to succeed in an application for ABA accreditation than the San Diego campus. It was the main campus of the college, with better facilities, a deeper administrative structure and an impressive president. It enjoyed more community support than did the San Diego campus.

They would consider an application for the San Diego campus at a future date, after one or both Orange County campuses were accredited. He told me that they understood my desire to pursue accreditation and wanted to appoint me the dean of whichever Orange County campus was selected to apply. In that way, I would have the opportunity to lead a campus through the accreditation process and to teach at an ABA accredited law school.

Jack also said that the shareholders wanted to engage expert consultants to help them determine whether an application for either Orange County campus was feasible. They wanted me to find the consultants and to invite them to visit the two Orange County campuses, but not the San Diego campus, since that campus was no longer under consideration.

He concluded by urging me to think about what was best for the college as a whole. The first priority was to save the Orange County campuses. The San Diego campus would an opportunity to apply once the Orange County campuses were safe.

I told Jack that my commitment was to the San Diego campus, which we had been working to bring into compliance with the ABA standards for more than three years. I had no interest in serving as the dean of an Orange County campus. Further, while both Orange County campuses might need the approval, neither was ready to apply. The San Diego campus had been preparing for this moment since 1991, was ready to apply now, and could lead the way for the other campuses, setting a favorable precedent for the accreditation of a proprietary law school, while the other campuses took the necessary steps to achieve compliance with the standards. Finally, excluding the San Diego campus from consideration was a terrible idea. If I was right that only the San Diego campus was ready, then any application on behalf of an Orange County campus would fail, causing the shareholders to abandon the pursuit of ABA approval without ever knowing that they could have succeeded had they permitted the San Diego campus to apply first. I also noted that the additional cost of evaluating the San Diego campus would be small compared to the value of the information that the evaluation might provide. Jack told me that my argument made sense and that he would urge the shareholders to allow the consultants to visit all three campuses, although he still believed that the decision would have to be between the two Orange County campuses. Meanwhile, he wanted me to start looking for consultants.

I began calling all of the accreditation experts with whom I had been speaking during the past several months in search of possible consultants. I spent hours interviewing candidates. Ultimately, I found three extraordinary consultants.

Jack Grosse, the former dean of the Salmon P. Chase College of Law at Northern Kentucky University, had served on the Accreditation Committee for nearly a decade, including in the 1980s when WSU had applied unsuccessfully for provisional approval. Because Kentucky is my native state, we found immediate common ground. Jack became our official consultant and regularly provided absolutely invaluable advice until we obtained full approval. He helped us solve a number of vexing problems, gave me much needed support when I had to ask the shareholders for more money, and was, in a word, indispensable.

Joe Harbaugh, then dean at the University of Richmond School of Law, also agreed to serve as a consultant. Joe too had served on the Accreditation Committee during our unsuccessful application. Joe's responsibilities as dean limited the time that he had available, but he and I had numerous conversations throughout the process in which he always seemed to have exactly the right advice. He offered great counsel and strong moral support in our most difficult times.

Peter Winograd, the associate dean at the University of New Mexico School of Law, had a scheduling conflict and could not travel to California when we would need him, but he offered to serve as an informal advisor rather than a formal consultant. And he did. I called Peter for advice so often that we had a running joke that, if his phone rang after 7 p.m., he knew that it was me.

By the time that I had identified the consultants, Jack had persuaded the shareholders to allow them to visit the San Diego campus. On January 20, I sent Jack Grosse and Joe Harbaugh a lengthy memorandum with a long series of questions that I wanted them to address during their visit to the three campuses. The most general and pressing question was which, if any, of the three campuses was closest to complying with the ABA accreditation standards. The memo also included a number of other more specific questions dealing with areas where I feared that we might not comply with ABA standards without additional effort. These questions concerned matters such as our lack of an endowment, the small size of our library collection, and the credentials of the students in our entering classes. I wanted to know how much more needed to be done.

Scheduling problems at the last minute prevented Joe from traveling to California, but Jack came on January 29 and spent a day on each campus. In preparation for Jack's arrival, I wrote a 123 page, single-spaced document that assessed the extent to which the San Diego campus complied with each one of more than 40 ABA standards. Joe read all the materials that we sent him and consulted with Jack about what the latter had seen. At the end of his visit, on February 2,

Jack Grosse met with a group that included the shareholders and top administrators. Joe joined us on a speaker phone. Jack Grosse gave us his oral report, which Joe endorsed completely. Then the two of them answered our questions.

Jack and Joe reported that the San Diego campus was ready to apply for accreditation immediately. They believed that our application would be successful on the first attempt. Neither Orange County campus was ready. They told us that the Orange County campuses did not have the atmosphere of an ABA approved law school. In particular, insufficient members of the faculty were engaged in scholarship. Our consultants' recommendation fully vindicated our efforts to hire faculty with scholarly promise and to change the atmosphere in San Diego. On March 31, Jack Grosse sent the college a detailed memorandum setting forth the steps that would be necessary to bring WSU into compliance with ABA standards and reiterating his conclusion that the San Diego campus was the closest to satisfying those standards.

Changes in the ABA Accreditation Standards

Meanwhile, more good news arrived in February when the ABA, at its mid year meeting, abolished its prohibition on the accreditation of proprietary law schools. As already noted, the ABA had suspended the rule in 1977, but had not repealed it. In the meantime, the ABA accreditation process had come under assault from several different directions. First, on November 23, 1993, the Massachusetts School of Law, which had been denied ABA accreditation, filed an antitrust action against the ABA, alleging that it was conspiring to stifle competition from nontraditional law schools and to force all law schools to comply with a single model. That model involved the hiring of full-time faculty engaged in research, the creation of expensive research libraries, and the charging of high tuition to pay the costs of research. The complaint by the Massachusetts School of Law prompted the Antitrust Division of the Department of Justice in July 1994 to commence a civil investigation of the ABA's accreditation process, particularly its prohibition on proprietary law schools. Meanwhile, on April 23, 1994, Congressman Marty Meehan of Massachusetts introduced H.R. 4285, which would have required states to permit graduates of both ABA accredited and state accredited law schools to sit for the bar exam. That same month, a group of 14 deans of national law schools, including Harvard, Stanford, Chicago, Virginia and Pennsylvania, launched an attack against the ABA standards as intolerant of diversity in legal education and called for the formation of an organization of deans to address the problems in the ABA accreditation process.

Another of the targets of the antitrust actions was the ABA's standard relating to faculty salaries. The Justice Department's argument was that the accreditation process was dominated by law professors who took turns conducting site evaluations of each other's campuses and demanding that salaries at the evaluated campuses be increased, a kind of price fixing scheme by law professors. The ABA repealed the standard relating to salaries at its midyear meeting as well.

Julie Greenberg, who was the elected faculty chair during the 1994-95 academic year, believed (correctly) that an application for ABA approval would require that we have a permanent dean in place. She approached me one day in the spring to ask whether I would be willing to remain in the dean's office. I told her that I would be willing to stay in order to keep alive the movement toward ABA accreditation, but only if the faculty recommended it. I had been appointed acting dean by the administration, but I would not accept a longer appointment unless I had the complete support of the faculty.

Julie Greenberg served as the elected faculty chair during the critical year when the law school decided to apply for ABA accreditation and served as associate dean for faculty development from 2003 to 2005. She is pictured at the 1996 commencement exercises, where Jan Dauss is assisting her with her gown and hood.

Deciding Not to Apply

After Jack Grosse's visit, it seemed as if our drive toward ABA accreditation had unstoppable momentum. And then our momentum stopped. In late February, Jack Monks called me with the bad news. The shareholders had discussed the issue of ABA accreditation extensively and had decided not to pursue it for any of the campuses. Perhaps someday they would reconsider, but for the foreseeable future the decision that they had made in 1988 never again to apply for ABA approval still stood.

The bad news continued. Jack also said that, because of the declining enrollment, the shareholders had decided to eliminate six faculty positions in San Diego at the end of the academic year. Three of these would be the positions of the new legal writing instructors that we had hired at the beginning of the year. The other three were to be the positions of faculty members that I was authorized to select entirely at my discretion. If I declined to select them, then Jack would do so. Further, Jack told me that another two or three full-time faculty positions would be eliminated at the end of the next academic year as well.

*Marybeth and I share a laugh with alumnus Randy Grossman at
one of our semi-annual receptions for our graduates who passed
the bar exam. Randy, a highly successful sports attorney whose
clients include Dave Winfield, a former San Diego Padre inducted
into the Baseball Hall of Fame, served as president of the Alumni
Association and would later become our third alumnus to serve on
the Board of Trustees (after Denise Asher and Marc Adelman). Julie
Greenberg used the occasion of the spring 1995 reception to speak
with Jack Monks about the need for a permanent dean.*

Our next faculty meeting was grim. I reported the news that the
shareholders had decided not to apply for ABA accreditation. We
discussed what we should do next. It was really gratifying to see a
faculty that, as recently as a year ago, had been badly divided over the
issue of ABA accreditation now unified in its support for an application.
After several suggestions were made, Ellen Waldman offered her
solution. "The problem," she said, "is that we need new owners."

Searching for New Owners

Ellen was right. The time had come to find new owners for the law school.

I began looking for private colleges and universities in the region that lacked a law school. My pitch was that the San Diego campus was profitable and would be more so as an ABA approved law school. The shareholders thus owned an asset that was worth less to them as a state accredited law school than it would be to a parent institution that allowed it to obtain ABA accreditation. A new parent could pay the shareholders the full amount that the law school was worth to them as a state accredited law school and thereby acquire an asset that, following ABA approval, would be worth far more than the new parent had paid. I believed that the shareholders would be willing to sell the San Diego campus in order to raise funds to finance a bid for ABA accreditation of an Orange County campus or to start a new campus in another location where no competition from an ABA approved law school existed.

In March, I met with Dean Joseph Olszewski of Webster University, a Missouri-based university with a branch campus in San Diego. After some internal discussion, however, Webster decided that my proposal did not fit within its long range plan. In July, I met with the president of Point Loma Nazarene University, James Bond, whose name I could not say without smiling. Point Loma had a very strong Christian identity and we both concluded that it was not a good home for a law school the faculty of which represented a much broader spectrum of perspectives on religious faith. I continued to look for other potential parent institutions.

Meanwhile, as I continued to search for new owners, the shareholders held a retreat in Palm Springs on April 7 and 8, 1995, to discuss the future of the college and, in particular, its declining enrollments. By the time of the shareholders' retreat, enrollment in San Diego had fallen to 601 students and was projected to decrease again in the fall. In fact, it would drop to 571 in the fall, compared with 734 in fall 1993, just two years earlier, when the National students arrived, and 673 in fall 1992, the year before the National students arrived. We still had a significant number of National students enrolled, which meant that, once the remaining National students graduated, our enrollment would fall even more.

I was invited to attend the morning session of the second day of the retreat. When I arrived, I was directed to a seat around a quadrangle of tables on which were spread innumerable reports and papers with enrollment and financial data. I listened to a discussion already in progress, saying nothing. Finally, Dick Leavitt turned to me and said, "Ken, you always have a lot to say. Why are you so quiet? What ideas do you have?" Everyone turned and looked at me. I started to talk about the need to apply for ABA approval, but Dick cut me off. "No, no," he said. "We don't want to talk about ABA approval right now. What ideas besides ABA approval do you have?" I replied, "You are meeting here because you have a serious enrollment problem. I've already told you how to solve your problem and you've rejected my solution. There is no other solution. If you don't want to take my advice and save the school, then I have nothing left to say." Then I fell silent. The entire room stayed quiet for several seconds as everyone continued to stare at me. Finally, Dick said, "OK. Tell us one more time why we should apply for ABA approval." I launched into a monologue, pouring out every argument I had. The shareholders asked me a number of questions and then excused me.

Deciding to Apply After All

The next day, upon arriving at the office, I found a message to call Jack. When I reached him, his first words to me were, "Ken! You did it!" "Did what?" I asked. "I don't know how," he replied, "but you talked them into it. We are going to apply for ABA approval. It may not happen right away. It may not happen this year. But we are going to do it. It is going to happen." Then he cautioned me to tell no one. I hung up the phone and called Marybeth to tell her.

One of the immediate benefits of the Palm Springs decision was that the order to fire six faculty members was suspended, pending further deliberations about the timing of the decision to apply for ABA approval. I had not told the faculty that six of them were two months from being fired, fearing that it would generate both a panic and a general bloodletting as everyone scrambled to avoid being one of the six whose position would be eliminated. I kept hoping that somehow I could change the shareholders' minds.

Although we now had a decision in principle to apply for ABA approval, the college was not taking any immediate steps toward an application. Nor was it clear when we would take any such steps. Rather, the focus was on cutting costs to deal with the immediate budgetary crisis attributable to declining enrollments.

At the end of May, we held our customary reception for our graduates who had passed the bar exam. Jack drove down from Fullerton, as he always did, to attend. I drew him aside and reminded him that I had agreed to serve as acting dean for only one year. I had not pressed the issue because we were actively discussing an application for ABA approval and a search would have broken our momentum. But now the year was up and it was time to start the search for a new dean, whom we needed to have in place prior to filing our application for ABA approval.

I also sent a memo to the faculty saying that it was time to begin the search for Mary Lynne's successor. Meanwhile, Julie Greenberg spoke with Jack at the same reception about the need for a permanent dean if the law school were to apply for provisional approval. Julie was thinking a few moves ahead and wanted a permanent dean in place in the event that the shareholders did agree to an application.

In June, Jack notified me that the possibility of terminating the positions of the three legal writing instructors was still under consideration. He invited Linda Berger and me to travel to Fullerton to meet with the shareholders and to plead for the jobs of the three legal writing instructors. The tragedy was that the legal writing instructors were very poorly compensated and thus eliminating these positions would save very little money, while disrupting three lives, substantially reducing our teaching capacity, and destroying our first year legal writing program. Linda collected data on the legal writing program, which she gave me. I studied the data and thought of an idea for a chart that would provide an argument for retaining the program.

When Linda and I arrived, we found that the shareholders had also invited members of the Orange County faculty to plead the case for their counterpart program. When our turn to speak came, I pulled out a single piece of poster board with two bar graphs. One showed our attrition rate before we created the legal writing program and the other our attrition rate after we created the legal writing program. We made a single brief point: in the year since we hired the legal writing instructors, our attrition rate had fallen enough that the money that we had saved by retaining these additional students had paid for the instructors' salaries and had increased the college's profits. The difference in attrition rates actually amounted to only a tiny handful of students (and, to be candid, we could not prove that the reduction in attrition rates was attributable to the legal writing program). The legal writing instructors, however, were so poorly paid that even a handful of students contributed enough tuition to cover their salaries. Thus, we argued, if the college eliminated the program, its earnings would diminish. After the faculty members left the meeting, the shareholders decided to leave the San Diego program fully funded.

Julie continued to be concerned about the need for a permanent dean, in the event of an application for ABA approval. I was unwilling to accept the deanship, however, unless I had full faculty support. Julie, as faculty chair, polled the fifteen members of the faculty and found that ten members of the faculty wanted to recommend that I be appointed the permanent dean immediately, while four members wanted the faculty to meet to discuss the matter before making a recommendation and one did not respond to the poll. No one was opposed to the appointment. The four who wanted a meeting felt strongly that a meeting should occur, however. Accordingly, on June 22, Julie sent a memo to the faculty calling a special meeting to discuss what the faculty should report to Jack about the deanship. On July 6, while I was absent from the room, the faculty voted unanimously by secret ballot to recommend that I be appointed as the permanent dean. Julie reported the faculty's vote to Jack Monks and to me.

Meanwhile, the discussion of the budget continued. I was invited to travel to Fullerton for a meeting on June 30, the last day of the fiscal year, at which the final decisions on the next year's budget would be made.

As it happened, three days before the meeting, on June 27, the Justice Department announced that it had entered into a consent decree with the ABA resolving the antitrust investigation. The consent decree required that the prohibition on accrediting proprietary schools and the standard relating to faculty salaries both be abolished, although in fact the ABA had already eliminated both in February. Including these prohibitions in the consent decree precluded the ABA from restoring the prohibited standards later. Another term of the consent decree required a review of the entire ABA accreditation process.

When we assembled in Fullerton on June 30, we started working through the budget, looking for costs that could be reduced. After a time, we took a break. As everyone milled about, I asked the shareholders if they had heard about the consent decree. Everyone had. Then I said, "We are missing our opportunity here. You are all worried that the ABA does not really want to accredit proprietary law schools, but now for the first time ever you have the Justice Department watching over the ABA to make sure that proprietary law schools are treated fairly. If you are ever going to get a fair hearing, it is now." I also reminded them that the ABA could no longer consider faculty salaries in connection with its accreditation decision. The WSU faculty was paid well below the faculty at ABA accredited law schools and the shareholders did not wish to award enormous raises to the entire faculty in order to apply for ABA approval. Now they would not have to spend hundreds of thousands of dollars on salary increases as the price of applying for provisional approval.

Everyone stopped what they were doing and began looking around the room at each other. They all realized that I was right. In an instant, the entire mood of the room changed. With almost no discussion, the shareholders quickly reached a decision to allow the San Diego campus to separate from WSU and to apply for ABA approval immediately. I sat in stunned disbelief as the shareholders, Jack Monks and Joel Goodman discussed the details of how and when the announcement would be made. June 30 was a Friday and so Independence Day was the following Tuesday. The consensus was that many people would be on vacation during the upcoming weekend and that the announcement should be made on July 5, when more people would notice it.

On July 5, as planned, Jack announced internally that the San Diego campus would separate from Western State University, adopt a new name, and apply for ABA approval in the fall. The college made a public announcement on July 6. On July 10, Jack announced that

I had accepted an appointment as dean of the San Diego campus. I asked Marybeth to remain as associate dean and she agreed to do so.

The student newspaper announces our 1995 decision to apply for ABA accreditation.

One of the ABA standards limited the use of adjunct faculty. Jack Grosse had told us that we should have no adjunct faculty teaching any first year courses and that we should ensure that at least two-thirds of our courses in both the day and the evening divisions were taught by full-time faculty. Marybeth went through the schedule with an axe, eliminating adjunct taught courses and in some cases replacing them with sections taught by full-time faculty. We had no one to teach a section of Civil Procedure scheduled to be taught by an adjunct on Friday night and so I volunteered to teach it. I was already scheduled to teach a section of Constitutional Law during the day on Tuesdays and Thursdays. As a result, I would be teaching a large section of two different required courses during our application for ABA approval. In other words, I would be carrying more than the equivalent of a full-time teaching load at most ABA approved law schools, while continuing to serve as dean during the accreditation process. On July 7, two days after we had announced our decision to apply for ABA approval, we sent a letter to the students notifying them of Marybeth's revised schedule, which effectively required many of them to reregister for their fall courses.

The student reaction to the announcement was wildly enthusiastic. We saw none of the criticism that accompanied WSU's announcement in 1984 that it was seeking ABA approval. When classes resumed in the fall, I held two open fora for students. An article in a fall 1995 edition of *The Advocate* reported that "the theme dominating both sessions was the status of the school's ABA application." As *The Advoctate* described the meeting, "the tone of both questions and answers was positive and upbeat, reflecting the enthusiasm that both administration and students share as together we all work toward making the campus of Thomas Jefferson School of Law an ABA campus prepared to compete nationally."

10

Adopting a New Name

The same day that we announced the new fall schedule, we also announced that we were conducting a contest to name the law school. Because only one Western State University College of Law would be ABA accredited initially, I had argued to the shareholders, we needed to rename one of the campuses to avoid confusing potential applicants. I insisted that the ABA would disapprove of two identically named law schools, only one of which was accredited. While it clearly was important to avoid consumer confusion and the ABA would be concerned about that, I had additional reasons for wanting us to change our name. One was that, like our accrediting agencies, I was never comfortable with a name that implied that we were a state supported institution and that we taught disciplines other than law. Our name seemed misleading. Further, the WSU name was well established in San Diego as the name of a state accredited law school. I thought that a new name would give us the opportunity to create a new identity as an ABA accredited law school. Holding a contest would be a fun way to give everyone at the law school an opportunity to feel personally involved in the great adventure that we were undertaking and might well produce a better name than any other process.

Because the shareholders were proud of WSU, openly criticizing the name did not seem like the best approach. So I rested my argument for a new name solely on the genuine need to avoid confusion. At one point, one of the shareholders suggested that the San Diego campus keep the WSU name and that we rename the Orange County campuses, but I argued that WSU had longer, deeper roots in Orange County than in San Diego and that the WSU identity should be preserved in Orange County. The shareholders accepted that argument.

Although the shareholders regarded any decision about a new name for the law school to be within their sole discretion, they had no objection to receiving suggestions. Consistent with creating a more participatory atmosphere, I wanted everyone to have an opportunity to suggest names. The contest to name the school offered that opportunity.

Our most important challenge in coming years would be to recruit strong entering classes. We had begun our revolution in San Diego by transforming the faculty. The next step was to transform the student body. We would need stronger entering classes to meet ABA standards and to raise our bar passage rate, which was also necessary to satisfy ABA standards. Thus, in my mind, the most important criterion in choosing a new name was its usefulness in recruiting students. Law schools generally are named after an individual or a location. I thought that few students were likely to attend a law school merely because it was named after a particular individual, but they would be drawn to a particular location. For that reason, I wanted a name that emphasized our beautiful San Diego location. I suggested San Diego College of Law. Jack Monks told me, however, that most of the names that included geographic references sounded too much like the names of other law schools already in existence, including the University of San Diego, California Western and a number of state accredited or unaccredited law schools.

By July 25, we had received suggestions of about 70 names. Many of the names did emphasize geography and used terms such as San Diego, California, Pacific, Southern, Western, Frontier and even San Andreas in various combinations. Others identified the law school with a particular person, including James Madison, Earl Warren, Sandra Day O'Connor, William Rehnquist, Roger Traynor, Stanley Mosk, Clarence Darrow, Richard Henry Dana, Juan Rodriguez Cabrillo, Vasco Nunez de Balboa, Clara Shortridge Foltz, and Oliver S. Witherby. Three or four people suggested naming the law school after me or after both Marybeth and me. One student noted that if we named it after Bill Slomanson (William Slomanson University), the initials could remain the same. Another student suggested "Bolt Hall," a name that both invited comparison to the law school at UC Berkeley (Boalt Hall) and honored the San Diego Chargers. My favorite suggestion came from Aaron Schwabach. Satirizing the admonition that we avoid confusion with other law schools in the region, he cleverly suggested California Western State University of San Diego.

The student newspaper, *The Advocate,* published its own list of about 70 names, one of which was Jefferson School of Law. *The Advocate* even ran a poem called, "The Contest." The poem read,

There once was a Dean that so dared,

To unmask a dream that we've shared;

The time has now come, to give him the thumb,

We're ecstatic that he really cared!

The *Advocate's* "the" place to state,
The names that have surfaced to date;
Back from vacation, on accreditation,
I am pleased to resurface this date.

We've been asked to dispense a creation,
A name that will sound through the nation;
We must tender our best, in this appellation contest.
As we move now toward Application.

One of the best that has nary
A doubt that is contrary,
Providing some pomp, with a name that would romp.
Is the College of Kenneth and Mary.

Then there's the best of them all,
For those who cherish football;
Would it be such a fad, like the school hailed by Had,
To bring to the south a Bolt Hall?

And now that I've tendered this rhyme,
Make certain that you take the time,
To consider my musing, with serious perusing,
Your entries will make the school chime.

The poem captured the spirit of that time. So many people had dreamed for so long of obtaining ABA accreditation for the law school. At last we had the opportunity to prove that we were as capable as we claimed to be. Like the contest, our impending drive for accreditation would be a shared venture, drawing faculty, staff and students alike into participation in a common enterprise.

Jan Dauss, my executive assistant, forwarded all of the suggested names to Jack Monks as we received them and I tried to obtain as much information as I could about the names that were most under consideration. At one point, I attended a meeting with Jack and Joel Goodman at which we discussed the name of the law school. Joel suggested the names of Thomas Jefferson and Benjamin Franklin, because both were revered Founding Fathers who had no law school named after them. I said regarding Franklin that I thought it would be odd to name a law school after a man who was not a lawyer. Jefferson was both a lawyer and the founder of university-based legal education in America, to say nothing of his authorship of the Declaration of Independence, his two term presidency and his founding of the University of Virginia. While Jefferson had owned slaves, so had Franklin (although not remotely as many).

Jack apparently liked Joel's idea of naming the law school after Jefferson and began to use Jefferson's name on internal planning documents. On April 4, Jack circulated a memorandum suggesting "Jefferson Pacific School of Law," believing that we should name the law school after a famous individual and refer to the law school's location as well. I was pleased to see a name with a geographic reference.

Dick Leavitt had always greatly admired Thomas Jefferson and, by coincidence, he independently urged the other members of the board to name the law school after Jefferson. With Dick strongly advocating adoption of the name and with support from Jack and Joel, a consensus among the shareholders to name the law school after Jefferson quickly formed.

Even our colleagues in Orange County were drawn into the exhilaration of our impending accreditation application. After the shareholders chose our new name, the faculty at the WSU Irvine campus gave us a portrait of Thomas Jefferson in honor of the occasion. We hung the portrait of Thomas Jefferson at the entrance to the law school as a daily reminder, as we embarked on our historic quest, that we had claimed the legacy of a revolutionary.

We adopted our new name for internal purposes effective August 15, although it was not publicly announced until later because we needed time to order stationery and change the signage on the building. The year before, as a cost saving move, WSU had eliminated the position of receptionist in San Diego and our telephones now were answered by someone in Orange County. Prior to the public announcement of our new name, we also needed to hire a receptionist who could answer the telephone in San Diego using our new name.

On August 16, I circulated a memo announcing internally that the board had approved a new name. The choice, however, drew some criticism. The principal objection was to the fact that Jefferson had owned slaves, one of whom was widely believed to be the mother of some of his children. Many expressed the concern that African-American students would not want to attend a law school named after a slave owner and I have no doubt that the name did discourage some potential applicants. As it happened, however, I would later discover, in speaking with prospective students at recruitment conferences, that the Thomas Jefferson name also was a draw for some applicants who admired his political philosophy or other aspects of his life.

Because people often asked about the name, I created materials that described the ways in which Jefferson's legacy reflected the values of our law school. Jefferson's name was synonymous with intellectual accomplishment. His Declaration of Independence, with its appeals to liberty, equality and democracy, articulated the fundamental values that underlay our political and legal systems. He was a practicing lawyer and he had been responsible for the appointment of the first law professor in the United States.

The geographic names that I preferred all had been rejected because they were thought to be too similar to the names of other area law schools and might cause confusion. The supreme irony, however, was that, after the name Thomas Jefferson School of Law was chosen, we learned that a correspondence law school with the very same name had operated in California from 1970 to 1987. When we formally notified the CBE of our name change in October 1995, a CBE official advised us that the CBE already had received phone calls from the public asking for clarification of the relationship between our law school and the correspondence school. To make matters worse, some graduates of the correspondence school were still doggedly taking the California bar exam, without passing. So, for a couple of years, we had to endure the humiliation of seeing another Thomas Jefferson School of Law listed semi-annually as having a 0 percent bar pass rate, until the last of these graduates eventually abandoned their efforts to pass the bar exam.

11

Preparing for the ABA Site Evaluation

Despite all the work that had been done since 1991 to bring the San Diego campus into compliance with ABA standards, the reality was that, at the moment that the decision was made to apply for ABA approval, the campus was not yet compliant with many of the standards relating to the academic program, the campus, and finances. With a site evaluation only months away, we would have in essence one semester to cure all of these deficiencies and to resolve any issues relating to our separation from the main campus or to our proprietary status.

Drafting the Self-Study

Our application for ABA approval required that we draft a very detailed self-study, describing the law school and critically analyzing its program. Prior to our 1994 WASC inspection, Mary Lynne had appointed a faculty committee to draft a self-study several months before it was due. The committee met regularly but discovered that it was extremely difficult for a committee to draft a document. A few days before the self-study was due to be submitted to WASC, the committee produced the document. Mary Lynne took it home to read and then called me to say that the document that emerged from the faculty committee was not usable in its existing form. Some members of the committee had not adequately researched their areas of responsibility nor had they really attempted to evaluate the law school's program critically. Rather, the document read like a student recruitment brochure – descriptive, self-congratulatory and not very detailed. Over the next few days, Mary Lynne sequestered herself in her home, revising the self-study and periodically calling Shari, Jan or me to obtain some bit of information that she needed.

The ABA self-study would need to be far more detailed than the WASC self-study, would need to address the ABA's standards rather than WASC's, and would need to represent our very best effort because it would form the site evaluation team's first impression of the law school. Further, we would have only a single semester to produce it. We could not risk having another document that would need extensive revision at the last minute. So, in early September, I set aside a few days, stayed home and wrote a complete self-study, a document of more than 250 pages in length, from cover to cover.

The self-study was supposed to be the product of collective deliberation. Accordingly, I appointed a self-study committee, chaired by Julie Greenberg and Shari O'Brien and comprising four faculty members, four staff members and four students. On September 14, I transmitted my draft to the committee and told them that the document was merely a proposed first draft. The committee was invited to make any changes it wished. It could add, delete, or modify the language in any way that it chose. It could rewrite the self-study entirely if it wished. Changes would be given directly to Jan to be inserted into the document without my knowledge or approval. By providing the committee with much or all the information that it would need in written form, however, I hoped to expedite the research process and to allow the committee to focus on evaluation rather than description.

Jan modified the document as she received the changes from the committee members. Once the committee had revised the document to its satisfaction, the entire document was made available to the faculty, which was invited to suggest to the committee other changes. When this process was completed, the faculty voted to adopt the self-study. I sent the self-study to Jack Grosse, who said that it was excellent and one of the best that he had ever seen.

The process was not perfect, but it did produce a successful document that seemed to reflect the consensus of the faculty. More than 15 years later, the document that I wrote in 1995 remains in use. It has been revised and updated prior to each subsequent inspection, but no one has ever proposed that we discard it and write an entirely new one using a different process.

The application process also required that we produce a feasibility study, demonstrating that the law school would be successful academically and financially as an ABA approved law school. We had no money to hire a consultant to produce the report and time was short. Fortunately, we had as a model the study that Tony Santoro had sent me and so we at least knew what such a study needed to include. I performed the necessary research and wrote a 48 page feasibility study that met ABA requirements.

Day after day, Jan worked late into the evening compiling the massive collection of documents necessary for our application. These included the self-study, the feasibility study, an annual questionnaire, a site evaluation questionnaire, and two volumes of attachments to the site evaluation questionnaire. The stack of documents was about six inches high and she would have to repeat the process of preparing these documents each year for the next five years.

Meeting with the ABA Consultant

During the summer, I had notified Jim White informally of our decision to apply for ABA approval. He told me then that he would like to schedule a visit to our campus in September. I called Jack Grosse for advice about the visit and Jack told me that Jim's purpose in coming was to evaluate me. He said that Jim might look at the facility and speak to a few people, but that he was there mainly to take the measure of the dean.

Jim came on September 27 and 28 and fulfilled Jack's prediction. I gave Jim a tour of the campus and offered to introduce him to members of the faculty and staff, but he did not want a structured schedule and he met few other people. Rather, he spent most of his time talking with me, asking questions about the law school and answering my questions about the accreditation process.

Because Jim had been the ABA consultant when WSU applied unsuccessfully in 1986, I wanted to hear his perspective on that application and to know what had gone wrong. He told me that the problem in the 1980s was that the ABA had the impression that WSU was too concerned with profits and not concerned enough with the quality of the education. He told me an anecdote about his pre-inspection visit to the Fullerton campus, when he had been met at the airport by Bill Lawless. Lawless was driving an expensive car, a Cadillac or a Lincoln, and Jim, trying to make small talk and break the ice, had praised the car. Lawless, however, had objected, saying that the owners of the school had promised him a "luxury car, like a Mercedes," but had instead provided him with what he regarded as a lesser car. When Jim finished the story, I was glad that I had met him at the airport in my 15 year old Fiat.

Jim told me that he was very impressed by the scholarly productivity of the faculty, that our academic program was well structured and that our academic policies would not be an issue. The scholarly productivity of the faculty and the structuring of the academic program, of course, all were the product of the efforts from 1991 through 1994 to transform both the faculty and the academic program. Jim said that he was also impressed by our dedication to the night program, which was taught extensively by full-time faculty rather than adjuncts, the result of Marybeth's massive revision of the schedule in July.

The major issues during our inspection, he said, would be whether Thomas Jefferson was truly independent from WSU and whether Thomas Jefferson had adequate resources to provide a program of legal education that met the standards. Jim urged me to make sure that the separation was complete and said that our application would be denied if it appeared that Thomas Jefferson was being managed by WSU, even if indirectly. Rather than trying to discourage us, Jim urged us to do everything right the first time and to obtain accreditation on the first application. He warned me that nothing would be worse than to be rejected.

ABA standards required that a law school own its campus and that it have adequate space for future expansion. Although we had expanded our campus as recently as the year before, when we took over the third floor of the building, our library was still quite small and unable to accommodate the significant expansion of our collection that would be necessary to gain ABA approval.

As luck would have it, located at 2120 San Diego Avenue, on the east side of San Diego Avenue directly across the street from our campus, was an office building called the Gann Professional Building. It was owned by Ed Gann, who had built a fortune in the tuna fishing industry. In the 1990s, he owned 25 percent of the Chicken-of-the-Sea tuna company. Gann operated his tuna fleet out of the building and leased some of the space to tenants. Then in his 70s, he was ready to sell the building as he began to move toward retirement. The Gann building had been on the market for more than a year.

The building was configured as a quadrangle around a charming courtyard and was ideal for our use. We needed the space desperately and the courtyard would provide an outdoor gathering place where students could enjoy the wonderful San Diego weather. One of the most interesting features of the building was a chart room, where Gann kept navigational charts and radio equipment for communicating with his fleet of some 50 tuna boats. Gann's enormous, wood-paneled office featured a private bathroom, a wet bar, and a spectacular view of the San Diego skyline.

The charming courtyard of the Gann Professional Building provided an ideal gathering place for students, faculty and staff. Seated on the bench next to the planter are Marybeth Herald and K. J. Greene.

As early as my first meeting with them in September 1994, I had told the shareholders that we needed to buy the building. During Jim's visit, he toured the building and he agreed. He told me that we must complete the acquisition of the building before the site evaluation team arrived.

Jim and I discussed the fact that the law school had no tenure plan. He said that we must have a tenure plan in place before the inspection. We also discussed the fact that, as a proprietary law school, we had never sought alumni donations. Jim commented that it would be important to demonstrate alumni support and urged us to establish a nonprofit foundation that could accept alumni donations. Because the law school was for-profit, the nonprofit foundation could not be under the control of the law school or operated for the benefit of the law school, but it could engage in legitimate educational activities that might indirectly benefit the law school, such as awarding scholarships to students or purchasing books that would be available for use by students and faculty.

After Jim left, I asked Art Toll's son, Danny, who served as our outside legal counsel, to establish a nonprofit corporation that could accept tax deductible alumni donations. Danny did so and named it the Jeffersonian Law Foundation. I invited Hadley, Karla, Marybeth and one of our most distinguished alumni, Denise Asher, to serve along with me on the board of the foundation. Hadley was our longest serving faculty member and every alumnus or alumna of the law school knew him. Karla headed the library, which we expected to be a primary beneficiary of foundation expenditures. Denise, of course, represented the alumni. Marybeth and I were on the board so that we could keep track of what it was doing, particularly since its existence and activities were accreditation related.

Expanding the Faculty

Another potential obstacle to a successful application for accreditation was the small size of our faculty. As the fall 1995 semester began, we had only 17 full-time faculty members, including the dean, associate dean and librarian, which was very small for a law school with both day and evening divisions. Our four legal writing instructors had excellent credentials and carried the same teaching load as the full-time faculty, six courses per year. They did not have faculty appointments, however, and all but Linda were paid well below what the faculty was paid. I proposed that we grant the four of them faculty rank, which would address the problem of faculty size. The shareholders recalled how at the time of the failed 1986 application for ABA approval the faculty had resisted any reduction in the number of faculty and so they were reluctant to add faculty members who might need to be terminated in the event that this application failed. I told the shareholders that the size of the faculty could be a critical issue and that we could solve it quickly by giving these four individuals faculty appointments and salary increases. The irony was that, only weeks before, the shareholders had been ready to terminate the legal writing program. Now the legal writing instructors might be an indispensable element in our accreditation. We argued at length and finally the shareholders said that I could grant the instructors faculty appointments, but under no circumstances could I increase their salaries. I replied that this was enormously unfair. During our inspection, we were going to count the four legal writing instructors as full-time faculty members, while refusing to pay three of them as such. The shareholders reminded me that the ABA could no longer ask about salaries during an inspection. That, of course, did not change the unfairness.

With great embarrassment, I told the legal writing instructors about the compromise and promised that I would fight again for higher salaries the following year. All of them said quite graciously that they understood the situation.

Faculty appointments required faculty approval and so I proposed that the faculty approve appointment of the legal writing instructors to the faculty. Several faculty members objected that this was inconsistent with our policy of nationwide recruiting, which Mary Lynne and I both had advocated for so long. It was indeed inconsistent with that policy, but our immediate situation was extraordinary. The debate stretched over a period of months as the legal writing instructors wondered what was taking so long. At one point, we lost a critical vote. When Marybeth and I met to discuss the next step, I told her that the only solution was to vote again. We put the issue on the agenda for the next meeting and continued to argue our case. At the next meeting, we had the votes we needed and I was able to appoint all four individuals to the faculty.

Many law schools were known to treat very poorly those instructors who taught legal writing and so, during the inspection, our legal writing faculty would be asked about their treatment by the law school. The team was impressed by our program and praised us for using full-time faculty members to teach all legal writing courses. Apparently, none of the legal writing faculty mentioned how shabbily we had treated them with respect to salaries. After we received provisional approval, I told the shareholders about the loyalty of our legal writing faculty and insisted that they be paid the same salaries as the rest of the faculty. This time, the shareholders agreed and we cured the salary disparity that year.

The fact that our legal writing program was taught by full-time, tenure-track faculty members distinguished us from most law schools and earned our program much praise from ABA site evaluation teams over the years. We continued to add more full-time faculty to teach legal writing and by 2004 *U.S. News and World Report* ranked our legal writing program sixteenth in the nation.

Although we have continued to this day to use full-time faculty to teach legal writing courses, the model of using such faculty exclusively became unsustainable very quickly. As early as the fall of 1996, only a year after the legal writing instructors received faculty appointments, I sent a memo to the faculty noting that, as our enrollment grew, we would need more sections of legal writing than we could staff with the four legal writing faculty members that we had. One solution was to add more legal writing faculty, which was the preferred solution of most of those who taught legal writing, but adding enough such faculty to cover every section would have precluded us from hiring faculty to teach other subjects. As will be discussed below, however, the ABA regarded the narrowness of our curriculum as a serious accreditation concern. Plainly, we could not ignore every subject but legal writing. In order to avoid having any adjuncts teach a first year subject, I proposed that the faculty reschedule Legal Writing II as a course to be taken in the second year, so that it could be taught by adjunct faculty. We had enough full-time faculty at that time to teach all of the Legal Writing I courses. Another advantage of the proposal was that, in combination with the upper level writing requirement, it would give students a significant writing experience in each of their three years of law school. The suggestion was vociferously opposed by most of the legal writing faculty, who noted, quite correctly of course, that students should master the skills taught in Legal Writing II during their first year. The faculty as a whole, however, accepted my argument that we could not afford to staff all the sections with full-time faculty and we could not have adjuncts teaching in the first year. After we received full approval, the faculty would return the Legal Writing II course to the first year, but, even with the hiring of several additional legal writing faculty members, we did not have enough full-time faculty members to teach both Legal Writing I and Legal Writing II. Thus, we continued to use adjuncts to teach Legal Writing II.

Linda Berger proposed a legal writing program that we inaugurated in 1994 and that, exactly ten years later, was ranked 16th in the nation. Yet, less than a year after the program began, she and I had to travel to the main campus to persuade the shareholders not to terminate the program.

Adopting a Tenure Plan

Jim White had made clear during my meeting with him that we needed to adopt a tenure plan. This requirement, however, raised a number of politically sensitive issues. When WSU applied for ABA approval in 1986, it adopted a tenure plan that would take effect upon receipt of provisional approval, which, of course, the college never received.

Some of those who were on the faculty at the time later insisted that they had complained to the shareholders about the lack of tenure and had been told that they should not worry because they had "*de facto* tenure*.*" These senior faculty members believed that they had employment rights arising out of those assurances and they did not want to adopt any tenure plan that gave them less than they believed that they already had. The shareholders, however, denied that they had ever told the faculty that they had any form of tenure.

After the failed 1986 application, the faculty in San Diego continued to look for ways to persuade the shareholders to adopt the tenure plan drafted in the 1980s. The faculty decided that one way to achieve that goal was to adopt the plan by faculty resolution and to operate under it. They hoped that, when the shareholders saw how well the plan operated in practice, they might be more amenable to adopting it formally. Accordingly, on January 11, 1991, the faculty passed a resolution adopting the tenure plan. They also declared that all who were on the faculty during the prior accreditation application process were tenured under the plan. This was the entire full-time faculty, except Maureen Markey, who had joined the faculty in fall 1990, and potentially me, who at that time was holding an offer and trying to decide whether to join the faculty. Because it was not recognized by the shareholders, the tenure plan provided the law school with a procedure for terminating the employment of faculty members hired in 1990 or later, without offering anyone any additional security. Adoption of the plan, however, did serve the valuable purpose of establishing a system of peer review. Further, the new tenure plan required publication and so it was a way of encouraging the faculty to publish. Four members of the faculty would eventually apply successfully for tenure under the plan, although, of course, the grant of tenure was not recognized by the college.

In the fall of 1995, when the issue of the tenure plan arose, the senior faculty insisted that the shareholders approve the tenure plan adopted by the faculty in 1991 and recognize the tenure of all of those senior faculty members who had been granted tenure by the 1991 faculty resolution. By this time, however, fewer than half of the faculty were covered by the 1991 resolution. Thus, most of the faculty had little stake in the plan adopted in 1991, although they recognized that some of the senior faculty felt strongly about the issue and they hesitated to divide the faculty over it. Accordingly, in fall 1995, the faculty adopted a resolution stating that the only tenure plan acceptable to the faculty was the 1991 plan. At the end of August, I sent a memo to the shareholders urging them to adopt the 1991 plan, noting that it had been in successful operation for four years, and that four members of the faculty had been evaluated under it.

The shareholders intensely disliked the 1991 tenure plan because they believed that, at 32 pages, it was far too long and far too complicated, and they feared that the plan, in the event of a tenure denial, would invite interpretive disputes, allegations of noncompliance by the college, and litigation. The shareholders said that they were willing to adopt a tenure plan if to do so was absolutely necessary, but they wanted it to be simple and easily understood by all. They also were adamantly opposed to granting tenure to anyone except as a result of peer review under the new plan. In other words, they refused to recognize the 1991 faculty resolution granting tenure to all of the senior faculty.

With the faculty refusing to consider any plan other than the 1991 plan, the shareholders decided that they would take the initiative to draft a plan. Mel Sherman was friends with Tom Brennan, the president of Thomas Cooley Law School, and asked him for a copy of the Thomas Cooley tenure plan. He also asked Jack Grosse for a copy of the Northern Kentucky plan. Then Mel drafted his own tenure plan, composed of provisions drawn from those two plans, although with important modifications. The plan was short and easily understood and the shareholders liked it.

Mel's efforts were laudable because they advanced the discussion, but his plan as drafted would not have been satisfactory to the faculty or the ABA. For example, it authorized the termination of a tenured faculty member for taking action disloyal to the law school. This provision could be construed as prohibiting members of the faculty from criticizing the law school, effectively destroying any possibility of faculty governance. It would also undermine academic freedom. For example, a faculty member might be terminated for counseling an applicant to attend a different law school that was better suited to the applicant's needs.

I asked Mel if he would object to my making some revisions to his plan and he very graciously said that he would not. I removed or revised the objectionable provisions. I also added language to address the concerns of the senior faculty. The new language exempted them from any obligation to apply for tenure and stated explicitly that adoption of the tenure plan did not affect any preexisting employment rights. In effect, the senior faculty could simply opt out of the new tenure plan, if they wished, refusing to apply for tenure under the plan and relying on the "*de facto* tenure" that they believed that they already had. The plan also provided that the senior faculty, if they did apply, would be held to a lower standard than the junior faculty with respect to scholarly publication, a recognition of the fact that most of the senior faculty had published little or nothing in their careers.

At a November 9 meeting, I presented my revision of Mel's plan to the shareholders. They really did not want to adopt any tenure plan. They believed that tenure was merely a shelter for the unproductive and the mediocre. I repeated Jim White's advice that we must have a tenure plan. Jack Grosse told them the same thing. I noted that all ABA approved law schools had a tenure plan and asked them whether they really wanted to destroy their chances of obtaining ABA accreditation over this one issue. With visibly pained expressions, they adopted my revised version of Mel's tenure plan.

To their credit, however, once they adopted the tenure plan, the shareholders implemented it with complete integrity. Over the next six years, until they sold the law school, they followed the recommendation of the faculty and the dean with respect to every single tenure recommendation, whether to grant or to deny tenure. They believed that the faculty and the dean were the best judges of the qualifications and performance of a faculty member. After they granted tenure to a faculty member, they always told me with utter sincerity to extend to that faculty member their warmest congratulations. They saw, from my memoranda recommending members of the faculty for tenure, that our faculty members were working hard and achieving distinction and they were pleased to acknowledge those accomplishments.

I notified the faculty that the shareholders had approved a tenure plan and circulated copies of it. This development should have been a moment of celebration. After a decade of discussion, the San Diego campus finally was one vote of the faculty away from a system of tenure. The reaction, however, was far from celebratory. Some senior members of the faculty were angry that the plan did not confer tenure on them immediately and that they would be required to publish before receiving tenure. I called a special meeting of the faculty at 11:45 a.m. on November 14 to discuss the tenure plan approved by the shareholders. The meeting ended without reaching a decision. A second meeting was called at 11:45 the next day and again it concluded without a resolution. The faculty reconvened at 9 o'clock that evening to continue the discussion. Various motions were made to exempt some or all of the senior faculty from at least some requirements of the tenure plan. For example, one motion would have permitted all who had been full-time members of the faculty for at least 15 years to apply for tenure without having to satisfy any publication requirement. All such motions were defeated. A motion that the faculty take no action regarding the tenure plan also was defeated. Finally, at 10:30 in the evening, the faculty voted to adopt the plan approved by the shareholders.

The new tenure plan allowed any member of the faculty who already met the requirements for tenure to apply immediately for tenure. Because we had no tenured faculty to review the applicants, it also provided for assembling a committee of tenured faculty from other law schools to make recommendations with regard to this initial group of applicants. Those granted tenure under that process would evaluate future applicants. This particular mechanism was Jack Grosse's idea. Six members of the faculty indicated that they wished to apply immediately. At its December 5 meeting, the faculty decided that it would conduct its own peer review of the six applicants.

The faculty also adopted a new promotion policy that I had proposed. Our existing promotion policy based promotion on time in rank rather than demonstrated achievement and could potentially subject us to ridicule. Because promotion was purely honorific and conferred no additional rights on faculty members, the shareholders were content to let the faculty adopt a new promotion policy without any further approval from them. The new policy based promotion to each rank on the applicant's teaching, scholarship and service since the prior rank was achieved. In 1998, Ellen Waldman would propose, and the faculty would approve, a revision to require that promotion to full professor be deferred until after receipt of tenure, meaning that additional publications and evaluations after tenure would be necessary for promotion to full professor. This brought our policies in line with those at many other law schools.

I met with the shareholders later in December and reported that the faculty had adopted the tenure plan. When they learned that the faculty wanted to conduct its own peer review of the applicants, they agreed that that was the best approach and said that they would rather have an evaluation from the faculty than from the outside committee called for by the plan. The shareholders decided to ignore the provision of the plan calling for the outside committee and to accept the recommendations of the faculty. They also told me that they wanted to grant me tenure immediately and they did so. Because Thomas Jefferson would be a separate corporation following the separation, they would grant me tenure again the next month, after the separation. Over the next several weeks, the faculty conducted a peer review process and recommended tenure for Hadley Batchelder, Karla Castetter, Marybeth Herald, Bill Slomanson and me.

At its January 15 meeting, the governing board formally adopted the tenure plan that the shareholders had approved in December. The board then very graciously adopted a resolution stating that "Whereas, Kenneth J. Vandevelde is the founding Dean of Thomas Jefferson School of Law and has performed outstanding service to this college in preparing it for ABA consideration," the board was granting me the honor of being the first tenured faculty member of the Thomas Jefferson School of Law. The board also conferred tenure on the other four individuals recommended by the faculty.

The tenure plan adopted by the faculty and the board during the 1995-96 academic year remains in operation without change. In the early years, several faculty members wanted to propose changes to the tenure plan, but I feared that if we started modifying it in ways to better suit the faculty, the shareholders might propose their own modifications that would not be in the best interests of the law school. The faculty and I recommended against tenure for three applicants during the last half of the 1990s and none of those applicants received tenure. All applications for tenure submitted since 2000 have been granted. The governing board has always followed the recommendations of the faculty and dean regarding tenure.

Expanding the Library

We believed that the single greatest barrier to obtaining accreditation was the size of our library collection. Immediately after the shareholders' decision to apply for ABA approval, Karla Castetter and I agreed to ask Professor Joan Howland to serve as a consultant to help us identify the steps that we could take to bring the library into compliance with ABA standards. Joan was the law librarian at the University of Minnesota, having previously worked as a librarian at Harvard Law School, Stanford Law School, and UC-Berkeley Law School. She was also the chair of the ABA Law Libraries Committee.

Joan served brilliantly. Before she arrived, we largely knew what our problems were and we had a number of ideas for addressing them, but we did not know which of our many ideas would best advance us toward the goal of ABA accreditation. Joan conducted an extensive site inspection of the library from August 10 to August 12, 1995. On August 14, she sent me a letter praising the work of our librarians and stating that the library met most of the standards, but noting that she had four areas of concern: the small size of the collection, the small size of the staff, the inadequacy of our information technology, and our lack of space. She proposed specific steps for addressing each of the problems. For example, she proposed a detailed schedule of annual increases in our acquisitions budget, told us which technology to acquire immediately and which should be acquired over time, recommended the creation of particular positions on the library staff, and proposed a plan for expanding our library space. Joan's recommendations made tremendous sense. We sent her report to Jack Grosse, who concurred with it completely.

The shareholders believed that the inadequacy of the library had been the principal reason that WSU had failed in its 1986 application and they knew that our library would be a major vulnerability in our 1995 application. Joan had masterfully devised a set of recommendations that ensured that we did enough to earn provisional approval, while deferring some of the budgetary pain to future years. This was exactly the right approach for the shareholders and they agreed to everything that Joan proposed. Her advice provided us with our strategic plan for addressing our accreditation issues with respect to the library over the next six years. Building on Joan's recommendations, Karla developed a much more specific three-year plan for developing our collection, staff, facility and information technology. Every team that visited Thomas Jefferson praised Karla and her staff effusively for their ability to work wonders with the limited resources available to them. Thanks to Joan, Karla and the library staff, by the time we were ready to apply for full approval, the library would not be an issue at all.

One of the first steps in our effort to build the library was to lay claim to the books acquired from National University. As already noted, most of these had been stored at a facility in Mira Mesa for use in the event that WSU opened another campus somewhere. Our collection, however, was absurdly small, totaling only about 60,000 volumes, including microform equivalents, about 40,000 volumes smaller than we understood would be the minimum number acceptable to the ABA. The National University collection stored off campus included another approximately 20,000 volumes, although these almost entirely duplicated the collection on our campus. Thus, they would increase our volume count, but not our title count. Still, the volume count was important and anything we could do to raise it would improve our chances of gaining provisional approval. Accordingly, in our internal correspondence, I began to refer to the National University collection as part of the San Diego collection. Some in Orange County tried to lay claim to it as well, but I argued that the San Diego campus had assumed the burden of absorbing the National students on a moment's notice and had suffered the adverse impact on its bar passage rate of graduating those students and thus the San Diego campus was entitled to any benefit that derived from WSU's agreement with National. Gradually everyone recognized that obtaining provisional approval for the San Diego campus was in the best interests of all three campuses and they acquiesced in our claim to the books. This was the start of a phenomenal expansion in our collection, which grew from 60,000 volumes in 1994 to 225,000 volumes in 2001, when we received full approval. Our title count exploded, from 6,344 titles in 1994 to 119,000 titles in 2001.

The development of the library was one of the great satisfactions of the ABA accreditation process. When I first joined the faculty at WSU, the library collection was so small that I soon discovered that it was necessary to do all of my research at California Western. On one occasion shortly after my appointment to the faculty, I was in the WSU library and saw some books sitting in a trash can. They appeared to be current and in good condition. I asked Karla about them and she said that our shelf space was exhausted. Accordingly, whenever we acquired new books, we had to discard other books to make room on the shelves for the new books. The collection could change, but it could never grow. The memory of that moment and of the hours spent in the basement of the California Western law library served as a continuous reminder of some of what we were trying to accomplish in our efforts to obtain ABA approval.

Acquiring the Gann Professional Building

We clearly needed to acquire the Gann building. The ABA standards required that a law school have space for future expansion and our library already had insufficient space for its collection. We had considered a variety of alternative ways to store our books, such as storing them in closed stacks that we would create in the parking garage or storing them in an offsite location. All of these alternatives, however, would only accentuate just how inadequate our facility really was. Jim White had insisted during our meeting in September that we needed the Gann building in order to demonstrate that we had space for our future needs. In October, Jack Grosse sent word that he concurred with Jim White. Failing to acquire the building would have been a colossal error.

The shareholders were divided over acquiring the new building. Mel Sherman argued that we should not buy the building unless we absolutely had no choice and he still was not convinced that we had no choice. This was the same reaction that had greeted the tenure proposal: we will do this if we absolutely must do it, but first prove to us that we absolutely must do it. Mel worried that we would be denied accreditation and then would find ourselves the owners of a building for which we had no use. I sent a memorandum to the shareholders explaining why we needed to acquire the building immediately. In reaction to Mel's concerns, I said that he was attempting to hedge our bets. If the ABA saw that we were hedging our bets, it would perceive that we were not fully committed to obtaining accreditation. If we were not fully committed, then the ABA would doubt our intention to meet the standards over the long run. In short, anything less than a demonstration of a full commitment would undermine our application. I believed that it was precisely this kind of hedging of bets that had doomed WSU's 1986 application. Art Toll liked the building the moment that he saw it and argued that it would be a good asset for us. Dick Leavitt concurred. The two of them together persuaded Mel to agree to the purchase.

The law school acquired the Gann Professional Building in 1996 and renamed it the Courtyard Building.

By the end of the fall semester, we had reached agreement with Gann to acquire the building and an adjacent parking lot for $1.1 million, a bargain that I regarded as only slightly less favorable than

Jefferson's Louisiana Purchase. Only four years before, Gann had been asking $3.8 million for the building. In our self-study submitted in January, we were able to report that we were in escrow. When the site evaluation team arrived in February, the chair of the team asked me if we owned the building. The timing was perfect. I smiled and said, correctly, "The transaction closed this afternoon."

Creating an Endowment

Jack Grosse advised us that the ABA would expect the law school to have some kind of endowment or at least a quasi-endowment.[5] These kinds of funds provide a law school with sources of income other than tuition and thus contribute to its financial strength. Jack said that in his experience a fund of about $3 million would likely be sufficient, but under no circumstances should we have less than $2 million. During the 1986 application, the shareholders had attempted to meet this requirement by pledging funds that would be available in the event of an emergency, but the funds were not actually transferred to the college. The 1986 application had failed and no one believed that such an approach would suffice this time.

The endowment issue was a serious obstacle. Indeed, following Jack Grosse's visit in January, Jack Monks identified that issue as one of the three major barriers to our seeking ABA accreditation, the other two being the need to purchase a campus for the Irvine school

---

5   The term "endowment" in this context refers to funds the use of which is restricted, such that the income generated by the fund, but not the principal, is available for use by the institution. The term "quasi-endowment" refers to funds that have been set aside as a reserve, although no legal restriction prevents the institution from using them for other purposes if it so chooses.

and the need to raise admissions standards to such an extent that it might result in unacceptably small entering classes. Because the law school was proprietary, no tax deduction would be allowed for a contribution to the institution. This meant that creating an adequate endowment for all three campuses could require the shareholders to donate some $3 million in after-tax income to each campus in order for it to apply for ABA approval. Ultimately, an application for ABA approval for the three campuses could require them to forego the equivalent of more than $15 million in pre-tax income, a prohibitive requirement.

I suggested as an alternative that we generate a quasi-endowment from four sources. First, the value of the Gann building itself should be treated as part of our quasi-endowment because the building was rented to tenants and thus it functioned as an income generating asset. Essentially, it was a real estate investment. Second, we could pledge that all of the rental income generated by the building would be placed in the quasi-endowment rather than used for current needs, thereby increasing the amount of the reserve. Third, because at that time, we charged students tuition by the unit, we could pledge that henceforth $15 of the revenue generated by each unit of credit for which tuition was paid would be put in the same fund. Fourth, to boost the amount of the quasi-endowment fund initially, the shareholders would make an immediate donation of $500,000 to the fund. Thus, the quasi-endowment would have an initial value of $1.6 million (comprising the value of the Gann building and the initial cash reserve). The pledge of tuition moneys and rental income would add well over $300,000 a year to the fund annually, bringing the value to approximately $2 million within a year, at least by my accounting at the time.

The shareholders accepted my proposal. We included in the financial section of the self-study a description of the various assets that constituted our quasi-endowment and no question about it ever arose during our early inspections. In fact, as will be seen, by 1999, the ABA questioned the wisdom of putting money into a reserve fund when the law school had serious unmet needs and thereafter we contributed nothing further to the fund. At that point, we no longer included the value of the Gann building because it was in use as part of our campus and not producing income anymore, but the fund included about $1.6 million in cash.

Submitting the Application for Provisional Approval

On October 30, 1995, Thomas Jefferson formally applied for provisional approval. At Jim White's suggestion, we deferred submitting our application materials, other than our letter of application, until January in order to include a full report concerning the final details of our separation from WSU. In addition, our library expansion required some building renovations and we would not have our building permits until January. Jim wanted us to be able to report that the permits had been issued so that the team would know that the work would be done. Although the normal practice was to submit certified financial statements for the institution, because our finances in the past had been entwined with the rest of WSU's, we could not submit separate certified financial statements for Thomas Jefferson. Jim said that the ABA would accept certified statements for WSU, accompanied by estimates of the revenues and expenditures for the San Diego campus in recent years. I thanked Jim for accommodating our unique circumstances without compromising the substance of the standards.

12

Separating from Western State University

During his visit in September 1995, Jim White had emphasized the critical importance of effecting a clear separation from WSU. This presented a very difficult problem because the central administrators in Fullerton were accustomed to exercising control over the San Diego campus and did not want to cede that control entirely. I am sure that they believed that we needed their help and, in financial matters, we did, because we effectively had no financial officer. Further, because the purpose of the central administration was to coordinate activities among the campuses, a sharp separation among the campuses would diminish the need for a central administration.

The shareholders also had reason to support a continued role in San Diego of the central administration. First, they believed that consolidating some functions on the Fullerton campus was more efficient than replicating those functions on each campus. Second, they had worked with Jack, Joel and Vice President for Finance Ernie Hurguy for years, had confidence in them, and believed that their knowledge and experience would be valuable to us. Third, the duties of the dean at that time involved little more than supervision of the academic program and the shareholders were aware that I had little experience in other aspects of law school administration.

Jack Monks proposed a variety of organizational structures with different relationships among the campuses that would ensure that the central administration maintained some responsibility for the San Diego campus. Under one such structure, Thomas Jefferson would be separately incorporated, but would be a wholly owned subsidiary of WSU. Jack Grosse and I persuaded the shareholders that this structure would doom our accreditation application.

Another alternative was to incorporate each of the three campuses separately. The shareholders would create a fourth corporation that would perform the services that previously had been performed by the central administration. Each campus would enter into a contract with the fourth corporation for those services. I opposed this proposal as well. Many of the services had a managerial component to them and I feared that we would be paying the fourth corporation to continue to manage the San Diego campus. This arrangement could threaten our autonomy and drain our resources. For example, one of the services provided by the central administration was student recruitment. The recruitment of stronger entering classes would be the single most important element in our future success and I did not want that function in the hands of a corporation that we did not control. Another service provided by the central administration was budgeting and financial management. I worried that the fourth corporation would retain control over our funds, effectively giving the Fullerton campus supervision of every penny we earned and every penny we spent. Because the fourth corporation would be supported solely by its contracts with the three campuses, the shareholders might require us to pay too much for its services. Jack Grosse and I were able to persuade the shareholders to abandon this proposal as well.

Complete autonomy would require that we manage our own financial affairs. I asked the shareholders to approve my hiring of a controller for the San Diego campus. The shareholders refused the request and said that Ernie would continue to manage our finances. I liked, trusted and respected Ernie immensely, but I knew that having our finances managed in Fullerton would be regarded by the ABA, quite correctly, as an indication that we were not truly independent. As it happened, a couple of staff positions in San Diego were vacant and so I disregarded the shareholder's instructions and used the salaries from those vacancies to hire a controller. The next time that the shareholders were in San Diego, I introduced the new controller and told them that he was paid from funds already budgeted. They acquiesced in the hire and never again questioned our wish to manage our own finances. Ernie quickly adapted to working with our controller and performed magnificently and selflessly as he assisted us in achieving complete independence while ensuring that we never stumbled along the way. In so doing, he knowingly contributed to the obsolescence of his own position as vice-president.

After a year, our original controller left and we had the good fortune to hire the brilliant Nancy Vu as our controller, although I soon changed her title to chief financial officer. Nancy was born in Vietnam, moved to Paris as a teenager to attend high school, earned her M.B.A. from the Sorbonne, and then immigrated to the United States. She was working in finance at National University when we recruited her. Nancy and I developed a very close working relationship. I learned that we had exactly the same goals for the institution, her judgment was excellent, her work was flawless, she worked extraordinarily hard, and she could be trusted completely. Nancy's competence, dedication, and integrity quickly earned the complete confidence of the shareholders, allowing us to gain full control over our finances sooner than had seemed possible at the time of our separation from WSU. The high quality of her financial reporting would be invaluable years later when we sought to become a nonprofit and needed to borrow millions of dollars.

As the moment of formal separation approached, we continued to debate with the central administration the question of just how complete the separation would be. For example, during the summer, Jack informed me that the members of the Orange County faculty who wished to teach at Thomas Jefferson would receive priority with respect to filling any future vacancies on our faculty. Such a policy would have violated ABA standards, which provide that the faculty and the dean shall have responsibility for faculty appointments. It also would have undermined our claim to be a separate institution. After I drew Jack's attention to these problems, he abandoned his proposal that we be required to hire the Orange County faculty, but continued to encourage us to do so.

We needed to design a new logo for the new law school. Joel's wife was a graphic designer and created a logo that the shareholders approved. The logo showed Jefferson's profile encircled by the name of the law school. The central administration wanted our logo to indicate that Thomas Jefferson was formerly Western State University. The argument was that in this way we would capture all of the goodwill associated with the WSU name. I argued that in Orange County much of the bar had graduated from WSU and that the WSU name was highly respected there as the name of what for many years had been Orange County's only law school. In San Diego, however, WSU was in competition with two ABA accredited law schools and so the WSU name carried a stigma associated with the lack of ABA approval. Creating a new identity as an ABA approved law school was the most important reason for the name change and we would lose that benefit by linking ourselves back to WSU. After much discussion, we compromised by including the reference to WSU for a brief time.

Immediately following its renaming as the Thomas Jefferson School of Law, the law school adopted a new logo.

Ultimately, the separation was much simpler and more complete than Jack had originally proposed. The shareholders established a new corporation named "Thomas Jefferson School of Law." They sold to the corporation all of the assets that WSU owned in San Diego and the corporation paid for the assets by issuing all of its stock to the shareholders. Thus, Thomas Jefferson was not a true legal successor to WSU. Rather, it was an entirely new corporation that merely purchased certain assets from WSU and that was owned by the same individuals that owned WSU. On the day that it opened for business, however, Thomas Jefferson employed the same employees as had the San Diego campus of WSU, enrolled the same students, adhered to the same policies, and occupied the same premises. No material change in any aspect of the operation occurred. Thus, our accrediting agencies were willing to treat Thomas Jefferson as the successor to the WSU San Diego campus for purposes of accreditation and did not require us to seek accreditation anew. We also continued to regard the alumni of the San Diego campus as our own. WSU continued to claim our alumni as well and, to this day, its website lists as notable alumni several lawyers who received their entire legal education on the San Diego campus. As a result, some 3500 attorneys in southern California are claimed as alumni by two different law schools.

One of the most satisfying elements of the separation was the opportunity to change the signage on our building. The law school occupied a Spanish style stucco building with a red tile roof situated on a hillside. The building was readily visible from around the area. Attached to the building were three enormous orange illuminated letters that read "WSU." Although the letters were technically channel lit signs rather than neon, everyone called them neon lights because they glowed brightly at night. Students at the other area law schools referred to us derisively as "Neon U" law school. Thomas Jefferson students were embarrassed by the signage. Indeed, shortly after we announced our new name, a group of students circulated a petition signed by more than 65 of their colleagues requesting that any future signage be tasteful and avoid artificial illumination. During an open forum that I held with students in fall 1995, one of the first questions the students asked was "When is the new signage going to appear?" The name change gave me a rationale for removing the letters immediately, which I did without consulting Jack or the shareholders. Shari found a contractor who proposed to build a sign made of dignified metal letters that would be backlit for nighttime visibility.

Just before the separation, the shareholders took a distribution of earnings, leaving the San Diego campus with no cash. In addition, we were told that Thomas Jefferson would be required to pay WSU for the goodwill that it derived from its former association with WSU. Because Thomas Jefferson had no cash, we signed a note obligating us to pay WSU $300,000 over the next two years. Thus, we learned that on our first day of business as an independent law school, we would commence our operation with essentially no cash on hand, a heavily mortgaged campus, and hundreds of thousands of dollars of debt owed to WSU. But we would be free.

Part Two

Thomas Jefferson School of Law

1995-2005

13

Obtaining Provisional ABA Approval

On January 2, 1996, I distributed a memorandum headed "Thomas Jefferson's Declaration of Independence." The memorandum noted that, as of the close of business on December 29, 1995, the Thomas Jefferson School of Law had become an independent institution. We were governed by a board of trustees comprising the three principal shareholders, U.S. District Judge Earl B. Gilliam, Superior Court Judge (and Thomas Jefferson alumna) Ann P. Winebrenner, UCLA Vice Provost Edward "Ned" Pinger, and me. I concluded the memorandum by wishing everyone a "Happy New Year" and a "Happy New Era."

The two law schools remained linked in a number of ways by virtue of longstanding business arrangements. For example, both schools were covered by a single defined benefits pension plan, a single 401(k) savings plan, a severance plan, health insurance plans, various other insurance contracts, equipment leases, maintenance agreements, and even a common LEXIS contract. Both schools utilized the same mainframe computer, located on the WSU campus in Fullerton. Thomas

Jefferson entered into a service contract with WSU under which we paid WSU more than $200,000 per year for use of the mainframe computer and for our participation in these various shared arrangements. All of these shared arrangements were terminated over time, as were the annual payments.

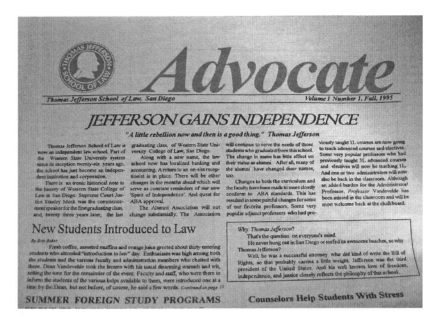

The student newspaper declares our independence.

Although the consent decree had helped to persuade the shareholders that the law school would receive a fair hearing before the ABA, it also greatly complicated our application. It prompted an extensive revision of the ABA accreditation standards at the very time that we were in the process of applying for provisional approval. We had to be prepared to meet the standards as they existed at the time we applied, as well as the standards as they might be modified while our application was under consideration. We monitored the debate concerning the standards vigilantly to ensure that we were in compliance with any new standards as they were proposed.

Hosting the Site Evaluation Team

The ABA site evaluation team was chaired by Dean Roger Dennis of the Rutgers-Camden School of Law. The other members of the team were Dean Michael P. Cox of Thomas M. Cooley Law School, Professor Ann Juergens of William Mitchell College of Law, Judge Manuel D. Leal, Dean John C. Roberts of DePaul University College of Law, and Professor Joyce D. Saltalamachia of New York Law School.

The team inspected Thomas Jefferson from March 3 through March 6. Roger Dennis was the first member of the team to arrive and so we spent a couple of hours together driving around the city. As we toured the area, he asked innumerable questions about the law school, especially its finances. Roger specialized in corporate finance and so he was particularly interested in the concept of a proprietary law school. He noted that proprietary law schools must pay taxes and a return to the shareholders, which puts them at an inherent disadvantage relative to nonprofit law schools that must pay neither. He wondered whether a proprietary law school ever could compete with nonprofit law schools that had, in effect, a lower cost of capital. His questions were not the least bit hostile. Ours was a historic application. We were on a path toward becoming the first proprietary law school ever to receive ABA approval. The ABA would need to formulate all of its policies with respect to proprietary law schools in the course of our application. Roger was trying to anticipate the implications of, and potential problems associated with, a law school that operated without the advantages of nonprofit status.

Thomas Jefferson School of Law, San Diego — *Magna est veritas et praevelabit* — Volume I Number 4, Spring, 1996

Major Expansion Set For
Thomas Jefferson School of Law

Some say there's a jacuzzi on the roof. Others whisper of a hidden sauna in a sumptuous penthouse suite. Still others confide that sauna and jacuzzi are nestled together, like sibling luxury appliances beckoning the privileged to relax.

We don't know.

What we do know is that our school is engaged in a major expansion with the scheduled purchase of the Gann Professional Center building located at 2120 San Diego Avenue, directly across the street from the current Thomas Jefferson School of Law facility.

The closing of the transaction is set for Monday, March 4. It will result in an approximate 40% increase in physical size of the Thomas Jefferson School of Law. The Gann building, built about the same time as our building, has similar architecture and Spanish style. It also has an outside parking lot upon which an additional building could be built in the future.

intended to provide Thomas Jefferson School of Law with long term future expansion room within the limited geographic confines that we find ourselves. After all, as Dean Vandevelde points out, we are not like schools which are a part of a giant, sprawling university

Gann Professional Center

another.

The first discernible changes for students and staff will be this summer, when the existing law library will expand directly upward to the second floor. This 3600 square foot enlargement of the library will displace the Earl Gilliam Moot Courtroom and the class-

low and casual. This will result in a very pleasant, open look and feel for research, writing, and study. The Moot Court and classrooms will then go to the third floor, and displaced offices will move to existing vacant offices across the street.

ABA Site Inspection Team to visit

Everyone at Thomas Jefferson School of Law is excited about our visit by the ABA Site Inspection Team, and the prospect of our school becoming approved by the American Bar Association.

All of us at Thomas Jefferson School of Law extend a warm welcome

The student newspaper announces the acquisition of the Gann Building while welcoming our ABA site evaluation team.

During the opening meeting with the team, I reviewed the reforms that had been occurring since 1991 and emphasized the ways in which the law school had subjected itself to a continuing process of critical self-examination that was by no means complete. Our renewal was generated by the faculty and would continue. I closed with a plea: "Please do not take the wind from our sails." They understood my meaning. Provisional approval would keep the process of renewal moving forward. Failure to achieve provisional approval would destroy it.

The first event in an ABA site evaluation is a tour of the campus. Just before the team arrived, Assistant Dean Shari O'Brien and I quickly walked around the campus to ensure that everything looked as it should.

We had only recently installed new carpeting, which required replacing the baseboards. Moments before I was to leave the campus to meet the team at its hotel, a piece of the new baseboard in the corridor fell off. Shari grabbed an Elmer's glue stick, smeared glue on the back, and stuck it onto the wall. The baseboard stayed on the wall for the duration of the tour, which was going well until our elevator car suddenly stalled, briefly trapping the team and me. I nervously joked about restarting the elevator in exchange for a favorable site evaluation report, while frantically pushing buttons. At last the elevator car restarted and our ascent began.

One feature of an inspection is a meeting with the students. The *Advocate* later published an article that reported extensively on what the students had told the team. Students said that the faculty was "quite good" and "were very positive about access to professors." Regarding the administration, the *Advocate* reported that "A number of students mentioned that they were surprised to find that most of their problems were answered swiftly and in writing by the Deans." Students were asked about a number of specific departments within the law school. The students conceded that the library collection was too small, but praised the collection as "improving" and the library as "very user friendly." They were "pleased" about the recent appointment of a new director of career services, Andrea Lamb, and gave testimonials to the assistance that they had received in finding paid and unpaid internships. They had "only positive things" to say about the financial aid office. Asked about the campus, students complained about the inadequate heating and cooling system, but said that the acquisition of the Gann building was "a major improvement." Regarding diversity, "students commented that the school was rich ethnically, age-wise, and in pre-law school life experience." One student did express concern that ABA accreditation would require the law school to deny admission to nontraditional students. The site team assured the student that it would not. Asked what they would do if they were dean for the day, several students said that they would add more specialized electives. The most common response, however, was, according to the *Advocate,* "Make this an ABA school!"

Jack Resigns

Two days after the team left, on March 8, Jack called and shocked me with the news that he had resigned effective June 30. He asked me to tell everyone at Thomas Jefferson how proud he was of what we had accomplished. I circulated a memorandum announcing his resignation and noted that "we could not have accomplished what we have without Jack's constant support."

I wrote Jack a letter in April expressing our deepest thanks for his "extraordinary efforts in connection with our successful separation from Western State University and our application for ABA approval." I told him that WSU was "not even remotely the law school that it was" when he arrived eight years before and that he had been "a friend beyond measure" to everyone at Thomas Jefferson School. The next month, as an indication of our respect, affection and esteem for him, at our annual commencement ceremony, we gave Jack the honor of being the first person ever to receive an honorary degree conferred by the new Thomas Jefferson School of Law.

At our 1996 commencement held at the Organ Pavilion in Balboa Park, assisted by Mary Lynne, I conferred an honorary degree on Jack Monks.

Less than a week after Jack announced his resignation, more surprising news arrived. On March 13, 1996, WSU announced that it was closing the Irvine campus at the end of the summer, after only six years of operation. The Irvine students would be transferred automatically to the Fullerton campus, which was preparing to apply for ABA approval. The irony was that only a year before, in March 1995, the shareholders and Jack had been scouting southern Orange County for a new location for the Irvine campus on the assumption that, if an application for provisional approval were made for one of the Orange County campuses, it would be on behalf of the Irvine campus. As late as December 1995, WSU had been in negotiations to purchase a new Irvine campus in preparation for an application to be made following the grant of ABA approval to Thomas Jefferson. The intention at that time was to acquire ABA approval of the Irvine campus, while continuing to operate the Fullerton campus as a state accredited law school, serving that segment of the market that could not gain admission to an ABA approved law school. The decision by Whittier Law School to open a campus in Costa Mesa, however, was drawing applicants away from the nearby Irvine campus, rendering that campus unsustainable. Although most of the Irvine students transferred to the Fullerton campus, some transferred to the San Diego campus, seeing this as their best hope of obtaining a degree from an ABA approved law school.

Although he did not tell me this at the time, I later learned that Jack had notified the governing board of his resignation many months before, in November 1995. At that time, with the Irvine campus planning to separate from WSU in order to pursue ABA approval and the Fullerton campus planning to remain a state accredited law school, Jack apparently recognized that there no longer would be a need for a president to coordinate the administration of multiple campuses. The decision to close the Irvine campus only made that fact all the more true. During the 1995-96 academic year, WSU had conducted a search for a new dean to lead the ABA accreditation process in Orange County and Jack certainly could have assumed that title and led the campus through the accreditation process, if he had wished to do so. His health had been poor, however, and he already had served as WSU president for eight years. He decided that the best course was to retire. Jack continued to serve on the WSU board for another year and as a marketing consultant to the college for a couple of years. He passed away in 2005 at the age of 75.

Appearing before the Accreditation Committee

Our appearance before the Accreditation Committee was scheduled for Friday, June 28, at the University of Wyoming College of Law in Laramie. Dick and Art attended as representatives of the shareholders. Following our separation from WSU, the shareholders had appointed me president, as well as dean, of the law school and thus I was also designated to meet with the committee. Because we expected the library to be a major issue, Karla joined us as well. I traveled to Laramie with Art and Dick, while Karla came separately. The three of us flew into Denver and rented a car to drive to Laramie. During the drive, the shareholders delivered the bad news: they had agreed that we would make only a single application for provisional approval. If we did not succeed on this first application, we would not be given a second chance. The future of the law school rested on our appearance before the committee the next day.

At the meeting, Art took the lead in speaking for the shareholders and, as one observer later told me, he "hit exactly the right note." Art told the committee that the shareholders had invested in the law school to make money, but that the institution was dear to their hearts. He was convincing because he was telling the truth. The law school was a business, but they cared about it and they were proud when it excelled.

When a law school appears before the committee, one member of the committee is designated as the "monitor" and takes the lead in questioning the school's representatives. Other members may ask questions if they wish, once the monitor has completed his or her questioning. Our monitor was Dean Len Strickman of the University of Arkansas. Len later confided to me that he had opposed our accreditation and his questions were very tough.

One concern raised by the Accreditation Committee was a complete surprise because it had not been raised by the site evaluation team. The committee questioned our practice of scheduling night classes in three hour blocs of time, which the committee thought was too long. Len asked whether the law school intended to continue this practice and I replied that we would reconsider it. He said he wanted a firm commitment that we would abolish it and I promised that we would. As soon as the meeting ended, I called Marybeth and told her that we needed immediately to revise the entire fall schedule to eliminate three hour blocs in the evening division. Marybeth completely revised the schedule over the weekend and on Monday we faxed the new schedule to the ABA consultant's office, which wanted to verify that, in fact, we had abolished three hour blocs. We then notified the faculty and students that we had radically restructured the fall schedule, the second time in two years that we had revamped the fall schedule over the summer to meet ABA requirements.

On June 30, exactly one year to the day after the law school decided to apply, the ABA Accreditation Committee recommended provisional approval. The news came in the form of a 12 page letter faxed from the Accreditation Committee. Jan notified me when the letter started to arrive and we waited for a few excruciating minutes until the last page, indicating the decision of the committee, emerged from the fax machine.

After reading the fax, I called Jim White. He told me that the decision was "not by any means a unanimous decision." The committee had "great concern" about the library and about the small size of the faculty. Jim told me that we had made "a very good impression" on the committee and that, if we had not made such an impression, the decision "would have gone the other way." He also said that it was common for the committee to deny provisional approval on the first application in order to give a school an additional incentive to improve, but that the committee had decided not to deny our application because it was clear that we were completely motivated to meet the standards and that no additional incentive was necessary. He warned me to be fully prepared for the council meeting in August and to be sure that at least two shareholders attended that meeting.

The Accreditation Committee had found that Thomas Jefferson was "in substantial compliance" with the standards and had given assurances that it would be in full compliance within three years, the findings that were necessary for a grant of provisional approval. The committee was concerned, however, that the law school achieve significant progress in five areas: the breadth of its upper-level curriculum, the breadth and depth of its library collection, the bar passage rate of its graduates, its continued demonstration of financial soundness, and the comprehensiveness of its self-study, particularly regarding its academic priorities. This last concern was a little opaquely worded but essentially reflected a fear that our faculty was too small to provide adequate curricular breadth for a dual division law school.

Appearing before the Council

We were scheduled to appear before the council on August 1, at its meeting in Orlando, Florida. Karla had been asked very little at the Accreditation Committee meeting in Laramie and so the shareholders decided that she need not travel to Orlando. Mel Sherman wanted to participate and so he attended in lieu of Dick Leavitt. Art Toll came as well. As it happened, Art and Dick were on a cruise in the Mediterranean with their wives and transporting Art from the cruise ship to Orlando required an incredibly complicated series of airline connections.

At the end of the meeting, Jim White told me that he would call later in the day with the council's decision. Art and Mel left for the airport. I sat in my room for several hours, awaiting a phone call that never came. As time passed with no word, I became increasingly anxious. Finally, in the late afternoon, well after the council meeting was scheduled to end, I decided to go for a run. At that time of the day, the temperature was registering 93 degrees and the humidity was at 100 percent. I ran about five miles and then returned to the hotel, my clothes soaked and my skin drenched. As I was riding the elevator up to my room, the car stopped, the doors opened and Jim White entered, accompanied by his wife, both dressed very elegantly for a formal reception and dinner that they were attending. Jim and I made eye contact and he quickly introduced his wife, who shook my very sweaty hand. Then there was an awkward pause as, I believe, Jim slowly realized that he had never called me and that I obviously wanted to know the decision of the council. As I stood staring expectantly at him and an elevator full of strangers watched, Jim said, "The council recommended you for provisional approval." I blurted out some kind of noise of appreciation and exuberance and then Jim continued, "But it was a closely divided vote. A lot of people wanted to make you wait another year. You have your work cut out for you. Full approval is much more difficult to obtain than provisional approval. You cannot rest on your laurels. You must work very hard. Everyone is going to be watching you closely now." I promised Jim that we would not disappoint the council.

It had been my intention, when I accepted the appointment as dean, to remain in that position for only one year or for as long as was necessary for us to obtain provisional approval. I wrongly assumed that, once we had provisional approval, receiving full approval would be a kind of formality. At that moment in the elevator, I realized that I could not leave until we had received full approval, for which we would be eligible in three years. Jim had warned me that we had a great deal of work to do in those three years and that we could not relax for a moment. I was afraid that we would lose too much momentum while we conducted a search for a dean and the new dean became acquainted with the law school. Nor could we be sure that the new dean would have the ability to lead a law school through the ABA accreditation process. As I continued the elevator ride to my floor, I resigned myself to the fact that I would be in the dean's office for another three years.

Receiving Provisional ABA Approval

The House of Delegates, which makes the final decision on accreditation, was not meeting for several more days. I remained in Orlando to wait for the meeting. Our approval was placed on the consent calendar for August 6, the last day that the House would be in session. The consent calendar included items that were presumed not to be controversial and that could be addressed together in a single vote. The ABA's modified accreditation standards, drafted pursuant to the consent decree, were before the House and were expected to generate some controversy. Practicing attorneys, who compose the vast majority of the delegates, are perennially concerned that law schools are not doing enough to prepare students for the practice of law and the Justice Department's lawsuit had given critics an opportunity to call into question the standards that governed legal education.

I was sitting with a group of officials from the Section on Legal Education awaiting our moment and listening to the extensive floor debate on the ABA standards. Numerous delegations had proposed resolutions relating to the revised standards. One of the resolutions, proposed by the Illinois State Bar Association, would have mandated that all law schools be required to offer live client experiences. The Council of the Section on Legal Education opposed the resolution, believing that the standards should permit law schools some discretion in how they structured their programs and that live client experiences, while desirable, should not be required. The resolution was adopted, however.

Ellen Waldman's mediation program provided us with the live client experience that we needed to satisfy a new ABA requirement adopted only minutes before the final decision on our accreditation application.

Moments later, the incomparable Norman Redlich, who was then the section's liaison to the house, rushed over and asked to speak with me in the corridor. Norman said to me, "I have a very important question and you must think carefully about your answer. Do you offer your students any live client experiences?" I replied that we did, and described the mediation program founded and supervised by Ellen Waldman. "Great! That's all I need!" he said. Thanks to our mediation program, we were in compliance with the new standard adopted only moments before and now applicable to us. A few minutes later, the House of Delegates, without debate, approved the items on the consent calendar. The Thomas Jefferson School of Law at last was a provisionally approved law school.

The student newspaper, which was briefly named The Declaration, announces Thomas Jefferson's receipt of provisional ABA approval in August 1996.

The shareholders, needless to say, were thrilled that we had obtained provisional approval. Dick and Art sent a congratulatory telegram from their ship somewhere at sea. Seeing that it was possible for a proprietary law school to obtain ABA approval, upon their return they appointed a new dean for the Orange County campus, Dennis Honabach, whom Jack Grosse had recommended to them and who would lead WSU through the process of gaining provisional approval in 1998. In preparation for the application in Orange County, the shareholders approved the construction of a new library building on the same four acre plot where the law school had been located since 1974.

In San Diego, the Board of Directors adopted a resolution commending the faculty, staff and me for our exemplary work in obtaining ABA approval. They offered me a raise effective in 1997 and asked me for a commitment to remain for three years. I had no contract as dean and could be dismissed at any time, although I was also free to resign at any time. I assumed that they asked me for a commitment in order to ensure that I would not leave before we received full approval, which we all expected to receive at the earliest possible date, in 1999. I was a little nervous about making a commitment because to do so would remove a powerful weapon from my arsenal, the threat to resign. At the same time, however, having a contract would make it more difficult for the shareholders to fire me, if we ran into disagreements over the means of pursuing full approval. Ultimately, I gave them the commitment that they sought. As it happened, I eventually would threaten to resign, but not until four years later.

I was also happy to have the salary increase. My raise in 1997 was the last salary increase, however, that I would have as dean. In succeeding years, particularly during our long, difficult march to full approval, I decided to use whatever bargaining leverage I had with respect to salaries to obtain larger raises for the faculty and staff, rather than to seek a raise for myself. Until the faculty and staff were properly compensated, I would not request a salary increase. When I left the dean's office in 2005, my salary was the same as it was in 1997, although, of course, eight years of inflation had eroded much of its value.

Converting to a Nonprofit -- Almost

My effort to find new owners of the law school in the spring of 1995 had been unsuccessful. By June of that year, however, the shareholders had decided to seek ABA approval immediately and the urgency of finding new owners diminished. Still, at least one of the contacts that I made during that period had long term repercussions, although no permanent impact.

The oldest law school in San Diego, California Western School of Law, traces its origins to Balboa Law School, founded in 1927 as a proprietary night law school.[6] The Balboa Law School originally offered courses at San Diego High School under the auspices of the public school system, but during the Great Depression competitors pressured public school officials to terminate support for the proprietary school. Faced with the loss of degree granting authority, the Balboa Law School purchased the charter and degree granting rights of the San Diego Chiropractic College, founded in 1924, which was about to lose its charter for nonpayment of franchise taxes. In 1939, the founder of the Balboa Law School was convicted of fraud in a matter unrelated to the law school and the founder's brother assumed control. With enrollment down to four students, the new dean decided to shed the stigma attached to a proprietary night school. He converted the institution to a nonprofit, added other programs, offered courses in the day and evening and renamed the institution Balboa University. In

---

6   Two histories of California Western School of Law are available. *See* George N. Gafford, *Odyssey of a Law School: A Personal History of California Western School of Law, its Exotic Voyage Past Theosophy, African Gold and an Elks Hall* (2001), and Robert K. Castetter, *"Every Day Is a Good Day. . .": A History of California Western School of Law* (1996).

1950, Balboa University moved from Hillcrest to Point Loma. In 1952, the university changed its name to California Western University and suspended the operation of the law school because of low enrollment. The law library was given to the University of San Diego, which used the library to open its law school in 1954. In 1958, California Western University reopened its law school at a location on Fifth Avenue, offering only a full-time program. Enrollments were small. The first entering class included only 14 students, one of whom was George Kraft, who was elected president of the student bar association each of the three years that he was enrolled. When the class graduated in 1961, only six students remained in the class. In 1962, the law school received ABA accreditation and moved to the Point Loma campus. In 1968, California Western University was renamed United States International University (USIU) and the law school became known as California Western School of Law of United States International University. In the early 1970s, USIU was suffering severe financial difficulties. In 1973, USIU sold its Point Loma campus and moved to Scripps Ranch on the former site of Camp Elliott, a marine base famous for the Navajo Code Talkers program that originated there during World War II. The Point Loma campus was acquired by Pasadena College, which today is known as Point Loma Nazarene University. As the rest of the university was heading toward Scripps Ranch, the law school relocated to a building on Cedar Street, where it remains. In 1975, to escape the financial woes of the university, the law school separated from the rest of USIU and continued to operate as California Western School of Law. By the 1990s, USIU again was in severe financial distress. A Kansas City based nonprofit organization, HRS Group, had rescued USIU by purchasing the campus and leasing it back to the university. The sale of the campus gave the university the cash it needed to address its financial problems.

In the spring of 1995, as I searched for new owners, I wondered whether HRS Group might rescue us as well. I performed some research and discovered that one of the members of the USIU governing board was Ambassador Joe Ghougassian, who taught at Thomas Jefferson as an adjunct. I took Joe to lunch and asked him to introduce me to the USIU president. I then asked the USIU president for a meeting with Richard C. Hawk, the chairman of the board of HRS Group, the next time that he was in San Diego. By August 1995, when my meeting with Dick Hawk was finally arranged, the shareholders had decided to apply for ABA accreditation. Nevertheless, many of the faculty hoped that the law school someday would become a nonprofit and so I believed that Dick was someone with whom I should become acquainted. I met with him in the USIU president's office in August 1995 and described our circumstances. I told him that I believed that USIU and Thomas Jefferson had much to offer each other. Dick told me that he was very impressed by my presentation and hoped that we could stay in touch.

A year later, in September 1996, Dick contacted me and said that he wanted to make an offer on behalf of HRS Group to purchase Thomas Jefferson. I sent a memo to the shareholders informing them that I had received an offer to purchase the law school. They replied that they would be interested in selling Thomas Jefferson, but only in conjunction with a sale of WSU too.

The shareholders had been approached during the mid 1990s by several potential purchasers, but at the time that they decided to apply for ABA approval they also decided to defer any sale of Thomas Jefferson or WSU until both were ABA accredited. Because WSU had not yet acquired ABA approval, the shareholders were not ready to entertain an offer for WSU. They were concerned, in particular, that selling Thomas Jefferson would suggest to the ABA that they were not committed to the law schools on a long term basis, which they thought would undermine their application for ABA approval of the Fullerton campus. They wanted to wait until WSU was ABA approved and then sell both law schools together. I argued that the ABA would applaud a sale of Thomas Jefferson to a nonprofit organization and, far from damaging their credibility, the sale would demonstrate their readiness to act in the school's long term best interests. With that reassurance, they authorized Mel Sherman in March 1997 to contact Dick Hawk and commence negotiations.

The problem that quickly arose was how to value an asset when the returns were expected to grow significantly, but the amount of the growth could not be easily predicted. Thomas Jefferson was newly accredited and all expected that it would be more profitable than ever before, but no one was sure just how profitable it would be.

Dick Hawk suggested that HRS Group purchase the law school for a price tied to projected earnings and that the sale price be adjusted at a future date, based on actual earnings. Thus, if the law school proved to be more profitable in the future than projected, the sale price would rise to reflect the greater profitability. He offered to make an initial payment of about $6.7 million plus future payments that would bring the total purchase price to $25 million, if financial projections were met. The shareholders made a counteroffer and by May the two parties had reached agreement. HRS Group would purchase the law school for a down payment of $15 million, with additional future payments that could bring the total price to $33 million, if projections were met. Less than a year after we received provisional ABA approval, we were about to become a nonprofit law school.

Then problems arose. Apparently, the two parties miscommunicated about certain aspects of the deal. My understanding is that, most importantly, Dick Hawk had understood that HRS Group was purchasing the law school free of debt. The campus, however, was heavily mortgaged and for the shareholders to eliminate the debt would cost them millions of dollars. The shareholders had believed that HRS Group would assume the debt. In any event, on July 3, Dick Hawk called to tell me that the deal was dead. He and the shareholders had been unable to resolve their differences over the purchase price.

I had greatly enjoyed all of my interactions with Dick Hawk and had believed that he would give us the autonomy that we needed to build a great law school, free from the pressure to make a substantial profit in the short run and to pay income taxes annually. The collapse of the negotiations seemed at the time to be a real tragedy for the law school and to doom any chances in the foreseeable future of converting the law school to a nonprofit institution.

14

Improving the Strength of the Student Body

The single best argument for seeking ABA approval had been that it would allow us to recruit students nationally. The expanded applicant pool would enable us to raise admissions standards and thus improve the quality of our academic program, our bar passage rate, and our reputation, which would increase the professional opportunities available to our students. It would also ensure a sufficient number of qualified students to guarantee the financial viability of the law school and even to increase its profitability, which was an important concern to the shareholders.

Developing a National Recruiting Strategy

Recruiting a strong entering class became my top priority. The secret to student recruitment was simply reconciling supply and demand. We needed to ask two questions: what assets could we offer prospective students and what did prospective students want from a law school? If we could match what we offered with what prospective students wanted, they would apply.

I wanted to recruit students on the basis of our academic program. The mission that we had pursued in the past, one of providing access to a wide range of students, had given the law school certain academic strengths. We placed enormous importance on the quality of classroom instruction because we believed that our students needed good instruction if they were to pass the bar exam. Our faculty was accustomed to helping students outside of class and thus was remarkably accessible to students. The fact that most students were part-time required our scheduling to be flexible. Our declining enrollments, attributable to our lack of ABA accreditation, meant that we had small classes.

Our mission was changing, however. Increasingly, we were focusing on the quality of the education that we provided rather than the nature of the student body that we served. Thus, we also had academic strengths that derived from our new circumstances. The explosion in the size of the faculty that began in 1990 had brought in a large number of young faculty members who were enthusiastic teachers with interests in cutting-edge subjects. Looking ahead to the time when we would want to recruit students from around the country, I had tried since 1991 to ensure that our new faculty members were recruited from the most prestigious law schools in the country because someday we would need the credibility that a faculty with Ivy League credentials brings. A young, dynamic faculty with prestigious credentials and expertise in exciting new areas of the law became another critical asset that we could offer. At the same time, all of our faculty were former practitioners and thus had both the ability and the inclination to teach students the practical application of the law.

We added faculty biographies to the catalog and moved those biographies up to the front, although, admittedly, behind the pictures of San Diego that adorned the first few pages. A standard part of our recruiting appeal was to invite prospective applicants to compare the credentials of our faculty with the credentials of the faculty at any other law school that they were considering.

With time, we learned which of these assets appealed to prospective students and which did not. The small class size and accessible faculty had great appeal and we began to refer to those characteristics, along with our flexible scheduling, as our individualized approach to legal education.

The credentials of the faculty and their interests in cutting-edge subjects also appealed to prospective students. At the recruitment conferences, I asked every prospective student that I met about his or her subject matter interests and found that intellectual property and international law were by far the most commonly mentioned subjects, a fact that would influence my 1999 proposal, described below, to launch our three centers.

Our scholarship programs, under which every admitted applicant with an LSAT score of 150 or higher was guaranteed some kind of scholarship, appealed to prospective applicants as well. Over time, we modified the scholarship programs so that the amount of money varied according to factors in addition to the LSAT score, such as undergraduate grade point average or contribution to diversity, but it remained the case that every admitted applicant with an LSAT score of 150 or higher was assured of some kind of scholarship award and that the minimum amount of the award was published. We aggressively publicized our scholarship policies, which helped to attract many of our strongest applicants. Often, the scholarship offer merely piqued their interest. Once they applied, however, we had the opportunity to talk with them more extensively about why they should choose us.

Finally, we missed no opportunity to mention our location. At the beginning of my deanship, we purchased rights to a beautiful photograph of the San Diego harbor and skyline and used it on the cover of the catalog without change every year after that. Some members of the faculty and staff complained that our catalog cover never changed, but the vast majority of applicants would never know that it was the same cover that we had used for years before. Besides, I could not think of a better cover and it made no sense to switch to a worse one.

Telling our story to prospective applicants also entailed preempting other, less favorable versions of who we were. One such version was that we were a new law school that was not well-established. We preempted that by constantly referring to ourselves as the "up and coming" law school and emphasizing how much we had achieved already in very little time, suggesting that so much more would be achieved in the near future. If some saw risk, we emphasized opportunity, growth and dynamism. This was not mere puffery. We truly were a law school on the move.

Another potentially less favorable version of our story was that our campus was small and unimpressive. We preempted that by emphasizing that the quality of a law school is determined by the people rather than by the facilities. Our recruiting materials told potential applicants that if they wanted the law school with the most stained glass windows, we were not the right choice for them. If they were looking for a law school with a talented and dedicated faculty, then we were their choice. This became a cue to remind them of the credentials of our faculty and the individualized attention that students would receive. Again, the argument was not advertising puffery. The revolution at Thomas Jefferson had been fueled initially by the growth of the faculty and then by the changes in our entering classes. The value of Thomas Jefferson truly was in the people that it comprised.

That became the core of our recruiting message: We had an outstanding, committed faculty offering students an individualized approach to a cutting-edge legal education. Our wonderful location and our generous scholarships were additional inducements that we mentioned at every opportunity and events would show that they had powerful appeal.

In our efforts to preempt unfavorable images of the law school, we surveyed our entering students to determine which factors had weighed most heavily against attending Thomas Jefferson. The survey consisted solely of open-ended questions, so that the answers were not suggested by us. We were hearing the students' own words.

In one such survey, out of 112 responses from the entering class, 45 students mentioned our lack of reputation or low ranking as a major concern. Seven mentioned a related concern, that we were a new law school, while nine mentioned our lack of full approval, which was to some extent another way of expressing concern about our reputation, although it also reflected fears about the future portability of their degrees. Our reputation thus was by far the students' greatest reservation about attending Thomas Jefferson. These results underscored the importance of our emphasis on the recent strides we had made and our potential for future advancement. We wanted prospective students to focus more on what we would become than on what we were at the moment. As the strength of our program grew, the value of their degrees would rise.

Thirty-two of the respondents mentioned that we were far from home, obviously a problem that we could not solve. Twenty-one mentioned the high cost of both tuition and living in San Diego. The high cost of living, of course, was also beyond our control and was merely the corollary to our wonderful location. No other negative consideration was mentioned by even five students. We had been apprehensive about our modest facility, but only four out of the 112 respondents mentioned the campus as a negative consideration.

We also asked our entering students what had brought them to Thomas Jefferson. The single biggest factor was our location, mentioned by 58 students. After that, the individualized attention that we offered and our scholarship programs essentially tied, with 39 mentioning individualized attention and 38 mentioning scholarships. Thirty-five respondents mentioned small classes, essentially a variation of the individualized attention consideration. The other considerations frequently mentioned were the credentials of the faculty and our cutting-edge curriculum, which were mentioned with equal frequency. Because the questions were open-ended, the survey results indicated that students were hearing the message in our recruiting materials and that message was bringing them to the law school.

The success of our recruiting strategy required that we be what we claimed to be. In other words, our recruiting had to reflect who we really were and, as we evolved, we had to consider how the direction of that evolution would affect student recruitment. Always in my mind was how each event affected our account of who we were. For example, when the faculty, in an effort to improve our bar pass rates, decided in 2000 to start administering mid term examinations in many of our classes, a highly unusual practice at the time, we sent letters to prospective applicants explaining that our faculty cared so much about the success of our students that, unlike the faculty at most law schools, they administered midterm exams, giving students an opportunity to receive comments on their exam performance before the crucial final exams. This reinforced our claim to have an individualized approach to legal education as well as our claim to have a dynamic, innovative and dedicated faculty. I worried that the promise of more exams would drive students away, but applicants heard the message that I hoped they would hear and the announcement drove up applications.

Adopting a New Mission Statement

When it seemed as if our narrative had gelled, I decided that it was time to formalize it in a new mission statement. The WSU mission statement had declared that WSU's mission was to provide "educational opportunity of the highest caliber, at the lowest possible cost, to all possible qualified candidates for law study," particularly working students. That statement, however, no longer captured who we were. A new mission statement emphasizing our academic program would tell prospective students who we were now and also serve as a reminder to us of who we claimed to be. In addition, drafting and adopting the statement could serve to indicate whether a faculty consensus existed with respect to the claims that I was making on behalf of the institution. If the faculty did not agree with the way that I was presenting the law school, I needed to know.

In 1999, I drafted a new mission statement that was intended to capture those elements of our law school that I believed both reflected who we were and would draw students to us. My proposed statement read, "The mission of the Thomas Jefferson School of Law is to provide an excellent legal education for a nationally based student body in a collegial and supportive environment, with attention to newly emerging areas of the law, particularly those involving technological development, globalization and the quest for social justice."

I circulated the proposed mission statement to the faculty for comments. I wanted to show them the statement that I regarded as optimal for purposes of student recruiting, but I anticipated that the faculty would propose that the statement be referred to a committee for study and revision.

To my surprise, however, when I placed the matter on the agenda of our August 17 meeting, the faculty had virtually no changes to suggest. A process that I expected would take months was completed very quickly. The only objection concerned the word used to describe our education, which was "excellent." After a short debate about semantics, the faculty voted to change the word "excellent" to "superior" and then adopted the statement with that one change.

I had told the shareholders about my proposal for a new mission statement and they said that any new mission statement would require their approval. When the shareholders received the statement approved by the faculty, they changed "superior" to "outstanding." At its September 13 meeting, the board approved the statement with that one change, to which the faculty raised no objection.

Thereafter, each year, we published an attractive brochure that showed how we were advancing each element of our mission statement. The brochure was a way of keeping us focused on the link between appearance and reality and of ensuring that we remained the institution that we said we were. Our 1999 mission statement remains in use more than a decade later, although in 2006 at the suggestion of my successor the faculty added the word "diverse" to the description of our student body.

The change in our mission troubled some of our alumni, particularly those who had been nontraditional students and believed that our new mission signaled an abandonment of students like themselves. My response was that it was more accurate to say that nontraditional students had abandoned us rather than that we had abandoned them. In the 1970s and even the early 1980s, we could sustain the law school largely with a nontraditional enrollment. By the 1990s, however, we simply did not have enough nontraditional applicants to sustain a law school of any quality. If we wanted to survive, our only choice was to attract a larger number of traditional students and, to do that, we needed to adopt a different mission emphasizing the quality of the education that we provided, rather than the nontraditional nature of the student body that we served. Our mission had evolved, from providing opportunity to seeking excellence.

We would continue, of course, to admit many nontraditional students and we would provide a better education for those nontraditional students who did enroll. We would no longer admit many of the least qualified applicants, but those applicants, who were often traditional students, had rarely succeeded in any event. Occasionally, an applicant with poor credentials excelled beyond all expectations, but we could not sustain a law school on the basis of a few remarkable success stories. Without abandoning our commitment to nontraditional students, we needed to reduce the percentage of high risk students in our entering classes, whether these were traditional or nontraditional students.

Nationwide Recruiting Begins

Because of the importance of student recruitment, I wanted to become personally involved in the recruiting process. Jennifer Keller, our assistant dean of admissions, told me that the Law School Admissions Council organized recruitment conferences in major cities around the country attended by thousands of potential law students. As an ABA approved law school, we were allowed to attend each conference, occupy a table, distribute literature, and speak with the attendees. I wanted to attend as many of these conferences as I could. I assumed, correctly, that other law schools generally would not have their dean present and so this would distinguish us from the competition and it would reinforce our claim to have an individualized approach to legal education.

More important, however, was that I could use my conversations with these potential applicants as a form of market research. I could ask them what they were looking for in a law school and watch their reaction when I touted various aspects of our law school, to see which aspects appealed to them and which did not. Over the next decade, I spoke with thousands of prospective law students at these conferences and I learned how we could use our existing strengths to recruit a much larger and much stronger applicant pool.

The first conference of the academic year was in New York City in September 1996, only weeks after we received provisional approval. The deadline to apply had already passed, but Jennifer persuaded the organizers to let me attend, with the understanding that we would have a table, but no signage directing applicants to our table. As we were instructed to do, we packed hundreds of catalogs and other brochures into boxes and shipped them to the conference center, which would have them waiting for me at my table when I arrived. When the conference opened very early on Saturday morning, I found that our boxes had not arrived. I had put three catalogs in my carry-on bag and that was the only literature that I would have at the conference. I spent the next two days telling well over a hundred potential applicants who came to our table that we were America's newest ABA approved law school, that we were a rising star, and that they should examine carefully our wonderful catalog, but they could not take it with them because I had only three. On a couple of instances, while I was preoccupied talking with one potential applicant, another potential applicant wandered off with a catalog anyway. By the end of the first day I had only one left, which I held in my hand and used like a flipchart for the rest of the weekend.

After that inauspicious beginning, however, we became experts at attending the conferences. Members of our admissions office and I fanned out across the country to recruit students. One fall, I was out of town on five out of six consecutive weekends, trying to recruit students from all over the country. Many of the members of our admissions staff, including Jennifer Keller and our admissions counselors, also spent weeks traveling around the country every fall. Jennifer and the rest of our admissions staff were among the many heroes of our revolution. Over the course of a decade, they learned to process a more than tenfold increase in the number of applications for the fall entering class, with no increase in personnel. Jennifer had exceptional organizational skills and was able to generate quickly and accurately the volumes of statistical reports that I requested weekly throughout the year so that I could monitor closely the progress of our student recruitment and admissions process. Our ability to evaluate empirically everything that we did would be critical to the law school's phenomenal success in attracting a stronger, more diverse student body.

One of our problems was that, as a newly accredited law school, we were not in any of the published guides to law schools or, if we were, we were listed as unaccredited. We needed a way for prospective students to hear about us. Joel Goodman suggested that we hire a company to place posters for us on college campuses around the country. This would be an efficient way to announce our accreditation and create name recognition, until we appeared in the guides. Although I wanted to brag about our academic program, I needed to grab their attention. So, I decided that the poster would focus on our location in San Diego. I asked our designer to create a poster urging prospective applicants to attend "Law School in Paradise." The poster featured a full-length photo of the beautiful San Diego skyline with boats in the harbor, over which was placed type that announced the arrival of America's newest ABA approved law school. Smaller type described our academic program. More than fifteen years later, that slogan can still be seen on some of our admissions materials.

This 1995 poster reflects the law school's first effort to create name recognition immediately following its receipt of provisional ABA approval. The same image appeared on the cover of our catalog every year for a decade. During that decade, admissions applications would increase more than tenfold.

The Law School Admissions Council sold address labels of those who took the LSAT. One could order labels for potential applicants who met certain criteria, such as location or LSAT score. After I had attended a few recruitment conferences, I composed letters that we mailed to every person who had taken the LSAT and achieved a score sufficient to gain admission. I did not think it ethical to send recruiting materials to a prospective applicant whom we knew that we would not accept and so we never did so. The letters were highly effective and began to generate thousands of responses a year. In our first year as an ABA approved law school, the number of applications we received for our fall entering class more than tripled. By the time that I left the dean's office, we were receiving more than ten times the number of applications for the fall entering class that we had received in fall 1994. For our fall 2005 entering class, we would receive more than 4000 applications, compared with fewer than 400 for our fall 1994 entering class.

After an applicant was admitted, we wanted him or her to experience directly the kind of individualized attention that we claimed that we offered. I sent a personal letter to each applicant welcoming him or her. This letter was followed by additional letters, each talking about a different aspect of the law school. To reinforce the theme that we dealt with students as individuals, I personally signed every single letter that appeared over my name. During my time as dean, I signed more than 100,000 letters to newly admitted applicants.

I also called each of our admitted applicants on the telephone, a practice that entailed making hundreds of telephone calls a year, including both the fall and spring entering classes. Because I was most likely to reach applicants in the late afternoon or early evening, I would start calling applicants on the East Coast around 3 p.m. and then work my way west as the hour grew later, ending with the West Coast applicants, whom I would call until about 8 p.m. I thought that a call after 8 p.m. would seem a little desperate or even creepy and, having missed dinner with my family nearly every evening for weeks at a time, I wanted to see my wife and young daughters at least briefly before they all went to bed.

Recruiting Our First Post Accreditation Entering Class

As we set out to recruit the first entering class following our receipt of provisional approval, I realized that, while I was hoping for an immediate improvement in the quality of the class, the shareholders were looking for an immediate improvement in profitability. They approved a budget for the 1996-97 academic year that assumed a spring 1997 entering class of 100 students, compared with just 57 spring entering students the year before.

Unfortunately for us, we were attempting to build an entering class at a time of declining demand for legal education. For example, the number of LSATs administered peaked at 152,685 in 1990-91 and then went into a long decline. By 1995-96, the first year in which we were attempting to recruit a class as an ABA approved law school, the number of LSATs administered had fallen to 114,756. It was that very decline, of course, that had impelled the shareholders to consider an application for ABA approval. During the next two years, the number of LSATs administered would decline to 103,991. Thus, we would be initiating our effort to recruit a stronger entering class during an era in which the number of applications to law school would drop by 32 percent over a period of seven years.

Because it took some time for us to spread the word that we were now accredited, applications for the spring 1997 entering class increased by only about 17 percent. We nevertheless reached our enrollment target of 100 students, bringing in the largest spring entering class in five years, but the median LSAT score fell from 148 to 147.

Within a few months, however, the news of our accreditation had spread and applications for the fall entering class soared. Ultimately, we would receive more than a thousand applications for our fall 1997 entering class, which, as already noted, was about triple the number that we had received the year before. We tripled the number of applications despite the fact that the number of law school applications nationally fell in that one year by more than 10 percent.

The pool of applications that we attracted was not only larger, but demographically quite different, than any we had ever seen. In the past, many of our applicants were nontraditional students, that is, local residents whose job and family responsibilities precluded them from attending law school outside San Diego. If we made them an offer, they were very likely to accept it. We also received applications from traditional applicants, but many of these were applicants who had been denied admission to other law schools and so they too were likely to accept our offer. Now we were receiving applications from much stronger traditional applicants with the ability to gain admission at many law schools and the geographic flexibility to attend any of them. We could only guess at the percentage of our offers that would be accepted.

The 1996 action letter from the ABA that accompanied our grant of provisional approval had questioned the law school's financial viability. The shareholders, wishing to see some financial return from their investment in accreditation, pressed me to increase enrollment, arguing that higher enrollments would demonstrate the financial viability that the ABA wanted to see. In an ironic reversal of circumstances, the shareholders were using the ABA standards to justify the demands that they were making on me. We began to extend a significant number of offers without knowing with any certainty what our yield rates would be. By late spring, we had discovered that the difference between the acceptance rate of stronger and weaker applicants was greater than we had anticipated.

We seated a class of 188 students, compared with 131 the year before. The most dramatic change was in the number of full-time students, which grew from 62 to 136 in just one year. In 1997, for the first time in its history, the law school admitted more full-time than part-time students. Never again would Thomas Jefferson be predominantly a part-time law school.

About 30 percent of the entering class were students of color. This was by far the highest percentage of minority students in an entering class in our history up until that time. It was also about 10 percentage points above the national average at the time.

Approximately 40 percent of the class came from outside California, compared with 20 percent in fall 1996 and 10 percent in prior years. They represented 33 states, compared with about seven in past years.

Seeing the explosion in the number of students from out of state, I became concerned about the ability of these students to find housing. I asked Lisa Ferreira, Jane Barnhart's successor as our director of student services, to create a housing office within her operation, which consisted only of herself and a part-time assistant. Lisa responded brilliantly. She quickly acquired a large array of materials to assist students in finding housing and worked long hours to assist them, while continuing to perform her usual duties. On some occasions, when an out-of-state student was attempting to decide about a particular apartment, Lisa would drive to the apartment and inspect it for the student.

Lisa exemplified what was true of so many of the staff during the revolution at Thomas Jefferson, which was that the profound changes in the institution required sometimes radical changes in their work responsibilities, usually in the form of many new tasks to perform. I was continually finding new things for Lisa to do in order to create a more nurturing environment for our changing student body and Lisa was taking the initiative in this regard as well. She took on each new task with enthusiasm and relentless good humor as we continued to build an atmosphere that by the end of the decade, as will be discussed below, brought us a ranking of fifth in the nation for the quality of life on campus. Lisa was only one of many talented and dedicated staff members.

The successful revolution at Thomas Jefferson owed much to a talented and dedicated staff. Pictured here, having fun at the 1993 Barristers Ball, are, clockwise from the bottom, Kay Henley (academic administration), Lisa Ferreira (student services), Jan Dauss (dean's office), Julie Miller (human resources), and Mary Retoriano (admissions).

Unfortunately, the credentials of the two 1997 entering classes were weaker than those of the smaller classes admitted the year before. For example, the median LSAT scores of the two classes that we admitted prior to receiving provisional approval were 148 and 150. The median LSAT score for both the spring and the fall 1997 entering classes fell to 147.

Raising Admissions Standards

The fall 1997 entering class was a step in the wrong direction. We sought ABA approval so that we could raise admissions standards and instead they had fallen, even if unintentionally. The fall 1997 class, however, had taught us a great deal about yield rates in various segments of the class. We put the knowledge to good use and, as a result, our spring and fall 1998 entering classes were much stronger. To illustrate, the average LSAT score climbed an astonishing four points in one year --from 147 in fall 1997 to 151 in fall 1998.

Particularly impressive was the improvement in the top of the class. The percentage of the entering class with LSAT scores of 155 or higher grew from 10.6 percent in fall 1997 to 28.8 percent in fall 1998. Our LSAT score at the 75th percentile in fall 1998 was higher than that at 65 ABA approved law schools, including our neighbors California Western, McGeorge, Southwestern, Golden Gate and Whittier. (We did not have figures for Chapman or WSU). Over all, the admissions statistics of our fall 1998 entering class indicated that we now had stronger entering classes than 27 fully approved law schools, although we were only provisionally approved.

By 1998, we had essentially stopped taking students without undergraduate degrees. In spring 1995, the last semester before we applied for ABA approval, more than 20 percent of the class lacked a baccalaureate degree. Even as late as spring 1997, more than 11 percent of the class lacked such a degree. By fall 1998, less than one percent of the entering class was admitted without an undergraduate degree.

We were able to achieve this dramatic improvement in strength without a significant reduction in the size of the class. In fact, the fall 1998 class was only 11 students smaller than the fall 1997 class. The class size fell from 188 to 177.

By the next year, the major surge in applications from our receipt of provisional approval had ended. Applications for fall 1999 rose by 15 percent, but the shareholders approved a budget requiring a 15 percent increase in class size, to 200. Thus, the slightly larger applicant pool did not permit us to be any more selective. In fact, much of the increase in applications was among weaker segments of the applicant pool with the result that the fall 1999 entering class was slightly weaker than the fall 1998 entering class.

Our First Post-Accreditation ABA Site Evaluation

Our first ABA site evaluation after we received provisional approval, conducted on April 13-16, 1997, found that we had made "substantial forward progress" in all five areas where the ABA had called for action: financial viability, long range planning, the breadth of the upper level curriculum, the size of the library and bar passage rates. In fact, the first three of these concerns seemed to have been eliminated entirely as a result of steps we had taken during the prior year. The team's "overall impression" of Thomas Jefferson was "one of optimism and energy in a time of rapid and profound change." The law school had "enthusiastic and loyal students, a committed and unified faculty, sound administration, a solid demand for places in its classes, and a good financial base."

The 1997 site evaluation team, however, found new concerns, notably with regard to our physical facility. In particular, the team observed that traffic noise was audible in the classrooms on the west side of the building, overlooking the Interstate 5 highway. In two classrooms, the line of sight from certain seats was blocked by pillars. The team noted that the law school was aware of deficiencies in its facility and was already contemplating the construction of a new building on the parking lot adjacent to the Gann building.

The 1997 Accreditation Committee found that the law school was not yet in full compliance with the accreditation standards in three respects. First, our library collection was still too small, a problem of which we were well aware and which we were addressing with annual increases in the acquisitions budget. Second, our classrooms were inadequate. Our proposed solution was to move our classrooms to the Gann building, where the highway noise would not be audible. Third, the dismissal rate of our minority students was too high and the number of minority faculty was too small.

The committee also expressed concern about our bar passage rate and, because the team wrote its report before we admitted our excellent 1998 entering classes, about our failure to raise admissions standards following receipt of provisional approval. The committee, however, did not find us out of compliance in those regards. These two concerns were related, of course. The only way to improve bar results significantly was to improve the strength of the entering class. At the same time, low bar passage rates would impede our ability to attract stronger entering classes.

In just a year, we had eliminated the ABA's concerns about our financial viability, our curriculum, and our long range planning. The size of the library and the bar passage rate remained issues, however, and now our physical plant, admissions policy, faculty diversity and minority student dismissal rate were new issues.

Lowering Our Dismissal Rate

Somewhat different concerns about our dismissal policies also came from the shareholders. They were troubled by the fact that we were dismissing students after the first semester, arguing that the law school was not giving students sufficient time to prove themselves. WASC had expressed similar concerns as early as 1981. In response to the WASC concerns, the law school had abandoned the practice of first semester dismissals. Faced with continuing low bar pass rates, however, the faculty in San Diego had reinstated the practice in 1990, when about 15 percent of our students earned an average grade below 1.51 at the end of the first semester. Under the rule adopted in 1990, a student with a grade point average below 1.51 at the end of the first semester would be dismissed.

In March 1998, I sent the faculty a memorandum reporting that the shareholders wanted us to cease the practice of dismissing students after one semester. The following August, I formally proposed abolishing first semester dismissals. Admittedly, some of the impetus for the proposal was to buy peace with the shareholders. We had raised admissions standards dramatically in both the spring and fall of 1998, resulting in smaller entering classes than the shareholders wanted. Abolishing first semester dismissals would earn some goodwill that could be used to maintain higher admissions standards.

Adopting the proposal would also address the longstanding WASC concerns. Further, students would be pleased because many of those dismissed with a low first semester average felt, as did WASC, that they had not really been given a fair chance to prove themselves and they complained bitterly about such an early end to their legal studies. Moreover, we had raised admissions standards so dramatically that, by 1998, only about one percent of the entering class was dismissed after one semester and we were unlikely to have any such students in future classes. Thus, adopting the proposal would likely have no practical impact, although it would send a helpful signal to WASC, the shareholders and the students. The faculty approved my proposal in November.

As already noted, the Accreditation Committee had expressed concern about our minority student attrition rate in 1997. By 1999, the ABA's concern about our attrition rate for minority students would broaden to include our attrition rate for all students, not just students of color. The ABA saw our high attrition rate as proof that our admissions standards were too low. WASC, of course, had been making the same point since 1976. The 1999 site evaluation team also noted that high attrition rates would frighten prospective applicants, impairing our ability to attract better students.

The concern about our dismissal rates reflected the fundamental tension that had underlain the mission of the law school since its founding, between providing access to a broad range of students and earning respect for a high quality academic program. Our traditional mission of providing access rested on the assumption that everyone who was not clearly unqualified should have the opportunity, if they so wished, to pursue a legal education. The law school's only obligation was to inform them fully of the risks and, in fact, as dean I redesigned our admissions materials to provide prospective applicants with a better understanding of the risks that they would be assuming. If applicants chose to assume those risks, the shareholders believed, they had that right. Many applicants would choose unwisely and so it was appropriate for the law school, once it determined that they did not have the requisite ability, to dismiss them. The law school saw a high attrition rate as an unfortunate price of providing access to a broad range of students. Further, from a purely institutional perspective, the law school could not survive with a low bar passage rate, as National University had demonstrated. If the law school admitted students with weak credentials, its survival would demand a high dismissal rate.

The law school's desire to create a well-regarded, high quality academic program, by contrast, militated in favor of a lower dismissal rate. A law school known for dismissing large numbers of students would have difficulty attracting a really strong entering class or building a reputation for academic excellence. WASC long had criticized the morality of accepting applicants with a very low likelihood of success, taking their tuition for a year, putting them in debt, and then dismissing them. During my two years as associate dean, I dealt with numerous students who were heartbroken and desperate over their shattered dreams of becoming a lawyer. While it was true that they had freely chosen to attend law school despite their low LSAT scores and poor undergraduate records, it was also true that many of them had genuinely deceived themselves about their ability to succeed. The essence of the whole person admissions policy was the claim that the numbers did not matter much and our touting of that policy fed the students' self-deception. Having encouraged our students' hopes and taken their money, we should not dismiss them simply to protect our bar passage rate. Instead of relying on a high dismissal rate, we should raise admissions standards and accept only those with a reasonable probability of success. Adding to these longstanding moral concerns was the fact that the ABA now had joined WASC in insisting that we lower our dismissal rates (preferably by raising admissions standards so that a high dismissal rate would be unnecessary). If we lowered dismissal rates too much, however, we would nullify the effect of higher admissions standards and our bar passage rate would never rise.

As it happened, the issue of whether to lower our dismissal rates resolved itself without a conscious collective decision by the faculty. As one might have predicted, the improvement in the strength of our entering classes led naturally to reduced dismissal rates. Of our weak fall 1997 entering class, some 25 percent were dismissed at the end of the first year. For our much stronger fall 1998 entering class, the dismissal rate plunged to 9.5 percent. For our very next class, the spring 1999 entering class, the dismissal rate fell to 5.8 percent. These lower attrition rates resulted less from a deliberate policy to lower them than from the faculty's natural reaction to stronger entering classes.

We also cured our problem with the dismissal rates of our students of color. In fall 1997, the minority student dismissal rate was 32.1 percent, compared with 22 percent for white students, a gap of more than 10 percentage points. By fall 1998, the gap had fallen to six points. By spring 1999, the minority student dismissal rate was actually lower than the dismissal rate for white students.

We were well aware that the lower dismissal rates for all students would have an adverse impact on our bar passage rates, perhaps eliminating some or even all of the gain in bar passage rates attributable to our higher admissions standards. The consolation was that, by the end of 1999, when our dismissal rates for all students had achieved consistently low levels, we knew that the classes with lower dismissal rates would not sit for the bar exam until after our deadline for obtaining full approval. As long as we gained full approval by the 2001 deadline, the adverse impact of the lower dismissal rates on our bar passage rates would be felt only after we were already fully approved and thus would not affect our accreditation application. Our hope, of course, was that we would be able to raise admissions standards enough to more than offset the effects of our lowered dismissal rate and that our bar passage rates would rise despite the lower dismissal rates.

15

Building a Stronger Campus Community

In February 1998, WASC sent an interim inspection team to evaluate the law school's progress with respect to areas of concern identified in the 1994 WASC inspection. The special visit originally was scheduled to last for two days. The first day would consist of fact gathering. On the second day, the team was scheduled to meet with the shareholders to discuss its findings and concerns. At the end of the first day, however, the team came to my office and told me that they were so impressed by the progress that we had made in the past four years that they could see no reason to meet with the shareholders. After giving me a brief outline of what they had seen, they left, a day earlier than originally planned.

The team's report offered the following summary evaluation:

Thomas Jefferson School of Law is a well operated entity providing quality legal education for its students. It enjoys a very dedicated and able faculty and staff and strong and effective leadership by the dean. The students interviewed were very supportive of their overall experience at Thomas Jefferson.

The report went on to note the increase in the strength of the entering classes as well as the law school's increased disclosure to its applicants' of their prospects for success. It cited in particular a decline in the number of applicants admitted without a bachelor's degree from 20% in fall 1994 to fewer than 2% in fall 1997. It also noted with approval the law school's falling attrition rates.

It found that the institution "continues its strong commitment to student diversity and involves students from different backgrounds in recruiting activities." It found a "striking increase" in the number of minority students in the most recent entering class and observed that the percentage of minority students at Thomas Jefferson placed it above the national average.

The longest section of the report dealt with the morale of the faculty and staff. The 1994 team had been concerned that some members of the faculty did not feel at liberty to speak their opinion about institutional governance. The report noted that the team had asked members of the faculty explicitly about this concern during the 1998 visit. It observed that

> The faculty members' response to this point was clear and convincing in affirming that there was no restriction on the freedom or right to express oneself, and further, that the climate at the University allowed for the unfettered and unrestricted expression of different points of view. There simply was no evidence of any sense of restriction in this content.

> This sense of significant improvement in faculty morale since the last WASC visit was in part produced by greater involvement of the faculty in decision making and active reaching out by the administration (Dean) to communicate

directly with the faculty. The separation from the LA campus and the establishment of Thomas Jefferson as a free standing institution provided the opportunity for the faculty, administration and staff to forge a commonly agreed upon direction including the active seeking of ABA accreditation. Even the senior well established faculty who were initially reluctant to seek ABA accreditation are now actively participating in the process and see it as possible while in the past they viewed this as both impractical but also "out of their reach."

The team found improvement in staff morale as well:

Just as was the case with the faculty, the staff issues have been directly addressed by the administration. A formal "Staff Liaison Committee" whose members receive release time hears complaints from across the institution and works to resolve complaints in timely fashion. [I]t was the reaction of staff with whom we spoke that the establishment of this group as well as other steps taken by the administration have resulted in significant improvement of morale as well as improved the relationships among the faculty, staff and administration.

The Commission, after reviewing the report, sent the law school a letter recommending continued attention to the attrition rate, while "encouraging the institution to continue its very impressive record of recruiting minority students and sustaining their enrollment." The Commission also noted its pleasure with respect to the "significant improvement in faculty morale."

Receiving National Recognition for the Quality of Life on Campus

Our efforts to improve the quality of the entering class received a major boost during the summer of 1998. Earlier in the year, the *Princeton Review of Law Schools* had requested permission to come onto our campus to survey our students about their attitudes toward the law school. In August, we received the results. We were thrilled to discover that, based on the survey of students, the *Princeton Review* had ranked Thomas Jefferson sixth in the nation for the quality of life on campus. The quality of life ranking considered the sense of community on campus and the relationship among the students and between the students and the faculty.

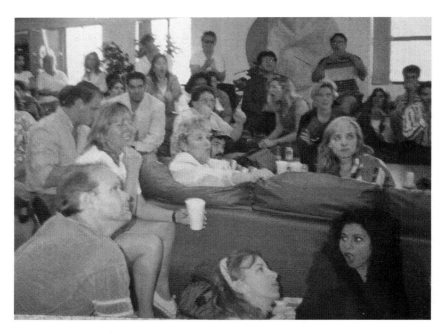

We worked hard to build a strong sense of community on campus. Here, a group of students gathered in front of a television in the student lounge to hear the verdict in the 1995 murder trial of former football player O. J. Simpson.

The results were profoundly gratifying because creating a more humane institution had been one of my two goals as dean, the other being the improvement of our academic program. Our receipt of ABA approval had indicated that we were achieving the academic improvements that we sought. WASC had noted the improvement in faculty and student morale. Now we had evidence that our students recognized our efforts to change the culture of the institution. In subsequent editions, we were ranked fifth in the nation.

Naming and Renovating the Gann Building

The Gann building also provided us with an opportunity to build a stronger campus community. It featured a charming courtyard that could provide an outdoor gathering place for students. I wanted to locate the student lounge, the deli, the student mailboxes, the bookstore, the student organization offices, and the moot courtroom around the perimeter of the courtyard so that it would be convenient to those places where students would likely go when not in class and would become a kind of crossroads where students routinely would find each other. I also wanted to locate the admissions office adjacent to the courtyard to increase the likelihood that prospective students would encounter our enrolled students. Student morale was high and I believed that virtually any contact between our students and our applicants would increase the probability that the latter would enroll.

At the time we purchased the Gann building, much of it was occupied by tenants with leases of various terms. As has been seen, we were using the rental income to build a quasi-endowment and to address ABA concerns about our dependence on tuition revenue. Thus, rather than attempting to occupy the entire building immediately, we decided initially to occupy it in stages, as the various leases expired.

The timing of our occupancy, however, was not entirely within our control. As already noted, in 1997, the Accreditation Committee found that the condition of our classrooms constituted a violation of ABA standards, necessitating that we relocate some of our classrooms to the new building as a prerequisite to receiving full ABA approval. As a result, we began to encourage our tenants to leave early so that we could begin the renovation as soon as possible.

Our existing classrooms had been in place essentially without change since the law school moved to Old Town in 1983. This would be our first chance in more than a decade to rethink classroom design. Moreover, the furniture in the classrooms had been in use at the law school since it opened its doors in 1969, almost 30 years before. The chairs were uncomfortable, hard-shell plastic chairs. The tables were too small to hold both books and a laptop and were not wired for laptop use.

Because classroom design can affect the quality of instruction, I wanted to be sure that the faculty designed the classrooms. In October 1997, I called a meeting of the faculty to discuss the design. By then, we had identified a list of issues that would need to be resolved, such as the location of aisles, the configuration of the seating, and the type of furniture and equipment to be used. The faculty discussed each of these issues and, where there was disagreement, we conducted straw votes to ascertain the majority view. After the meeting, I circulated a memorandum summarizing what I thought was the consensus and calling for further faculty comments. To facilitate that process, we also circulated a memorandum to the faculty asking a series of open-ended questions intended to elicit the widest range of comments about classroom design.

Everyone wanted the new classrooms to be wired for laptop use. I was convinced, however, that hardwired Internet connections would become obsolete in a few years and so we decided to skip that stage in the technological evolution and bring a wireless Internet connection into both buildings. The first WiFi network had been built only a couple of years before, at Carnegie-Mellon University, and so the decision placed us at the cutting-edge of campus technology. We did, however, bring a hard-wired electrical power connection to every seat because it did not appear that battery technology would soon reach the point at which students could operate on battery power all day.

Room 200, by far the largest classroom in the law school, illustrates the new design of our classrooms and our new furniture, the first new classroom furniture since the law school opened in 1969. The room is more spacious, the tables are angled, and the aisle is in the center rather than at the sides. Although the entire classroom had wireless Internet access and all seats were wired to provide power, as is evident from the photograph, very few students were using laptops in 1999, when the building renovation was completed.

Ultimately, all of the new classrooms were designed on the basis of the faculty comments. We operated under a number of constraints, including the fact that we were renovating an existing building rather than constructing a new building and the budget for renovation was very small. Within those constraints, however, we built classrooms that conformed to the wishes of the faculty.

The relocation of the student lounge, the deli, the bookstore and the moot courtroom to the new building allowed us to expand the library to fill the entire second floor of the main building. A few classrooms were moved to the third floor of the main building, on the east side away from I-5. This required that all of our administrative offices be relocated to the new building as well. As a result, the main building would house the library on the first two floors, while faculty offices and some classrooms would occupy the third floor. Everything else would be located in the new building.

Several members of the faculty and staff suggested that I relocate the dean's office to Ed Gann's former office, but I thought that to isolate the dean's office from the faculty offices would create an unhealthy distance between the faculty and the dean. Further, Gann's office was such a beautiful space that I wanted everyone to be able to enjoy it. We converted it to a conference room that was available for use by faculty, staff and students.

I show the plans for the renovation of the Courtyard Building to my daughter Shelly, the skeptical one on the left, and my daughter Jenny, on "Take Your Daughter to Work Day."

In December 1996, we would rent the room to a Hollywood production crew that was filming a movie set in San Diego called *When the Cradle Falls,* which starred actresses Linda Gray, famous for her role as Sue Ellen Ewing on the long-running television show *Dallas,* and Cathie Lee Crosby. Gray played an attorney involved in kidnapping babies for black market adoptions. Gann's office was used to shoot scenes taking place in the law office of Gray's character. I lent the crew the law books from my office to give the scene a realistic appearance.

As we prepared to renovate and then occupy the new building, everyone increasingly recognized that it needed a name other than "the new building," "the other building," or the "Gann building." Wanting again to build on the sense of participation at the law school, I decided to hold a contest to name both buildings.

In the spring of 1998, we held our contest and received about 40 suggested names reflecting a broad array of ideas. Many of the suggested names bore some connection to Thomas Jefferson or his contemporaries. Suggestions included Monticello, Shadwell, Tuckahoe, Richmond Hall, Hamilton Hall, George Wythe Hall, Madison Manor, Adams Place, Benjamin Banneker Building, Hemings Hall, Independence Hall, Freedom Hall, Liberty Pavilion, and Jefferson West and Jefferson East. Some were slight variations of these names. Others were more obscure names that we would have spent years explaining to people. A frequent suggestion for our original building was "Main Building." A couple of people suggested what became my sentimental favorite, Vandevelde Hall. One of them also suggested renaming the Gann building as the Herald Building.

Ultimately, because our main building would be occupied principally by the library, we named it the Law Library Building. Many people had suggested names with the word "library" in it and so this name adopted a variation on all those suggestions. The name was highly descriptive of the building's use, it emphasized the importance we placed on library development and scholarly research, and the initials, LLB, were the initials for the degree in law conferred by universities prior to the mid twentieth century, when the Juris Doctor degree displaced the Bachelor of Laws degree. At the suggestion of our former dean, Mary Lynne Perry, we named the new building the Courtyard Building, in honor of its most distinctive feature, the beautiful courtyard in the center of the building. The reference to courtyard also conjured the image of a judicial facility.

While we were conducting our contest, Jim White came to San Diego to meet with me and to evaluate our progress since his visit more than two years before. Jim told me that we would not receive full approval until the renovation was completed and urged us to start on it as soon as possible.

The Courtyard Building was not zoned for academic use and so the relocation of our classrooms to that building would require that we obtain a conditional use permit. Knowing that obtaining the permit would take some time, I had initiated an application for a permit at the beginning of 1997, expecting that the permit would be granted within about six months and construction could begin by summer 1997. Four local residents, however, decided to oppose the permit because they were angry that our students had been parking on the street, sometimes preventing them from parking in front of or near their homes. As a result of their opposition, the city required the law school to perform a parking study, a traffic study and an environmental impact study. Some of the neighbors argued that all on-street parking in the area should be for the exclusive use of the residents and their guests. In other words, parking on the public streets should be allowed for anyone except those affiliated with the law school. Thus, they argued, our enrollment should be limited to the number of parking spaces on campus.

Not all of our neighbors opposed the permit, however. One called the city in support of our proposal and others sent us expressions of support. They understood that we were trying in good faith to address the parking problem.

In July 1998, we submitted to the city a report that showed that our enrollment had fallen from 724 in fall 1983, when we moved to Old Town, to 588. That is, we had significantly reduced the demand for parking created by our students. Because of our desire to increase the selectivity of our admissions process, we did not anticipate that our enrollment would ever exceed the size that it was in fall 1983. At the same time, our purchase of the Courtyard Building had increased the number of parking spaces available on campus from 127 to 183.

We also sought to lease a parking lot north of the Courtyard Building, which would add another 20 spaces. I had first inquired about purchasing the lot in 1997, but it was the subject of a title dispute. By summer of 1998, the title dispute had been resolved and I proposed to the shareholders that we purchase the lot at that point. Mel Sherman hesitated because he believed that the law school should construct a new building elsewhere that would be designed specifically for our needs. Buying more land in Old Town would only sink deeper roots in a location that he did not much favor. I noted that the shareholders had been looking for a suitable site for years without success and that, until we found a better location, we needed to address our needs in our current location. Mel relented and in early 1999 we made an offer to purchase the lot for $150,000, an offer rejected by the seller. Mel then proposed that we negotiate to lease the lot, with a right of first refusal in the event that the owner received an offer to buy it. Those negotiations were successful. The owner would later receive an offer and we would exercise our right of first refusal and purchase the lot, which had been appraised at $300,000, for about $280,000.

We took other steps to mitigate the impact of our students' on-street parking. In the past, we had charged our students $20 per semester to park in our garage. Some students, rather than paying the fee, chose to park on the street. To encourage them to park in the garage, we abolished the parking fee, costing us about $20,000 a year in lost revenue. Some students were reluctant to park in the garage because they feared that their cars might be vandalized. Accordingly, we contracted for security guards in the garage, at an annual cost of about $50,000. Kay Henley, our hard working and highly capable director of academic administration, modified our course schedule in order to spread the demand for parking evenly throughout the day, avoiding peaks that would force large numbers of students to park on the street.

In July 1998, our application was reviewed by a citizens' advisory board known as "Uptown Planners," of which Maureen Markey was a member, although, of course, she recused herself in connection with our application. I attended the meeting as an observer and, after a couple of local residents complained about our students' parking on the streets, a representative of our local City Councilman, Byron Wear, rose and joined in their condemnation of the law school. I was disappointed that the councilman's representative was taking a position without having heard our perspective. After the meeting, I spoke to the two neighbors who had criticized our proposal. I described our efforts to purchase more land for parking and the other steps that we were taking. One of the neighbors told me that he would oppose any solution that we tried to adopt. The only resolution that he would accept was for the law school to relocate to another part of the city. His goal, he said, was to create so many problems for the school that it would relocate simply to be rid of him.

After the meeting, I called Wear's office and asked the staff member why he had attacked us publicly without speaking with us first and reminded him of the contributions that our law school made to the community. He apologized immediately and invited me to brief him on our view of the situation. He called me later and told me that Councilman Wear would support our efforts to improve our educational program. Over the next few months, the councilman was very helpful at times when the process seemed to stall.

When the shareholders learned about the problems that we were having with our neighbors, Mel Sherman recommended that I contact Trish Butler, a consultant who handled land use planning issues. Trish was a gem – smart, effective and easy to work with. She made some calls on our behalf and our permit began to move its way through the bureaucracy.

I also tried to learn as much as possible about the city planning process. As the city reviewed our application for construction permits and the conditional use permit, I met personally with each of the city officials involved, stressing that our campus expansion was intended to improve academic quality, that we had no plans to increase enrollment beyond the level that it was in 1983 when we were allowed to occupy the Old Town location, and that we had taken substantial steps to improve the parking situation.

The city staff respected our efforts to improve the quality of the institution and acknowledged our efforts to provide more parking for students. They told me that the city understood the value of our enterprise and that it would never impose conditions on us that would prevent us from operating or that would cause us significant damage. Further, the neighbors had no right to the exclusive use of on-street parking. The streets were public streets, maintained by taxpayer dollars and available to all on the same basis. The city staff said that they would need to give the neighbors a hearing, but that in the end all that the city would ever ask from us was a good faith effort to reduce the impact of parking where we could. Although some of the neighbors were demanding that the city cap our enrollment, the city staff told me that they would not do that to us.

As time passed, I became increasingly concerned about whether we would be able to finish the construction by summer 1999, when we would be eligible to apply for full approval. I spoke candidly with the city staff about our accreditation concerns and told them that the delay was imperiling the law school. They told me that under the circumstances they would approve the issuance of building permits, to allow the work to begin, even though the building could not be occupied until the conditional use permit was granted.

Our entire budget for the renovation of both buildings was only $375,000. As construction progressed, city building inspectors discovered countless instances where our buildings were out of compliance with the building code, which had changed after the buildings were constructed. Now that we were requesting permission to alter our campus, the city was entitled to require us to bring everything into compliance with the current code. All of the restrooms in the Courtyard Building needed to be gutted and rebuilt entirely. The elevator shaft needed to be enlarged, but we persuaded the city to grant us a hardship exemption for that requirement. The Law Library Building had two front entrances, but the code required them to be just a few feet farther apart than they were. So, we had to cut an entirely new entrance into the front of the building, a few feet away from the existing entrance, and construct a fire-rated corridor to the new entrance. By February 1999, the cost of construction had reached $485,000.

On September 9, 1998, the city planning office notified me formally that it would recommend that we be granted the conditional use permit. The next step was for the office staff to prepare a report for submission to a hearing officer, who would conduct a public hearing on our application and make the final decision.

The hearing was scheduled for February 1999. Many of our students attended, as did our neighbors. The neighbors went to the microphone one by one to denounce our students as rude and noisy and to complain about students' parking on the street. Many of the students wanted to rise in their own defense, but we asked them not to speak because we had established an excellent rapport with the city staff and we were confident that the result would be in our favor. The hearing officer, as we anticipated, granted us our permit, although with a proviso that we conduct annual parking studies to permit the city to monitor the situation.

Construction was substantially completed by May 1999, just in time for the meeting of the Accreditation Committee. In June, city inspectors noticed that our entire second floor was allocated for use as library stacks, but that the floor had not been reinforced to meet the code for library stacks. They notified me that the floor would need to be reinforced, at a cost of $225,000.

By this time, our efforts to address the parking situation and our candor about our operation had established considerable credibility with the city staff. As a result, I was able to persuade the city to allow us to operate the library without reinforcing the floor, provided that we promised that the load we would place on the floor would not exceed a designated limit. I met with our library staff and we designed a plan to ensure that the load would remain within that limit.

After completion of a construction project, the owner typically examines the work, looking for instances where the work was not performed satisfactorily. These instances are compiled into a list called a "punchlist." The owner generally withholds a portion of the contract price, which is paid to the contractor only when the punchlist items are completed. We produced a punchlist, but our contractor was slow to complete the items. At a certain point, we realized that we had not seen him in quite a few days and no progress was being made. I called his office and reached his wife on the telephone. When I asked for him, she began to cry. Unbeknownst to me, a few days before, the contractor had been in a Las Vegas casino when he collapsed suddenly and died. He was the only person who really knew the details of his company's operation. His wife asked me for some indulgence while she tried to sort out the company's commitments. I extended my condolences and hung up the phone. No one from the company ever came to complete the punchlist items. With an Accreditation Committee meeting looming and wanting to be able to report that we had completed the renovation, I directed our facilities staff to complete the few remaining items and we retained the unpaid portion of the contract amount.

Once we began to occupy the Courtyard Building, we had the problem that students, faculty and staff were crossing the street between the two buildings continuously all day. Students in particular would step out into the street in the evening after dark, sometimes without looking for approaching cars. I came very close to hitting a student with my car one evening and many others had the same complaint. As early as October of 1996, Robin Lee, our director of facilities, had requested that the city install a stop sign at the corner and a crosswalk between the two buildings so that everyone would have a safe place at which to cross. The city denied her request, however.

As time passed, the problem continued and this became another source of the neighbors' complaints. The neighbors and I both thought that it was only a matter of time before a student was struck by a car. In 1999, I called the traffic engineer's office to discuss the problem and was told that the city opposed crosswalks because they increased the danger to pedestrians by giving them a false sense of security, leading them to step into the crosswalk without looking for approaching traffic. Without a crosswalk, people realized that they were in danger and were more careful. Our problem, however, was that we did not have a crosswalk and students still were not being careful. I did not see how a crosswalk could possibly make the situation worse.

After much discussion, the traffic engineer agreed to send someone to the campus to observe the situation. The inspector asked me to meet him on the street corner at 11 a.m. on a designated day. We sent a notice to everyone on campus that the inspector was coming and asked them to please cross the street at that time. I also asked the faculty to release their classes exactly on schedule. The response was remarkable and demonstrated the strong sense of community that existed at the law school. At 11:15 sharp, a flood of students, staff and faculty gushed into the street. A number of students crossed the street, went into a building and then came out moments later and crossed it again. A sight impaired student who usually navigated the campus without a cane emerged from the Courtyard Building, white cane in hand, and tapped it on the pavement as he walked across the street with no stop sign or crosswalk to protect him. By 11:30, we had a promise of a crosswalk, which the city quickly installed.

16

Struggling to Raise the Bar Passage Rate

During the first two years following our receipt of provisional approval, we believed that we were making great strides in our quest for full ABA approval. In the midst of the building renovations, Thomas Jefferson hosted its 1998 ABA site evaluation team from February 8 to 11. The team reported that the law school was addressing all of the issues raised by the Accreditation Committee in the past.

At the end of February 1998, as already noted, Jim White returned to campus for two days, apparently to assess our progress since our grant of provisional approval. He told me that we were heading in the right direction in every respect and praised in particular our development of the library, our use of technology, and the expansion of the full-time faculty. He could not think of any way to improve upon our building renovation plans. He did make clear, however, that we would not receive full approval until we completed our occupation of the Courtyard Building. Assuming that we completed our renovation and continued our expansion of the library and faculty, he believed that the only issues that could cause us not to receive full approval were the related issues of the quality of our entering class and our bar passage rate. As we would learn later in the year, however, those issues were emerging as a severe obstacle to our receipt of full approval.

At the time of Jim's visit, our most recent bar exam results were those of the July 1997 bar exam, on which our first time pass rate of 45.9 percent was 34 percentage points below the statewide pass rate for graduates of ABA approved law school, results that were no better than those we had achieved prior to our receipt of ABA approval. Of course, the graduates who were taking the bar exam in 1997 and 1998 were admitted prior to our receipt of provisional approval, when our admissions standards had been quite low. We were paying for our past sins of admission.

Jim acknowledged that raising the bar passage rate could take many years, because of the time required for stronger entering classes to graduate and sit for the bar exam, and thus the best way to address the issue of the bar passage rate was to demonstrate improvement in the quality of the entering classes. This we had done with the spring 1998 entering class and would do so again with the fall 1998 entering class. Our two 1998 entering classes, after they graduated, would prove that Thomas Jefferson could produce a class capable of succeeding on the bar exam.

A Pounding by the Accreditation Committee

As we could have anticipated from Jim's remarks to me, the Accreditation Committee, at its meeting on June 26-27, 1998, found the law school out of compliance with ABA standards in three respects: admissions, the bar passage rate and, because the building renovations at that point were not yet completed, the physical facility. The committee directed us to submit a plan by September 10 for bringing the law school into compliance with the standards in those three respects.

In November, Art Toll and I traveled to San Francisco to appear before the Accreditation Committee at its request. The committee members were deeply concerned about our low bar passage rate and troubled that the shareholders had recently taken a distribution of profits while the law school still had unmet needs. They made clear that, as long as the law school had such poor bar results, it had serious unmet needs and profits should not be taken. Art justified the distributions on the ground that the money was not needed for the law school, noting that I had not asked for additional funds. I greatly disliked that response for two reasons. First, the only effect of the response was to damage my credibility with the committee, which was not helpful to our cause. Second, the response did not adequately portray the situation. The shareholders told me each year the approximate size of the surplus that they expected in the budget. They would approve additional funds for the academic program, as long as I admitted additional students to cover the cost and generate the expected surplus. Admitting additional students, however, would require lowering our admissions standards and would result in a lower bar passage rate. So, I did not ask for more money because I was trying to raise our admissions standards and our bar passage rate, the very thing the committee wanted me to do. My frugality was cause for praise, not criticism. The impact of blaming me for the distributions became clear when, near the end of the meeting, one of the members of the committee turned to me and said, "Someone needs to hit you over the head with a 2 by 4 because you just don't get it." When we were excused, Art and I walked to our car in silence.

The action letter generated by the November 1998 meeting of the committee found the law school to be out of compliance with the standards in two respects: our low bar pass rates and our failure to complete the renovation of the building. The committee reminded us that a law school has only five years to achieve full compliance and said that it was "imperative that the School fully comprehend the significance" of the deadline and "take all appropriate action necessary to bring the School within compliance of all Standards."

In January 1999, I had lunch with Jim White at the AALS annual meeting to discuss the accreditation process. Jim told me very bluntly that our bar passage rate was too low and that it was not reasonable for the shareholders to expect to make money during the first few years of accreditation. Jim said that the reason that our reception at the November meeting had been so hostile was that the members of the committee were angry that the shareholders were taking distributions of profits at a time when our admissions standards were still too low, our library collection was still too meagre, and our faculty was small for a dual division law school. If the law school had money remaining at the end of the year, it should be used to address these problems. The shareholders should take no distributions, other than an amount to cover their tax liabilities for any surplus generated by the law school, until the needs of the law school were fully met. Although he was not explicit, I understood Jim to mean that there should be no distributions of profits until the law school received full approval. Later that year, to address the ABA's concerns, the shareholders returned the distribution of profits that they had taken in 1998.

We also discussed the fact that the law school was eligible to apply for full approval in 1999. Jim observed that, while the standards allowed an application after three years, few law schools achieved full approval after three years. The norm, he said, was five. He told me not to expect full approval in 1999. Rather, we should be working toward full approval in 2001, the year in which our provisional approval would expire.

I left the lunch deeply dispirited. We were not yet close to receiving full approval and I would very likely need to remain in the dean's office until 2001.

Focusing on the Bar Passage Rate

Our brutal November 1998 meeting with the Accreditation Committee had made clear that our bar passage rate was the central issue in our accreditation and thus the key to our survival as an institution. The only other issue resulting from our 1998 site evaluation was the condition of our facility, which we were addressing through our building renovations. We thus began a relentless focus on raising our bar pass rate.

Several faculty members immediately asked to place the problem of the bar passage rate on the agenda of the December faculty meeting. They circulated a five page, single-spaced memo with their own recommendations for addressing the problem. Their suggestions generally focused on changes in our instructional program to better prepare students.

Aaron Schwabach volunteered to collect ideas from the rest of the faculty and eventually compiled a three page, single-spaced list of proposals for raising the bar passage rate. The multitude of suggestions that Aaron collected fell into three categories: ways to improve the strength of the entering class, ways to better prepare our students to pass the bar exam, and ways to encourage our graduates to study for the bar exam in the right way. Ultimately, we would try virtually everything proposed by members of the faculty and we would learn that the only thing that substantially improved our bar passage rate was raising our admissions standards.

Our strongest students would pass the bar exam even without any additional help, as long as they took a bar review course and studied very hard. Our weakest students had such severe skill deficiencies that we were not able in just three years to improve their performance sufficiently to pass the exam. A curriculum focused on preparing students for the bar exam might improve the performance of some students in the middle of the class just enough to earn them a passing score and raise our bar passage rate modestly. Only higher admissions standards, however, would provide the kind of dramatic improvement necessary to save our ABA accreditation.

Obviously, one alternative to higher admissions standards was more rigorous retention standards. A law school can have an open admissions policy and still achieve a high bar passage rate, as long as it dismisses a large enough percentage of the entering class before graduation. That had been the WSU strategy in its early years, although once applications declined after the mid 1970s the college no longer could afford the kind of dismissal rates required. Thus, after the mid 1970s, the strategy had consistently produced disappointing bar passage rates. In any event, we could not in good conscience radically modify our retention policies and apply the new policies to students who had already enrolled. If we wished to embrace higher attrition rates as a substitute for more rigorous admissions standards – and we did not wish to do so – even that solution would take time to implement and thus it would not have an immediate impact on our bar passage rate.

The problem, however, was that we had only two years left to receive full accreditation. No matter how much we raised admissions standards or attrition rates, the classes sculpted by those changes would not take the bar exam until after the 2001 deadline for obtaining full approval. We had no choice but to try to improve the performance of the students whom we had already admitted.

My first action following the November 1998 meeting with the Accreditation Committee was to create a new full time position of director of diversity affairs and academic support. The law school for many years had had a first-year academic support program (ASP), intended to prevent first year students from being academically dismissed. The problem with the program was that it helped students to improve their performance enough to survive the first year, but not enough to pass the bar exam. In a sense, the more successful the first year ASP was, the lower our bar pass rate would be, because we were graduating, rather than dismissing, students who did not have the skills to pass the bar exam. Thus, the first priority of the new director was to design a second and third year academic support program to assist students in passing the bar exam.

The new director would also assist in our efforts to attract and retain students of color, to prepare students of color to succeed in law school and on the bar exam, and to create a multicultural environment on campus. Although there is no reason in principle to link academic support with diversity affairs, the ABA's 1997 action letter had found that our minority student attrition rate was so high that we were not in full compliance with the standards. Thus, combining academic support with diversity affairs made sense under the circumstances. Further, I wanted to have a director of diversity affairs because I thought that we needed someone to spearhead our efforts to further diversify the student body, but funds for new positions were very difficult to obtain. Combining the diversity affairs position with academic support helped to justify the position to the shareholders.

In January 1999, I invited Steve Klein to make a presentation to the faculty about how to improve our bar passage rate. Steve was a psychometrician with the RAND Corporation who served as a frequent consultant to the Committee of Bar Examiners. He was regarded as the leading expert in the state on bar passage. Steve made a presentation to the entire faculty about the structure and grading of the bar exam. He reviewed the bar results of our students and said that they had deficiencies in every area of exam performance. After the presentation, he met individually with each member of the faculty (who wished to do so) to review that person's exam questions and to offer advice about how his or her exam questions could be modified to better test the same skills that the bar exam was testing.

Cheryl Lee, our new director of diversity affairs and academic support, arrived in January 1999 and began to create a comprehensive second and third year academic support program. Members of the faculty agreed to administer mid term exams in Contracts, Torts, Property, Constitutional Law and Evidence. Second year students were invited to attend a weekly course on exam writing. Third year students were invited to attend a semester long bar review course provided free of charge by the law school on the weekend. Each week, a different instructor would lecture on a different bar tested subject. At the end of the lecture, students would take a practice exam covering the material in the lecture. The following week, their exam answers would be returned to them with comments. The instructors asked to deliver the lectures were those whose classes had waiting lists, those whom we knew that the students would want to hear. To supplement the weekend lectures, we placed in the library review tapes created by the faculty covering every bar tested subject, so that students could review problem areas identified by the weekend course.

In December 1998, Jan Dauss, my executive assistant, had called every graduate who had taken the July bar exam and asked him or her a series of questions about how he or she had studied, whether he or she had worked while studying for the exam, and what portions of the exam he or she had passed or failed. She also asked the students who failed why they thought they had failed. We collected the results in order to construct a profile of the wrong and right ways to prepare for the bar exam.

In February 1999, I sent a letter to the entire student body describing what we had learned from the survey. The letter told them that they must take a bar review course, that BAR/BRI had by far the highest bar passage rate among our graduates, that they must not work while preparing for the exam, and that students who passed reported that they had studied between 70 and 98 hours per week. Those who failed had studied an average of 52 hours per week. The letter also told them that, unless they followed all of this advice, they had almost no chance of passing the bar exam.

In April, I sent a memo to the faculty about the bar exam. I noted that for the past five years we consistently had posted bar results lower than those of every ABA approved law school in the state. We were behind WSU. We were behind Chapman, which had just produced its first graduating class. I called the situation a "disgrace" and a "humiliation."

That month, I asked each member of the faculty to mentor at least one third year student at risk of failing the bar exam. The mentor would stay in constant contact with the student, ensure that the student was studying in the right way, review and critique practice exams, and work with the student on problem areas. Because at that time we had so few students in our graduating classes, helping even another 10 students to pass would substantially improve our passage rate. The other benefit of this process would be that, by working closely with at risk students as they prepared for the bar exam, we would ascertain exactly where their problems lay and could try to devise ways to overcome those problems.

In May, we received the report on our 1999 ABA site evaluation. The team liked our building renovations and praised our efforts to increase the diversity of the faculty and student body. The law school at that point had, for the first time in its history, members of the full-time faculty who were African-American, Asian-American and Latino. We had a director of diversity affairs and the percentage of students of color in our entering classes was above the national average. Our minority student attrition rate was below that for white students.

The report then focused on our central problem. We had raised admissions standards, but not enough. Our bar pass rates were still too low. The team urged us to stop putting money aside in our quasi-endowment fund and to spend every available penny on recruiting stronger entering classes.

At the end of the semester, I met with the shareholders to discuss the ABA site evaluation team's report. We all understood that the bar passage rate was now the central accreditation issue. When the shareholders learned that 20 percent of our graduates had taken no bar review course prior to the July 1998 bar exam and that all of them failed the exam, Dick Leavitt proposed a solution that the other shareholders quickly approved. Following the meeting, I sent a memo to our graduating class with the shareholders' offer. If a student enrolled in the BAR/BRI course, which among our graduates had the highest success rate, and passed the California bar exam on the first attempt, the law school would pay the student $1500.

None of this worked. None of it did. When we received our July 1999 bar results, they were catastrophic. Our first time pass rate was 31.3 percent, compared with 68.5 percent for all California ABA approved and 33.3 percent for all state accredited law schools. We were not even above the average for the state accredited law schools. The terms "disgrace" and "humiliation" that I had used in the spring did not seem strong enough now. We had been provisionally approved for three years, but the students taking the bar exam were still those recruited before we received ABA approval and our bar passage rate had not improved at all.

The weekend bar review course had started off very well. Forty-one students attended the first lecture. Only eighteen came the second week, however. Attendance dropped each week until eventually we discontinued the course because we had at most six students attending and most of them had grade point averages so high that they were certain to pass the bar exam even without any assistance.

Faculty mentoring of our graduates had failed as well. Most faculty members reported that their assigned graduates did not return their phone calls and did not show up for scheduled meetings. Of the thirty-two graduates assigned a faculty mentor, only three passed, a pass rate of fewer than 10 percent.

Even the shareholders' financial offer had not worked. Our top graduates, who would have passed anyway, passed the exam and collected a windfall of $1500. Everyone else failed. All we had really done was award a nice parting gift to our best graduates.

We now had only three administrations of the bar exam left before the end of our provisional approval. If we did not raise our bar passage rate in the next three administrations, the law school seemed certain to lose provisional approval, with calamitous consequences.

Further, our poor bar passage rates seemed to be infecting the ABA's view of everything at the law school. Although the 1999 site evaluation team was impressed by the "credentials, diligence and enthusiasm" of the faculty, it said that it found a lack of intellectual rigor in the classroom. The Accreditation Committee commented that the law school's bar results were "abysmal" and suggested that this might be attributable to the lack of rigor.

The allegation that our teaching lacked rigor was ridiculous. Three consecutive ABA site evaluation teams had visited the campus and all three had written reports that praised our teaching. Those reports were written, however, before our pass rate dropped to just above 30 percent. A low bar pass rate licensed our site evaluation teams to find academic deficiencies wherever they wished.

The criticism of our teaching and our bar pass rate was galling at times because some of our critics taught at law schools located in states with much easier bar exams than the California bar exam. Our graduates had excellent bar exam results in other states. Had we been located anywhere but California, the likelihood is that our bar pass rate would not have been a serious obstacle to our gaining accreditation. Our faculty was second to none in its ability to prepare students for a bar exam. As a California law school, however, we were held to a higher standard than law schools in many other states. Like other California law schools, we needed to achieve the right combination of admissions and retention standards to produce a graduating class capable of passing the California bar exam. We had not yet done so, however.

The committee noted the sharp correlation between admissions standards and bar passage rates. For example, graduates with an LSAT score of 155 or higher had a 71.4 percent pass rate, graduates with an LSAT score of 148 to 154 had a 44.4 percent bar passage rate, graduates with an LSAT score of 141 to 147 had a 32.3 percent bar passage rate, and graduates with an LSAT score of 140 or lower had a 25 percent bar passage rate. As was obvious to all, the problem needed to be addressed through higher admissions standards.

The committee was also concerned about our attrition rate. As already noted, by 1999, we had reduced our academic dismissal rate sharply. Now we had a new attrition-related problem, however. As will be discussed below, increasing numbers of our best students were transferring to other law schools after the first year, resulting in a lower bar passage rate than if these students had graduated from Thomas Jefferson and taken the bar exam as our alumni. This worried the committee and thus our attrition rates remained a concern, although for quite different reasons than before.

The one bright spot was diversity. Although the committee previously had worried about our minority student attrition rates, as already discussed, that concern had been completely eliminated by 1999. The committee found it "evident" that our minority students "felt that their needs were being met by the institution."

The committee found that the law school was out of compliance with ABA accreditation standards based on our high voluntary attrition rate and our low bar passage rate. It expressed concerns, but did not find a lack of compliance, with respect to the size of our library and our lack of long range planning, meaning essentially our inability to explain how we were going to solve our attrition and bar passage rate problems.

In December, Jan called the graduates who had sat for the July bar exam and spoke with 30 of them. She found that our hectoring about the importance of a bar review course had had some effect. All of the graduates she contacted had taken a bar review course. When she asked those who failed why they believed that they had been unsuccessful, they all gave the same answer. They said that they did not know how to write an exam answer. They had not had enough practice with exam writing.

Of course, we had offered students exam practice in both our weekend bar review course and in our bar exam mentoring program, but students, in effect, had declined both offers. It appeared that the only way to give them more practice with exam writing was to require them to practice.

Worried about our deteriorating circumstances, members of the faculty again began to circulate a variety of proposals to address our bar passage rate, just as we had done earlier in the year. One of the ideas was that we increase the number of midterms being administered. As it happened, I was scheduled to deliver a paper at a conference in Venezuela on the day of the December 1999 faculty meeting and so I missed the meeting. During the meeting, however, the faculty began to discuss midterms and, one by one, everyone pledged to give a midterm. The faculty did not adopt a mandatory policy in that regard. All had simply agreed that our students needed more practice with writing exam answers and that it was everyone's responsibility to provide the practice that the students needed. The faculty had come together to try to solve the problem. After that, the entire faculty began to administer midterms in at least one of their courses each semester, typically in whichever bar tested subject they taught.

As the spring 2000 semester began, our focus increasingly turned to working on students' exam writing skills. Believing that it was never too early to start, I decided to add to our orientation program for entering students a lengthy session on outlining their courses, analyzing legal issues, and writing an exam answer. To emphasize the importance of the session, I taught it myself, hoping that the entering students would pay attention to a program taught by the dean. Colin Crawford, one of our faculty members, offered later in the semester to teach a half day program on how to write an exam answer, open to all students, but targeted to those taking the bar exam.

The students were also alarmed about our low bar pass rate and its potential impact on our accreditation. During the spring, the Student Bar Association formed a committee to address the problem. The committee members met with me and told me that they believed that the reason that California Western's bar passage rate was so much higher than ours was that California Western had hired two psychologists who also had law degrees to design a bar preparation course. The two psychologists, Dennis Saccuzzo and Nancy Johnson, had written a bar review handbook. The students told me that their friends at California Western assured them that the secret to raising the bar passage rate was in the handbook.

I knew something that the students didn't, which was that the graduates sitting for the bar exam at that time were admitted to law school at a time when California Western had much higher admissions standards than did Thomas Jefferson. Thus, California Western's better performance could have been entirely the result of stronger entering classes, rather than the bar preparation program. We could not really know with any certainty.

In any event, I asked our students if they could bring me a copy of this handbook. A little later, the students returned to my office carrying an envelope. They handed me the envelope and told me that they needed the contents back in an hour. The California Western handbook inside the envelope contained a flowchart for each bar course. I thought to myself, "We can do this." I asked the faculty for volunteers to write summaries of bar tested subjects and soon had a volunteer for each subject. The legal writing faculty offered to provide materials on how to study and how to write an exam answer. By October, we had a 230 page bar examination handbook that showed students how to study and how to write an exam answer. It included an overview of every bar tested subject, explaining the core material that students needed to know to pass the bar exam in that subject and providing them with an approach to bar exam questions on the subject, although our handbook used outlines rather than flowcharts. We distributed a copy of the handbook to every third year student and continued to do so until the last year of my deanship.

As already indicated, by spring 2000, we were focusing our bar preparation efforts on developing exam writing skills. I believed that we needed to teach students these skills through individualized attention and that we needed to start early. I proposed to the faculty that we create a mandatory second year program for every student with a grade point average that put him or her at serious risk of failing the bar exam. Students in the program would be required to meet individually each week with a tutor and be required to remain in the program until the tutor certified that the student had acquired exam writing skills sufficient to pass the bar exam. These students would not be permitted to graduate until they completed the program. The idea was that we would not graduate any student with exam writing skills insufficient to pass the bar exam.

Over the summer, we hired four tutors – recent law graduates who had passed the bar exam and who had a particular interest in tutoring students in exam writing. In fact, some of them already were self-employed as part-time bar exam tutors. One of the tutors was taking a different bar exam every six months, to develop expertise in bar preparation.

The faculty had not liked mentoring graduates sitting for the bar exam and it had not worked. So, as of fall 2000, we abandoned the program and used the same tutors who were running the second year program to staff a third year bar preparation program. The third year program consisted of weekly practice with essay exams, performance tests, and multiple choice questions.

At the end of the academic year, we evaluated our new program with the bar tutors. We found that, of the students in the second year program, two-thirds saw an improvement in their grade point average after participation in the program for one semester and that the average increase after a semester was .288. One semester later, about

40 percent still were earning higher grades and the average increase was .498. It appeared that the program was working, but the question was whether the effect would persist until the students took the bar exam the next year.

We continued to use tutors to staff our second and third year bar preparation programs for the remainder of my deanship, eventually increasing the number of tutors to eight. The program of early intervention, mandatory individualized tutoring in exam writing skills, refusal to graduate students who could not demonstrate adequate exam writing skills, and the administration of midterm exams in all required courses became the heart of our efforts to better prepare our students for the bar exam.

In 2003, I would ask Steve Semeraro, by then the associate dean, to assume the supervision of the bar preparation programs so that we could ensure that its effectiveness was closely monitored. In 2004, Steve informed me that he had heard that Dennis Saccuzzo and Nancy Johnson were leaving California Western and asked for permission to offer them a contract to create a bar preparation program for us. Uncertain whether California Western's success was attributable entirely to its higher admissions standards or in part to the Saccuzzo-Johnson program, I authorized Steve to negotiate a contract for a one-year pilot program at Thomas Jefferson during the 2004-2005 academic year. Our plan was to evaluate the pilot program after a year in order to determine whether it was generating higher pass rates for our students. At the end of the year, however, I left the dean's office and the statistical evaluation was never performed.

All that lay in the future. Meanwhile, at its November 2-4, 2000, meeting, the Accreditation Committee found the law school still out of compliance with the standards. The committee found that our admissions standards must not be demanding enough because our attrition rate was so high and our bar passage rate was so low. The committee also continued to find that some classes still lacked the necessary rigor. We were nine months away from a decision on full approval.

Reducing Outward Transfers

One consequence of not having ABA accreditation for most of our history had been that our units would not transfer to an ABA accredited law school. Once a student enrolled at WSU, he or she was very unlikely to transfer to another law school, although occasionally a student forced for family or career reasons to relocate would transfer to another state accredited law school in California. Most of our students, however, were rooted in San Diego and did not wish to leave.

Our receipt of ABA accreditation meant that students could transfer to another law school at the end of the first year, if they wished. Further, because so many of our students came from outside of California, by the late 1990s a majority of our students had deep roots somewhere else. Students would arrive in San Diego, only to find that they missed their families, friends or lovers. Often students came because they were denied admission to a law school near their home. If they performed well at Thomas Jefferson, however, then the law school that denied them admission as a first year student often would accept them as a second year transfer student, giving many of our best students opportunities that they did not have before. In some cases, as will be discussed below, students who were admitted with a large scholarship failed to perform as expected and lost some or all of their scholarship, eliminating the financial incentive that had brought them to Thomas Jefferson.

The result of all of these factors was that, when the first fall entering class that we recruited following our receipt of ABA accreditation, the fall 1997 entering class, reached the end of its first year, we were surprised to see that more than 20 of the students transferred to other law schools. Many of them were the top students in the class.

Obviously, losing some of our best students would lower our bar passage rate. At one of my regular open fora with students, I had learned that one of the major complaints was that our grading curve was so low that even our top students had only B averages. In fact, the grade point average at the 90th percentile was approximately 2.85, meaning that some of the students in the top 10 percent of the class had below a B average. Our assistant dean of career services, Andrea Lamb, had voiced the same concern. We could argue that class rank was what employers really considered, but that argument was correct only within certain limits. An employer who saw that a highly ranked student had barely a B average might well conclude that the class as a whole must be poor and that this student was merely among the best of a weak lot.

The Law School Admissions Council annually provided us with a formula that predicted the first year grade point average of each of our entering students. When we compared our excellent fall 1998 entering class with prior classes, we saw that the formula predicted that the fall 1998 class would have a higher class average than the fall 1997 class, because of the stronger students. Accordingly, in October 1998, I proposed to the faculty that we raise our grading curve to allow higher grades. This would improve our students' employment prospects, increase the probability that they would remain at Thomas Jefferson, and boost our bar passage rate. Use of the LSAC formula to assist us in determining how much to raise our grades avoided any argument that the curve had been arbitrarily altered or that we had succumbed to grade inflation. We had empirical evidence that our standards were not changing and that we were merely accommodating stronger entering classes. The faculty adopted my proposal in November and this set a precedent under which in future years, as entering classes improved, we revised our grading curve to allow the stronger students to receive higher grades. Revisions of the curve, however, were always linked to data showing improvements in the quality of the entering class so that we were not simply raising the grades assigned to the same level of performance.

After we became aware of the transfer problem, I asked the faculty for their help in addressing it. In order to transfer, students typically needed letters of recommendation from some of their first year instructors. This requirement meant that we usually would know who was considering a transfer long before the transfer occurred. I asked the faculty to notify me anytime a student used the word "transfer" other than in a context relating to public transportation. The faculty responded wonderfully and I began to receive a flood of notifications about possible transfers.

I asked the students who were considering a transfer to meet with me to discuss their reasons for transferring. In some cases, I could not argue with their desire to transfer. For example, some students had compelling personal reasons, such as an ill parent, that necessitated their relocation. Some students had weak academic records and were likely to fail the California bar exam if they stayed. Transferring to a law school in a state with an easier bar exam made sense for them.

Many of the top students, however, told me that finances played a major role in their decision. At that time, we offered scholarships to our strongest incoming students, but these scholarships were for the first year only. We awarded scholarships to second and third year students, but these scholarships were based on their grades at the end of the prior year. In effect, no student ever received a scholarship commitment for longer than one year.

These policies, which dated from early in Jack Monks' presidency, were intended to encourage students to work hard throughout their law school careers in order to retain their existing scholarship or to earn a better one. Although encouraging and rewarding good performance was a laudable goal, the result for the students was constant insecurity. A poor performance on an exam could cost a student all or a substantial portion of his or her scholarship.

When students received their first semester grades, the top students realized that their grades might give them the opportunity to attend a different law school, one that was fully accredited and had a more established reputation. They had been lured to Thomas Jefferson perhaps in part by a scholarship, but the scholarship would expire at the end of the year and they had no guarantee that they would receive any kind of financial assistance for the second year. And, even if they received a good scholarship for the second year, they had no guarantee for the third year. Anxious about their future at Thomas Jefferson and aware of the new opportunities that they had, many of the top students decided to explore the possibility of transferring, often to a law school nearer their families, but sometimes to a more prestigious law school. Once students started the application process, their families, friends and lovers would become excited about the prospect of their returning home and, after they went home for the summer, they never returned.

I decided that the best way to discourage the transfer of our best students was to grant them scholarships for the second and third years before they had a chance even to think about transferring. We revised our scholarship policies so that we awarded scholarships to our top students at the end of their first semester. The scholarships were renewable, as long as the recipients maintained a B- average, which for students at their level, now that we had revised the grading curve, was a virtual guarantee of a renewal. We moved quickly to award the scholarships as soon as the first semester grades were final, so that by the time they started their second semester the top students effectively had a guaranteed scholarship for the rest of their law school careers.

Some of our top students considered transferring because they believed that transferring would improve their employment prospects. The problem that they did not anticipate, however, was that transferring would cost them their high class rank. They often had better career prospects as a highly ranked Thomas Jefferson student than as a student in the middle of the class at a better established law school. A number of transfer students wrote members of the faculty letters in which they regretted their transfer. In one or two instances, students actually transferred back to Thomas Jefferson. I collected this information and passed it on to students who were considering a transfer.

One of the problems was that the practice of transferring was self-perpetuating. After the first group of students from the fall 1997 entering class transferred out, students in the next entering class heard about it and concluded that transferring must be in their best interest. Each group of transfers inspired the next year's class to explore the same possibilities. As we drew closer to 2001, when students knew that our provisional approval would expire and as our bar results continued to disappoint everyone, fear that we would lose our accreditation swept through the student body, inspiring even more students to consider transferring, while the law school was still accredited.

Ultimately, however, the combination of our scholarship policies and our counseling of students solved the problem. In 2001, the year that we received full accreditation, I was able to report that out of the top thirty students in the first year class, only four had transferred to another law school at the end of the year. In prior years, we had seen as many as six of the top ten students leave. Further, those who transferred out, statistically speaking, were no longer our top students, but essentially a representative sample of the entire class. Losing a representative sample of the class would not lower our bar passage rate. As will be seen below, the ABA would conclude in 2001 that, by then, our outward transfer problem had been solved.

After 2001, we lost very few of our top students. The number of outward transfer students from all segments of the class continued to fall and, by 2004, the year of our last ABA inspection during my deanship, we were able to report that only three students out of the entire spring and fall entering classes combined had transferred to another law school. Outward transfers thus constituted less than one percent of the class. We had created an atmosphere in which virtually all of our students were choosing to remain.

17

Converting to a Nonprofit Law School

One day early in the spring 2000 semester, Art, Dick and Mel came to my office to speak with me privately. They shocked me with the news that they had decided to sell both law schools. During the fall semester, they had hired an investment banker, who was in the process of looking for a large, publicly traded company to acquire the schools. They expected to complete the sale by June at the latest.

I told them that I had always hoped that, when they were ready to sell the law school, they would sell it to a nonprofit organization, so that all of the resources generated by the law school could be used for the academic program, rather than to pay taxes and to provide a return to investors. I suggested that I investigate a sale to a university or another nonprofit institution. They said that they wanted to sell the school quickly and that I would not have sufficient time to find a nonprofit to purchase the law school. They directed me not to pursue that alternative.

I asked them why they had decided to sell at that time. Art replied that they were not getting any younger. Two of them were already over the age of 70. They had owned the law school for over 22 years. I later learned that Mel long had advocated selling the law school so that he could retire, but had needed years of discussion to persuade Dick and Art to acquiesce, at least in part because they enjoyed owning a law school. They told me that I must keep the sale confidential and that I could discuss it only with our chief financial officer, Nancy Vu.

Almost immediately after my meeting with the shareholders, I was contacted by their broker, Base Horner. He needed information about a variety of aspects of the law school. Nancy and I worked hard to assemble and transmit it. Over the next couple of months, the shareholders scheduled meetings with a handful of potential buyers. I attended each of the meetings and explained why I thought that the Thomas Jefferson School of Law had a glorious future. One of the potential buyers was Kaplan, Inc., a subsidiary of the Washington Post Company. Kaplan recently had founded the Concord University School of Law, the first online law school, and thought that a fixed site law school might complement its online program. In 2002, Concord would affiliate with William Mitchell College of Law, an ABA accredited law school in St. Paul, Minnesota.

By 1997, when this rare photograph of the shareholders and their wives was taken, they had already begun to consider selling Thomas Jefferson and WSU. From left to right are an unidentified man, Dick Leavitt, Bobbi Leavitt, Charlotte Toll (almost completely obscured), Sheryl Sherman, Art Toll, and Mel Sherman.

I did my best to assist the shareholders because I was grateful to them for allowing the law school to pursue ABA accreditation, but the prospect of a sale to a publicly traded company filled me with dread. Although the shareholders saw the law school as primarily a business, they took pride in the institution. Art and Dick were attorneys and so they felt a professional bond as well. Dick at one point visited

Monticello and returned with some Jefferson memorabilia that he gave me. They justifiably felt entitled to a return on their investment, but they also wanted the law school to be a respected part of the community. A publicly traded company would take no pride in academic excellence and would measure the law school solely by its profitability. I feared that a large publicly traded company would strip us of our autonomy, eliminate Nancy Vu's position, and place the financial management of the law school in the hands of a remote headquarters. Without control over our finances, we would never have the opportunity to find another buyer or to become a nonprofit. Everything we had achieved through our independence from WSU would be lost. Much of what we had hoped to achieve through ABA accreditation also would be lost. Our pursuit of academic excellence and the sense of community that we had built would be destroyed as we became just another profit-center for a multitude of faceless shareholders looking only for the highest return on their investment. We would never be more than the bare minimum of what the accreditation standards required that we be unless we could prove that some particular improvement would generate a higher return.

I began a feverish search for a nonprofit that could acquire us. My first call was to Dick Hawk. Dick said that he was still very interested in acquiring Thomas Jefferson, but that he was in the middle of major transaction that was tying up his resources and that he would not be able to make an offer for several months. That would be too late, of course.

I later learned that the transaction that prevented Dick from pursuing the acquisition of Thomas Jefferson was the merger of USIU with the California School of Professional Psychology, to yield on July 1, 2001, a new entity known as Alliant International University.

In 2010, Alliant would merge with San Francisco Law School, a state-accredited law school founded in 1909, creating an affiliation between USIU (through its successor institution) and a law school almost 15 years after I first met with Dick Hawk.

Meanwhile, I searched for potential partners as far north as Los Angeles. The shareholders had been right. Everywhere the answer was the same. No one could move quickly enough to acquire a law school before June.

I came to realize that the only nonprofit that could acquire the law school was the one that members of the faculty and I controlled – the Jeffersonian Law Foundation -- which we had established in 1995 at Jim White's suggestion to receive tax deductible alumni donations. From my work in the area of international investment law, I was familiar with debt-equity swaps in Latin America and I thought we needed to do the opposite: to swap equity for debt, replacing the shareholders with creditors. The problem would be to arrange the financing. I went to see Nancy, told her that I thought the foundation should buy the law school, and asked her whether, in spite of the shareholders' instructions, she would be willing to work with me to find a lender. Nancy said that, when she had been at National University, she had worked with an investment banker at Bank of America named Rick Chisholm, who specialized in raising financing for educational institutions. She found his number and we called him.

We told Rick that we were under instructions not to pursue the course that we were about to pursue and that we needed a promise of absolute confidentiality. Rick agreed and we explained that we needed to raise $10 to $15 million to buy our law school. We asked him if he could help us. He requested copies of our balance sheet and recent income statements and we sent the materials that he wanted.

Rick called us back and said that he believed that he could raise $12 million for us. The foundation would sell tax exempt community development bonds and use the proceeds to purchase the law school. The bondholders would be repaid over a period of 30 years from the income generated by the law school.

The Proposed Sale to Argosy

At that point, Nancy and I took the deal to the shareholders. We told them that we had found an investment banker who could raise $12 million for the foundation to buy the school. The shareholders told us that we were too late. They were in serious negotiations with Argosy Education Group, one of the potential buyers with whom we had met, and they expected to reach a deal imminently.

The ABA requires that an accredited law school obtain ABA acquiescence to any change of ownership before it occurs. WASC has a similar requirement. On May 7, 2000, Mel sent a letter to Jim White notifying him that the shareholders expected to receive an offer by Friday, May 12, to acquire all of the stock of both WSU and Thomas Jefferson. Further, the shareholders and the buyer intended to close the transaction by May 31, but no later than June 30. He requested that the ABA Accreditation Committee acquiesce in the change of ownership at its June 23-25 meeting. Jim replied that, in order for the matter to be considered at the June meeting of the committee, he would need to receive all relevant information and documents by June 5.

On May 22, Mel notified Jim that the shareholders had accepted a letter of intent on that date from Argosy Education Group to acquire both schools. Argosy was conducting its final due diligence while the final purchase agreement was in preparation. Mel believed that the due diligence and preparation of the purchase agreement would be completed within ten days.

Argosy was a publicly traded company the board chairman of which was a man named Michael C. Markovitz. On May 23, Markovitz came to San Diego to examine the campus carefully and to meet me. We went to lunch and he spent a couple of hours describing the new order that would be imposed following the sale.

Markovitz told me that as dean I would have enrollment and revenue targets to meet. If I met them, he would be very generous. If I did not, I would suffer the consequences. He also told me that the law school wasted too much money. He noted, for example, that members of the faculty each had his or her own office and then commented that "You don't make any money in an office. You make your money in the classroom." For the rest of the lunch, all we talked about was money.

It was just as I had feared. To Argosy, the law school was merely an income producing asset. The measure of our value would not be the quality of the education that we provided, the contribution that our research made to knowledge, or the significance of our service to the community, but the profits that we generated for Argosy. As we walked back to my office, I thought to myself, "I will never work for you and you will never own this law school."

I called Jim White. He was out of the country, but I reached Cathy Schrage, his executive assistant for accreditation. I mentioned Mel's letter about the sale to Argosy and she said that she had the letter. I told her that I had important information about Argosy's proposed acquisition of the law school and asked her to relay a message to Jim that the ABA must not acquiescence in the change of ownership without speaking to me first.

The next day, on May 24, Cathy notified Mel that Jim had conferred with the chair and vice-chair of the Accreditation Committee. They had determined that a limited site evaluation would be necessary before the ABA could acquiesce in the change of ownership and that time did not permit an evaluation prior to the June meeting. Consideration of the request for acquiescence thus would be postponed until the committee's next meeting, in November. That very same day, Art Toll replied with a letter expressing the shareholders' extreme disappointment at the decision not to follow the procedure set forth in the May 11 letter. He advised Jim that the result of the postponement would be, in effect, to terminate the possibility of the sale. He described the benefits of the sale. Argosy was the largest proprietary provider of doctoral degrees in the nation and thus had substantial resources available if needed. Further, sale to a publicly traded corporation would eliminate a problem that had concerned the ABA in the past, which was the absence of long range planning for the ownership of the law school in the inevitable event of the death of the shareholders. Art fought strenuously to put the matter back on the agenda of the June meeting, but to no avail.

The purchase agreement included a provision that, if the sale was not completed by June 30, either party could terminate the contract. The decision of the Accreditation Committee to postpone acquiescence meant that the sale could not be completed by the deadline.

I contacted the shareholders and told them that, inasmuch as the ABA's consideration of the sale had been postponed, the June deadline could not be met, and there no longer was any urgency to closing the deal with Argosy, I wanted to present the foundation's offer to them again. I also told them that I could not work for Markovitz and that I would fight ABA acquiescence to the sale to Argosy. They thus had a choice: they could try to sell to Argosy over my determined opposition or they could sell to the foundation with my full support. Finally, I told them that Marybeth, Nancy and I all had agreed that we would resign immediately if the law school were sold to Argosy. None of us would work for Argosy.

Our brilliant chief financial officer, Nancy Vu, was indispensable to our efforts to convert the law school to a nonprofit organization.

Meanwhile, our efforts to negotiate a purchase by the foundation were threatened by the emergence of other potential buyers. In June, I was contacted by one of the shareholders of Florida Coastal School of Law in Jacksonville, Florida, which had become the third proprietary law school approved by the ABA, after Thomas Jefferson and WSU. He asked me to notify the shareholders that he wished to purchase Thomas Jefferson.

I also received a telephone call from Tom Brennan, the founder and president of Thomas M. Cooley Law School in Lansing, Michigan. Thomas Cooley was a nonprofit, but Brennan had expressed regret in the past that he had not founded it as a for-profit, given how profitable the law school was. I was particularly worried about his interest in acquiring Thomas Jefferson because he was friends with Mel Sherman and thus might use his relationship with Mel to gain a sympathetic hearing from all three shareholders. Inasmuch as Brennan had gained ABA approval for Thomas M. Cooley, I would not easily be able to persuade the shareholders that the ABA would never acquiesce in a purchase by Brennan.

On June 29, I sent the shareholders a memorandum urging them to make a decision about our offer, arguing that we needed to complete the transaction before the ABA decided on our application for full approval. I was fending off competing offers from Argosy as well as from, potentially, the shareholder at Florida Coastal and Tom Brennan. I wanted the shareholders to commit to our proposal before any more purchasers appeared. After some discussion, they told me that they would be willing to look seriously at our proposal. Dick Leavitt said to me, "If you can match what Argosy has offered us, we will sell it to you." Years later, Art told me that the shareholders decided to sell to the foundation because of my threat to resign along with Nancy and Marybeth and to fight the sale to Argosy. Dick added that the shareholders also recognized that the law school would benefit more from a sale to a nonprofit than from a sale to Argosy.

Negotiating the Sale to the Foundation

The shareholders, Rick Chisholm, Nancy and I spent the summer working out the details of the transaction. The foundation originally had offered the shareholders $12 million for the law school, but the shareholders did not believe that $12 million was sufficient.

Eventually, we agreed on a figure of $14 million. Rick told us that the market would not allow us to pay a dollar more than that and that even $14 million would be difficult to raise. The transaction was considered so risky at that price that the bonds we were selling would not be rated.

We needed to borrow more than the purchase price. The law school already had more than $3 million in debt, which we would refinance on more favorable terms through the bond sale. There would also be costs of issuing the bonds, which would be financed through the bond proceeds as well. Finally, we wanted to create a cash reserve, to provide some financial stability for the law school. The result was that we would need to sell almost $20 million in bonds, of which $14 million would be paid to the shareholders and the rest would be used for these other expenses.

On September 11, 2000, I sent a letter to John Sebert, who had succeeded Jim White over the summer as the ABA consultant on legal education, requesting acquiescence in a change of ownership from the three shareholders to the Jeffersonian Law Foundation. John responded by appointing Professor Martin Burke to conduct a fact finding investigation with respect to the proposed change. Martin had chaired our February 2000 site evaluation team and thus was already intimately familiar with the law school and its finances. Accordingly, he conducted his fact finding through a series of telephone conversations with me. In December, Martin issued his report, finding that the change of ownership was feasible and would place the law school in a stronger financial position, although the long term prospects of the law school would depend upon its attainment of full approval.

Meanwhile, on December 4, I signed on behalf of the foundation a formal agreement with the shareholders under which the foundation would purchase the Thomas Jefferson School of Law. On December

8, the foundation board -- Hadley, Karla, Marybeth, Denise and I -- met and ratified the agreement. The shareholders' obligation to sell was conditioned upon the closing of the transaction by February 28, 2001.

On December 11, I sent the ABA a more detailed proposal for a change of ownership. In the proposal, I emphasized that Argosy remained interested in purchasing Thomas Jefferson and that the shareholders could rescind the purchase agreement with the foundation and sell to Argosy if the ABA did not acquiesce in time for the sale to close on February 28. I also informed the ABA that Marybeth, Nancy and I would resign immediately in the event of a sale to Argosy.

On February 7, 2001, John Sebert notified me that the Accreditation Committee at its January meeting had recommended acquiescence in the change of ownership. The council acquiesced at its February 17-18 meeting. The ABA thus accommodated our deadline. On March 6, I would learn that WASC also had approved the change of ownership.

As it happened, the sale did not close on February 28. The shareholders, however, chose not to rescind the agreement. The following month, the shareholders did sell WSU to Argosy, as had been agreed ten months before. After 32 years, WSU and Thomas Jefferson no longer had common ownership. In December 2001, Argosy was acquired by Education Management Corporation (EMC).

Under its new ownership, WSU suffered through some difficult times. WSU had received provisional ABA approval in 1998. In August 2004, three years after Argosy acquired it, WSU lost its provisional approval. WSU regained provisional approval in 2005 and then was granted full approval in 2009, eight years after Thomas Jefferson had received full approval. In August 2011, the U.S. Department of Justice and four states – California, Florida, Illinois, and Indiana – would file a civil action for fraud against EMC arising out of conduct by Argosy and other schools owned by EMC during the period from 2003 through 2011. WSU, along with other schools owned by EMC, would be named as a defendant in the action. The complainants would seek damages in the amount of $33 billion, approximately three times EMC's entire earnings during that period. EMC eventually would settle the claims against it by paying $95.5 million to the United States and the other complainants.

18

Obtaining Full ABA Approval

As the ABA examined our request for acquiescence in a change of ownership, we were also preparing our application for full ABA approval. In October of 2000, John Sebert paid a short visit, approximately 5 hours, to the law school. He toured the facility, spoke with a few members of the faculty that he happened to encounter, and then spent some time talking with me. As he departed, he told me that he was impressed by what he had seen.

Hosting the Site Evaluation Team

The ABA selected as the chair of our 2001 inspection team Dean Harry Haynsworth of William Mitchell Law School in St. Paul, an excellent choice. Other members of the team that would play a major role in the decision whether to grant us full approval were Professor Ralph Brill of the Chicago-Kent College of Law, Professor Susan Brody of John Marshall Law School, Professor Scott Pagel of George Washington University, and Ms. Kathryn Ressel of the Florida Board of Bar Examiners.

Prior to the visit, Harry told me that our bar passage rate would be the critical issue. He suggested that I prepare what he called a brief – an extended argument demonstrating that our bar results should be regarded as consistent with the standards. I conducted an extensive statistical analysis of our past performance on the bar exam and drafted a 29 page, single-spaced report that I supplied to the team prior to its visit.

The inspection on February 11-14 went very well. At the exit interview, Harry told us that it was "hard to believe that Thomas Jefferson had come so far" over the past five years. The law school had a "first rate" faculty that every member of the team would be proud to join. The team had seen none of the problems involving rigor in the classroom cited in prior reports. As the team was leaving, one of the members told me that he had been serving on ABA inspection teams for 40 years and that the trial practice class taught by Jeff Joseph was the best class that he had ever seen.

The team's report noted that Thomas Jefferson had "basically restructured the entire school" over the past seven years. The report summarized the extensive changes that had occurred since 1994, when the faculty and I first proposed to the shareholders that the San Diego campus seek ABA approval, and since 1996, when provisional approval had been granted.

Since 1994, the faculty had grown from 14 to 31, with the number of tenured faculty growing from none to 12. The number of books published by the faculty had tripled, from 7 in 1994 to 22 in 2001. The number of articles had almost quintupled, from 38 to 178. The library volume count had almost quadrupled, from 60,000 in 1994 to 225,000 in 2001. The number of titles, generally considered more important than the volume count, had soared, from 6,344 in 1994 to 119,000 in 2001. In 1994, our academic support program covered only the first semester and now it extended through all three years. The number of courses with midterm exams had grown from 2 to 20. In 1994, the percentage of minority students academically dismissed was 52.8 percent, while the percentage of white students dismissed was 34.3 percent. The minority student dismissal rate was now lower than the white student dismissal rate, tumbling to 6.7 percent, compared with 7.7 percent for white students. The number of employers interviewing through our career services office had grown from 10 in 1994 to more than 300 in 2001.

Appearing before the Accreditation Committee

Our application for full approval now became intertwined with our change of ownership. As the time for our appearance before the Accreditation Committee approached, the question arose as to who should appear as the representative of the law school's owners – one of the shareholders or an officer of the Jeffersonian Law Foundation. The shareholders agreed that a representative of the foundation should represent the law school at the meeting of the Accreditation Committee and the council

The original board of the foundation had been excellent for the foundation's original purpose, but it was not the board to manage the law school. So, in January 2001, we held a meeting of the foundation's board at which we elected a new board. Then all of us except Denise Asher, who had been elected to the new board, resigned en masse.

The new board had seven members, including Denise. The member whom I hoped would serve as chair was Sandy Kahn, a successful real estate developer and a graduate of the USD law school. Sandy's wife Suzanne was an alumna of the law school, whom Marybeth and I knew well. We were acquainted with Sandy through Suzanne.

The other members of the new board included Marc Adelman, an alumnus of the law school who had served as President of the State Bar of California in 1997-98; Bob Ames, a former partner of Gray, Cary, Ames & Frye, the largest law firm in San Diego; and Ted Graham, a partner at a major national law firm, Brobeck, Phleger and Harrison, which was then the third largest firm in San Diego. So that the board would have expertise in legal education, we also included Rudy Hasl, then dean of Seattle University School of Law, a former dean at two other law schools, and a former chair of the ABA Section on Legal Education, and Tom Read, then dean of South Texas College of Law and a former dean of four other law schools, including Hastings. Tom soon decided that he had a conflict of interest arising from an affiliation between South Texas and California Western and resigned.

On June 25, the new board of the foundation held its first meeting. It elected Sandy as chair and Denise as secretary. It then approved the various agreements necessary to obtain the financing for the acquisition of the law school.

The board also elected three additional members of the board. Two of these had served on the board of Thomas Jefferson School of Law, following its separation from WSU. One was Superior Court Judge Jesus Rodriguez and the other was UCSD Assistant Vice-Chancellor Elazar Harel. We had invited Elazar to join our board not long after the separation from WSU to replace Ned Pinger, who had resigned because he was moving to the East Coast. Elazar created a link to UCSD, the first of many that I hoped to create, and brought to our board enormous expertise regarding information technology. The third new member was Jim White, who had agreed to serve upon the end of his tenure as ABA consultant. Because Tom Read had resigned, the new board now totaled nine members.

In forming the new board, I had several goals in mind. The most immediate was to establish the credibility of the law school in the eyes of the local legal community and the ABA. A second was to ensure that we had the necessary expertise to manage the institution. A third was to provide adequate oversight of the dean, particularly by appointing members with whom I had few or no personal ties.

Alumnus Marc Adelman, center, who served as President of the California State Bar in 1997-98, joined the Thomas Jefferson Board of Trustees in 2001. A very loyal supporter of the law school, Marc had also served on the 1986 dean's search committee. Marc is pictured here at the 1994 Barristers' Ball with Pat Brown, who had left the campus in the late 1970s, and her date, Orville Redenbocker, the popcorn magnate.

As our June 29 appearance before the Accreditation Committee approached, we were making great progress with respect to the two most important aspects of our application. First, the first strong class that we admitted after our receipt of ABA approval, the spring 1998 entering class, sat for the February 2001 bar exam and earned a first time bar passage rate of 49 percent, compared with a statewide average for all ABA approved law schools of 50 percent. Our pass rate was higher than that of Whittier (28%), WSU (35%), Southwestern (43%), and Golden Gate (44%). UCLA and Loyola both had pass rates of 50% and California Western had a pass rate of 51%. We could tell the ABA with confidence that our higher admissions standards had produced higher bar passage rates. The bar pass rate had been the critical issue in our application and we had resolved the issue very favorably. Second, on June 12, the prospectus for our bond offering was mailed. We were able to tell the Accreditation Committee that we expected commitments to purchase the bonds by the end of the month.

Following our appearance, the Accreditation Committee recommended full approval by what the chair of the committee, Professor Michael J. Davis, and John Sebert both characterized in a July 12, 2001, memorandum to the council as "a closely divided vote." Those who opposed full approval would have voted to extend provisional approval for another year. No one thought that we should lose our provisional approval.

The Davis and Sebert memo noted that Thomas Jefferson had made "significant and substantial progress" during the five years in which it had been provisionally approved. Harry Haynsworth told the committee that the team had conducted the most extensive review of teaching by an ABA site evaluation team that he had ever seen.

The team found that the overall quality of teaching was "excellent." Further the team had observed "none of the problems with respect to rigor in the classroom that had been reported by some previous teams." The law school's curriculum had expanded significantly and the school had developed "a very strong academic support program." The Accreditation Committee thus found no concerns with the quality of the faculty or the law school's academic program. As a result of library expansion and significant improvements in information technology, the committee had no concerns regarding the library or information technology. The renovation of our two buildings had eliminated all concerns regarding the adequacy of the school's facility.

The committee's concerns focused on four matters: the quality of the entering class, the level of attrition, the bar passage rate, and the law school's financial resources. All four concerns, of course, were interrelated and mutually dependent. Improvement in the strength of the entering class would solve all four problems.

The committee found that since 1998 the law school had seen a "marked improvement" in the quality of the bottom quartile of students, the area of the committee's greatest concern. As reported in the brief that I gave the site evaluation team, the LSAT score of our entering class at the 25th percentile was now higher than that at 31 fully-approved law schools. The law school's most recent entering classes thus were of sufficient quality to meet the standards. The increase in outward transfers had become a subject of substantial discussion before the committee. The committee noted, however, that, based on the small number of students who had requested transcripts, the problem of outward transfers had been solved.

The committee had discussed our bar passage rate at length. Although we had poor results on the July bar exam in years past,[7] the committee had observed that the stronger entering classes that we began to admit in 1998 would not begin to sit for the bar exam until 2001. The first such class had sat for the most recent bar exam and had achieved a bar passage rate just 1 percent below that for all California ABA approved law schools. The committee believed that the stronger entering classes since 1998 suggested "a high likelihood" that the law school's bar examination results would continue to improve, a likelihood that was increased by our "strong" academic support program, which was based on individual tutoring. The law school already had entering classes that were very similar to those at a "substantial number" of fully approved law schools.

---

7   Throughout its history, the law school always performed much better on the February bar exam than on the July bar exam. Most elite law schools do not admit spring entering classes and thus they have small December graduating classes and very few graduates sitting for the February bar exam. Accordingly, our competition on the February bar exam comes principally from a small number of schools that have spring entering classes, such as California Western, Whittier, and WSU. Our students fare much better in competition with graduates from these law schools than they do in competition with graduates of Stanford, Berkeley and other law schools with much higher admissions standards whose graduates take the July bar exam. For these reasons, during the ABA accreditation process we reported the trend lines for our February bar exams separately from our trend lines for our July bar exams. The ABA gave much greater weight to the July bar results because far more graduates sat for that exam and because the results reflected the performance of graduates of a full spectrum of law schools. Thus, the committee was especially concerned about our poor performance in the past on the July bar exam and some members were not very reassured by our strong performance on a February bar exam.

Sandy Kahn, a San Diego real estate developer and graduate of USD law school, was elected chairman of the Board of Trustees of the Jeffersonian Law Foundation in 2001 just prior to its acquisition of the law school, the process that converted the law school to a nonprofit institution. We appeared together at the 2001 meetings of the Accreditation Committee and the Council of the Section on Legal Education at which Thomas Jefferson was recommended for full ABA approval. He is pictured here speaking at my farewell party in 2005, when I left the dean's office.

A significant minority of the committee argued for extending provisional approval for one more year in order to have time to determine whether the predicted improvement in bar passage rates actually would occur and whether the law school would change ownership as planned. The majority believed, however, that merely to extend our provisional approval would impair our ability to maintain the improvement. The memorandum also noted that the granting of full approval would likely facilitate the change in ownership, which would improve the law school's financial condition.

At the time of the Accreditation Committee meeting, we had expected the bonds to sell by June 30. The sale of the bonds, however, did not occur as planned. When the deadline to commit to a purchase of bonds passed, Bank of America had not received a single commitment. No one wanted to purchase our bonds.

The problem was that the potential purchasers believed that the risk was too high. We were a law school with virtually no assets. In the spring of 2000, once it became clear that the foundation would acquire the law school, the shareholders had begun taking distributions of profits in excess of their tax liabilities. Thus, we had almost no cash and our real estate was heavily mortgaged. We could expect future income, but that was jeopardized by the fact that our provisional ABA approval was about to expire.

Rick called a few of the most likely purchasers and asked them as a personal favor, in light of his longtime association with them, to travel to San Diego to meet with me. If after spending the day with me, he told them, they still did not wish to purchase the bonds, he would never trouble them about the deal again.

A few potential purchasers sent representatives to meet me in San Diego on different days. I gave them a tour of the campus and explained my business strategy for the law school. They peppered me with questions about our finances, our student recruitment strategy and ABA accreditation. Following the visits, each called Rick and told him that they were ready to commit to purchasing some of the bonds. Ultimately, we had commitments sufficient to purchase bonds in twice the amount that we were offering to sell. The only problem was that all of the potential investors wanted to wait until after the council meeting at the beginning of August to complete the transaction, in order to be sure that the law school obtained full approval before they completed the bond purchase.

Appearing before the Council

On August 3, Sandy and I appeared before the council in Chicago. The members questioned us very carefully about the sale of the law school. They told us quite bluntly their concern. It was that they would recommend full approval to the House of Delegates, the House would grant full approval, and then they would learn that the sale would not be consummated, that the shareholders who had not attended the meeting or made any kind of commitments to the ABA would now own a fully accredited law school, and that Sandy Kahn, who had offered his sincerest assurances of compliance with the standards, was the board chairman of a foundation with no connection to the law school. They wanted to be sure that they were dealing with the people who would be responsible for the law school following the grant of full approval, but they had no assurance that Sandy and I were those people. The bonds had been put on the market in June. They wondered why, if the deal was going to close, it had not closed already.

I explained that the potential bond purchasers were quite serious, but concerned that they were being asked to lend almost $20 million to a law school that might be on the verge of losing its accreditation. They were waiting to see what the council would do. The dilemma, in short, was that the council was waiting for the investors to purchase the bonds before granting full approval and the investors were waiting for the council to grant full approval before purchasing the bonds. I implored the council to have faith in us and to grant the approval. I told them that I genuinely believed that, if we received full approval, the bonds would be sold and the transaction would be consummated. I could not prove it, however. All I could do was to ask the council to trust me.

We were excused from the meeting. Sandy went to the airport to catch a flight back to San Diego and I returned to my hotel room to await the council's decision.

Late in the afternoon, the telephone rang. John Sebert was on the line. He came straight to the point and told me that the council had recommended full approval. He quickly added, however, that the council had accepted our representation that the law school was changing ownership and that Sandy represented the new owner. If the sale did not occur, the council would be deeply concerned and our accreditation would be called into question.

Elated, I called Rick Chisholm with the news so that he could pass it along to our potential bond purchasers. I had good news for Rick, but he had only bad news for me. The bond purchasers continued to worry about the risk. As proof that the investment was sound, they wanted the shareholders to assume part of the risk. More specifically, they wanted the shareholders to agree to take only $10 million in cash and to accept a note from the law school for the remaining $4 million. The note would be subordinated to the bonds. Because the shareholders would be lending us $4 million, the amount of the bonds we needed to sell was reduced to $15.75 million. If the law school encountered financial difficulties, the bondholders would be paid before the former shareholders. The willingness of the shareholders to accept that risk would be evidence that the shareholders truly believed that the law school could repay the bonds and would provide the bond purchasers the reassurance that they wanted. Rick told me that the bond purchasers initially wanted the purchase price reduced to

$12 million. They believed that $14 million was more than we could afford to pay. The idea of the subordinated note was a compromise in lieu of a reduction in the purchase price.

The Section on Legal Education had scheduled a reception for that evening at the ABA headquarters. Although I wanted to deal with this latest crisis, I thought that at this stage in our history it was important to be as visible as possible at ABA functions and so I made it a point to attend every reception that I could at any ABA or AALS meeting. When I arrived at the reception, the greeting that I received astounded me. Members of the committee and the council who, as recently as a year ago, were threatening to revoke our accreditation and who less than three years before had yearned to see me clubbed with a piece of timber now rushed to shake my hand, smiling and clasping my shoulder. Everyone was warmly congratulating me and telling me what a great accomplishment this was. One of the staff members who regularly attended meetings of the committee and the council came over and said to me, "We always knew that you could do it. Everyone really respects what you have done at Thomas Jefferson and they trust you. The personal credibility that you have established over the years is really what won them over."

After the reception, I returned to my hotel room to deal with the new proposal from the bond purchasers. I wrote a 17 page single-spaced memo to the shareholders reporting on this latest development and urging them not to walk away from the deal. My fear was that they would decide to sell the law school to Argosy instead. I told them that it was the best deal that they would ever get. If they turned it down, the council would reexamine our full approval. I warned them that, as a result of our reduced dismissal rates after 1998, despite our higher admissions standards we had what I termed a "freight train of bad bar results" on the way. If our full approval were called into question, the poor bar results would provide ample justification to return us to provisional approval or even to revoke our accreditation entirely. The shareholders might spend a couple of years just trying to regain provisional approval. Meanwhile, the value of the law school would plummet. I noted that, at $14 million, they were receiving 17 times our average annual earnings over the past four years, an excellent price for an education stock.

Approval by the House of Delegates

The House of Delegates was meeting on Monday, August 7, but it had a full agenda and, because the council had reached its decision regarding our accreditation late on Friday afternoon, we were not on the agenda. Unless we were able to change the agenda, our full approval would be deferred for another six months and the entire sale of the law school could unravel. Section officials lobbied vigorously to get our approval on the agenda. We learned on Monday that they had succeeded.

In the late afternoon on Monday, Normal Redlich took the floor to make a report and recommendation relating to our accreditation. In his remarks, he described how the ABA saw the Thomas Jefferson School of Law. He praised the strength of our faculty, the high quality of our classroom instruction, the cutting-edge curriculum that we had developed, and the individual attention that we gave our students. The council then moved that the House of Delegates adopt the recommendation of the council, which had two components. The first was that Thomas Jefferson be granted full approval. The second was that the consultant certify to the council on or before its December 2001 meeting that the proposed change of ownership had occurred. The motion carried unanimously. At 4:50 p.m. Central Daylight

Time on Monday, August 7, 2001, Thomas Jefferson School of Law received full ABA approval.

The shareholders were deeply unhappy about the last minute change to the terms of the purchase, but, in the face of the arguments in my memorandum and Rick's insistence that the bond purchasers would not agree to anything more favorable, they accepted the new terms. By August 8, we had firm commitments sufficient in amount to sell double the amount of the bonds that we needed to sell. That same day, John Sebert announced publicly that the Thomas Jefferson School of Law was fully approved.

Closing the Sale

Although the terms of the sale were by then fully agreed, there was considerable paperwork to be completed in order to effect the transaction. All of the formalities would take a few weeks to complete. The entire transaction was scheduled to close in New York on September 11, at 11 a.m. Eastern Time.

On the morning that the transaction was set to close, I was taking a shower and thinking that the law school would be a nonprofit entity in just a few minutes. Suddenly, my wife Lidia burst into the room yelling that terrorists had bombed the World Trade Center. I rushed to the television and saw the horrifying scene fixed in the memory of every American alive on that day. The news reports showed the unforgettable images of aircraft crashing into the towers, the World Trade Center in flames, and terrified victims jumping from the buildings to their deaths.

At some point, I heard a reporter say that the entire financial district around the World Trade Center had closed. With the markets closed, our bonds had not sold. We were still a proprietary law school.

Throughout the country, institutions were closing for the rest of the day in memory of the victims. When I reached the office, students, staff and faculty all were asking whether we should cancel classes and close the law school. I chose not to do so and then circulated a memorandum explaining my reasons. First, as a practical matter, we had no way to notify our students of the sudden cancellation of classes and thus most would have come to campus only to learn that they had made the trip in vain. Further, I thought that terrorism should be met by defiance. By keeping our doors open and our classes in session, we refused to bow to those who sought through violence to change our way of life. Moreover, I said,

> As a law school, we have a special responsibility. The most effective obstacle to the senseless violence of terrorism is the rule of law. We at Thomas Jefferson School of Law have dedicated our lives to promoting the rule of law and it is precisely at times of lawlessness that our work has its greatest importance. If the legal community is silenced or disrupted by terrorism, then all hope is lost.

Finally, I believed that we should maintain the life of our community for the sake of our students. In the face of national tragedy, we needed to assure for our students a place to gather with friends to offer emotional support and to talk about the events.

Trading on Wall Street had been suspended indefinitely. Eventually, Rick and I spoke on the telephone to discuss the prospects for our bond offering. Rick noted that, during times of crisis, there is a "flight to quality." He did not need to say the rest: we were not considered quality. Rick said that we should not be surprised if the bond purchasers revoked their commitments to purchase the bonds.

If that happened, the law school once again would be on the market, with Argosy the likely purchaser.

Over the next few days, he spoke with each of the bond purchasers and we were gratified that they still believed in us. Every one of the purchasers kept its commitment. On September 27, the transaction was completed and the Thomas Jefferson School of Law merged into the Jeffersonian Law Foundation, a not-for-profit corporation. Exactly six years to the day since I first met the shareholders, the Thomas Jefferson School of Law was an independent, nonprofit, ABA approved law school.

Aftermath of the Conversion

Because the Thomas Jefferson School of Law merged into the Jeffersonian Law Foundation, following the conversion the corporate name of the law school was the Jeffersonian Law Foundation. The name "Thomas Jefferson School of Law" was an alias under which the foundation was doing business. On June 9, 2005, we changed the name of the foundation to the Thomas Jefferson School of Law, which remains the official name of the law school.

To the best of my knowledge, none of the three shareholders ever returned to the campus after the sale. Mel Sherman passed away in December 2011, at the age of 85. Art Toll and Dick Leavitt are retired and living in Los Angeles.

Conversion to a nonprofit entity transformed the institution profoundly. As our students always understood, a for-profit law school exists to generate a return for the shareholders. Providing a sound or even an excellent legal education is simply a means to that end. A for-profit law school certainly can provide a sound program of legal education, but it is unlikely to provide a better education than the shareholders believe is necessary to generate the return that they want. Investments in improvements will be made only if they promise to generate a greater return than the shareholders would receive without the investment.

Even investments in quality that will generate a greater return may not be made if the return will occur only in the long term and the shareholders place more importance on their return in the short term. In my years as dean of a for-profit law school, I saw several instances where we took action that maximized short term returns, but that was inefficient in the long term. In so doing, we squandered our resources. The law school's single greatest accomplishment, obtaining the ABA approval that had eluded it since its founding, occurred only when the shareholders decided that they were willing to forego profits in the short term in order to build a stronger institution over the long term.

Once we became a nonprofit, no longer under pressure to generate an annual return for distribution to the shareholders, we were able always to consider what was in the institution's long term best interests and to make long term investments that would improve the quality of our academic program. For example, as our applications for admission increased, we raised admissions standards and stressed improving the quality of our academic program, rather than simply accepting more students and maximizing short term profits. As the quality of our program improved, we attracted even more applications. By the time I left the dean's office in 2005, our annual net income as a nonprofit was more than four times what it was in our best year as a for-profit law school. Because we were a nonprofit, however, we could retain the surplus for use in making long term investments in improving our program of legal education. Our ability always to think about the long term ultimately strengthened us both academically and financially. Everyone understands that academic strength requires financial stability, but our financial stability rested on our academic strength. The two were mutually dependent and mutually reinforcing.

19

Solving the Bar Passage Rate Problem

Following the August 2001 ABA meeting at which we received full approval, Marybeth and I went to lunch to celebrate our receipt of ABA approval and the bond commitments that appeared to have made the change of ownership inevitable. We reflected on the fact that in just six years the law school had been transformed from the branch campus of a state accredited for-profit law school to an independent, ABA accredited, nonprofit law school. The quest that we had begun when we arrived at the law school exactly one decade before had been successfully completed.

We agreed that it was time for both of us to leave the dean's office. In my case, I had been on the faculty for only one year when I became associate dean and for only three years when I became dean and I wanted the opportunity to engage in the long deferred teaching and research that had drawn me to academic life. Because our new governing board had little prior connection to the law school, we also agreed that we should not both leave at the same time, in order to ensure some continuity. Further, as part of our effort to sell the bonds, I had promised the bond purchasers that the current management would remain in place following the sale. So, I simply could not leave immediately. We decided that Marybeth would resign effective at the end of the spring 2002 semester and that I would resign effective at the end of the spring 2003 semester, giving me almost two years to orient the governing board to its new responsibilities and to reassure the bond purchasers.

With two years left as dean, I wanted to use my remaining time to ensure that Thomas Jefferson was well-launched in its new incarnation as an independent, fully-accredited, nonprofit law school. The law school's history had shown the fragility of its finances and the extent to which its fortunes were tied to changes in the applicant pool. As a law school without a well-established reputation, we were especially vulnerable to sudden changes in the demand for legal education. In times of a diminishing applicant pool, the elite law schools reach deeper into the pool, leaving fewer applicants for law schools such as ours. Further, even apart from demographic changes that periodically reduce the demand for our program, legal education as a whole undoubtedly would face new challenges in the years ahead. For example, the emergence of distance learning technology could substantially change the nature of legal education, while the growing size of student debt meant that law schools could not continue raising tuition in real terms indefinitely.

I wanted to take advantage of our newly achieved full approval and nonprofit status to secure Thomas Jefferson's place so that, in the face of future reductions in the size of the applicant pool or other challenges, we would never need to fear for the health of the institution. The best way to do this was to build the law school's reputation to ensure that our degree would always be desirable. This, in turn, required building a stronger law school. To do that, I wanted to focus, as I had for the past seven years, on pursuing academic excellence and creating a more humane institution for students, faculty and staff by promoting communication and a participatory form of institutional governance. If we focused on these core values, we would attract and retain the best people and that would strengthen both the institution and its reputation.

In April of 2002, as we planned, I announced Marybeth's resignation as associate dean. I praised her as utterly selfless and unrelentingly good humored throughout her eight years as associate dean. I thanked her for her wisdom, intelligence, humanity, and good judgment. Marybeth, as I noted then, had never sought any recognition for herself, but she had been a full partner in every step that we had taken on the long road to full accreditation. When faced with tough decisions, I could always seek her counsel because I knew that we shared the same values and that her advice would reflect those values. In addition to the constant advice and assistance that she gave me, Marybeth had supervised a number of administrative departments as well as the entire adjunct faculty. We were inspected by accreditation teams eight times during Marybeth's tenure as associate dean and every inspection report that we received treated the quality of the adjunct faculty as indistinguishable from that of the full-time faculty, a tribute to her success in selecting adjuncts.

I asked Steve Semeraro to serve as her successor. At the time, Steve was still a junior member of the faculty, but he had already impressed everyone with his excellent teaching and scholarship. He worked very well with people and was energetic, creative, capable, and committed. As a junior member of the faculty, he could serve as a link between the dean's office and the younger faculty. Steve accepted the appointment and performed an outstanding job for the next five years, three during my deanship and two working with my successor.

*Steve Semeraro served as associate dean following Marybeth's
resignation in 2002. I would ask him to assume special
responsibility for our bar preparation programs.*

The single most important way that we could improve our
academic program was to continue to raise our admissions standards.
Taking advantage of our receipt of full ABA approval, our fifth in the
nation ranking for the quality of life on campus, the high caliber of our
faculty, our individualized approach to legal education, our cutting-
edge curriculum, our beautiful location, and our generous scholarship
programs, we continued to recruit students aggressively over the next
four years.

For the fall 2002 entering class, the first fall class that we recruited
as a fully approved law school, we received 2171 applications, an
increase of 45 per cent over the prior year's 1510 applications, received
when we were still only provisionally approved. By fall 2003, news

of our full approval had spread more widely and applications soared to 3204, more than double the number that we had received just two years before as a provisionally approved law school. For the fall 2005 entering class, the last class that we recruited during my deanship, we received more than 4000 applications, compared with fewer than 400 in fall 1994, my first year as dean.

The explosion in applications occurred despite the lack of any significant growth in the national applicant pool. For example, in 1991-92, my first year on the full-time faculty, the number of applicants to ABA approved law schools was 97,720. As already noted, the number of applicants nationwide declined throughout the 1990s. By 1995-96, the year we obtained ABA approval, the number had fallen to 76,715 and it continued to decline through the 1997-98 academic year. At the end of the decade, the decline reversed, but the national applicant pool did little more than regain the ground lost during the 1990s. The number of applicants for the fall 2005 entering class was 95,760, which was still fewer than the number of applicants when I began teaching at the law school fifteen years before.

We wanted to use the explosion in our applications to improve the strength, rather than to expand the size, of the entering class. Thus, we became increasingly selective. In fall 2001, our last entering class before we received full approval, we extended offers to 69 percent of our applicants. The following year, our first after receiving full approval, we extended offers to 55 percent of our applicants. In fall 2003, following the surge in applications, we extended offers to only 36 percent of our applicants. By fall 2005, we were extending offers to only about 20 percent of our applicants. We were receiving approximately 23 applications for every seat in the class.

The increase in the number of applications and in our selectivity allowed us to strengthen our entering class considerably. In just two years, between fall 2001 and fall 2003, we raised our LSAT score at the 75th percentile from 153 to 157. Progress at the lower end of the class was a little slower, but ultimately more remarkable. Our LSAT score at the 25th percentile rose six points in just four years, from 145 in fall 2001 to 151 in fall 2005. By fall 2005, the median LSAT score had reached 153.

Despite the fact that our intention was to strengthen, rather than to expand, the entering class, the entering class grew as well. For the fall 2003 entering class, we actually reduced the number of offers of admission that we made, but a much larger percentage of students accepted our offers. The result is that enrollment soared from 673 in 2002 to 825 in 2003, an increase of more than 22 percent in just one year. At 825 students, we had about a hundred students more than we wanted. We continued to reduce the number of applicants that we accepted, but, even so, the yield rates continued to climb and, when I left the dean's office in 2005, enrollment was at 833, still about a hundred students above our preferred enrollment

We continued to draw our entering class from around the country. After 2001, two-thirds of our entering classes came from outside of California. This was the second highest percentage among all the law schools in California, behind only Stanford.

The higher admissions standards that we applied in spring 1998 had raised our bar passage rate just in time to bring us full accreditation. Between 1998 and 2001, as we pursued full approval, we were able to maintain those same admissions standards to a large degree, but our lower dismissal rates after 1998, counteracted some of the effect of the higher admissions standards. In round numbers, the higher admissions standards that we adopted in 1998, combined with the lower dismissal rates in subsequent years, narrowed the gap between our pass rate and the average pass rate for ABA approved law schools on the California July bar exam by about 10 to 15 percentage points. This was an improvement, but still a disappointment.

Full approval changed everything. As already noted, following our receipt of full approval, the quality of our entering classes began to improve markedly, while our dismissal rates remained constant. The result was steadily improving bar passage rates. The first class that we admitted following our receipt of full approval was the fall 2002 entering class, which when it graduated and took the July 2005 bar exam, had a pass rate of only 38.9 percent, which was typical of the classes that entered before our receipt of full approval. The class had been recruited, however, starting only weeks after we received full approval and the news of our approval had not yet spread. We were still offering admission to more than one out of every two applicants. By the next year, however, our applications were soaring and admissions standards were rising. As we admitted progressively stronger entering classes and they graduated, our bar pass rates rose, to 51.1 percent in July 2006, to 63.3 percent in July 2007 and finally to 75.2 percent in July 2008. Our February bar exam pass rates showed a similar upward trend during the same three years. Our three years of progressively stronger entering classes from 2003 through 2005 had produced three consecutive years of rising bar pass rates, from 2006 through 2008.

For some 35 years, Thomas Jefferson and its predecessor, the San Diego campus of WSU, had struggled with a nearly always disappointing pass rate on the California bar exam, widely regarded as the most difficult in the nation. In the late 1980s, as a result of higher admissions standards, we experienced a brief period of strong bar results, but the admissions standards were unsustainable financially.

In the years following full approval, however, we had found the solution. We had identified a combination of recruiting, admissions and scholarship policies that would produce strong bar results. The steady upward trend in bar results that began in 2006 and its correlation with our progressively stronger entering classes admitted beginning in 2003 were both unmistakable.

The bar exam is precisely the place where the basic tension underlying the founders' vision of the law school appears most starkly. The founders' goal of providing access to a wide range of applicants resulted in a low bar passage rate, which undermined their other goal of earning respect for the law school's academic program. Raising admissions standards improved our bar passage rate and earned much more respect for the law school, but the price was to deny admission to 80 percent of our applicants.

I left the dean's office in 2005 not knowing for sure what kind of pass rates the stronger classes admitted in 2003 and thereafter would have because they didn't start to graduate until 2006, a year after my departure. I knew that the bar results would be better, but could not be sure how much better they would be or whether still higher standards would be necessary to achieve the bar results we desired. As those classes graduated and we saw our pass rates rise, I took great satisfaction in seeing that our hard work to strengthen the entering class at last had solved the most intractable problem that the law school had ever faced. As long as we followed the admissions strategy that we had spent years developing and maintained the size of our applicant pool, the Thomas Jefferson School of Law need never again know the embarrassment of a low bar passage rate.

We had recruited stronger entering classes after full approval without having a high pass rate on recent exams to serve as a recruiting tool. As the stronger classes yielded higher bar passage rates, however, I anticipated that we would be able to use the higher pass rates to recruit even stronger entering classes, which would raise our pass rate still more. We were on a self-propelling upward spiral with no obvious end in sight.

20

Creating Institutional Governance for a Nonprofit Law School

Apart from raising our admissions standards and thereby improving our academic program, our bar passage rate and our reputation, the most urgent task ahead of us following our conversion to a nonprofit law school was to create a new system of institutional governance. In our days as a proprietary law school, everyone recognized the legitimate right of the shareholders to make most of the decisions about the management and operation of the law school, including the disposition of its resources. Under the applicable accreditation rules, the faculty and the dean were guaranteed some authority in matters of academic policy, but even that authority was severely circumscribed by the authority of the shareholders with respect to institutional resources.

Once the law school no longer had shareholders, the question was where the responsibility for fundamental policy making at the law school should lie. California corporation law requires that the law school have a governing board and vests ultimate authority over the corporate entity in that board, although maintaining the law school's accreditation requires deference to the faculty and dean on some issues. While corporation law settles the question of where ultimate legal authority lies, it does not determine, except at a very high level of generality, how that authority should be exercised. In particular, it does not determine the extent to which members of the board should collaborate with the other constituencies of the law school.

Members of a board of trustees owe a fiduciary obligation to the institution that they govern. As uncompensated volunteers, they can approach their responsibilities free of self-interest, pursuing only the best interests of the institution. Yet, the best interests of the institution can be consistent with a wide variety of choices. For example, a law school can choose to offer only a full-time program or both a full-time and a part-time program. It can seek to grow, in order to provide more material resources to students, or to remain small, so that it can provide greater attention to each individual student. It can choose to emphasize particular subject areas and thus to achieve excellence in those areas or it can choose to seek breadth and avoid too much concentration in one area. A mere commitment to promoting the best interests of the institution will not necessarily decide any of these or many other questions.

I believed that, in evaluating the best interests of the institution, the board should look principally to the faculty for guidance. The faculty has the expertise on which the law school's operation rests and it has the primary responsibility for the academic program of the law school. Members of the faculty have also, in general, made very long term commitments to the institution, unlike in many cases the members of the board or the dean. Further, ABA and WASC accreditation rules require a role for the faculty in certain areas of institutional governance.

The staff, students and alumni should participate in institutional governance as well. Many of the staff also make very long term commitments to the institution and many of them possess special expertise with regard to critical areas of the law school's operation. Students are the very reason for the existence of a law school and their resources fund its operation. Thus, they too have a legitimate claim to a role in institutional governance. As former students who supported the law school in the past and who have linked their careers to the law school's fortunes, alumni as well have an interest in the law school's operation and can contribute importantly to its success. A good system of institutional governance would ensure the participation in different ways of all of these constituencies. I had been seeking broader communication and participation since my appointment as acting dean in 1994 and our conversion to a nonprofit organization at last made it possible to achieve these goals to the extent that any academic institution can.

Denise Asher was an original member of the foundation board and remained on the board after it acquired the law school. She is pictured at our 1994 commencement exercises, where she was class valedictorian despite having attended Thomas Jefferson full-time while also working and raising a family. Her dedicated service to the law school demonstrated the invaluable role that alumni can play on the governing board.

My sentiments in this regard were shaped by my own experience at the law school. Neither our successful application for ABA approval nor our conversion to a nonprofit organization had occurred at the initiative of the shareholders or the board of directors. Indeed, the shareholders and their board initially had opposed both of these projects. Rather, the initiative had come from members of the faculty and from the dean whose appointment the faculty had unanimously recommended. Further, the staff, students and alumni had vigorously supported these projects from the inception. The truest understanding of the institution's long term best interests had not originated at the top.

Strengthening Faculty Governance

In May 2003, I sent a memorandum to the faculty arguing that the faculty should assume more responsibility for setting the fundamental direction of the law school. If the faculty were to assume greater responsibility for guiding the law school, then the faculty would have to achieve the institutional capacity to do so. To build that capacity, I proposed in the memorandum to give the faculty a detailed presentation on the law school's budget at its annual summer retreat. I had already given a more cursory presentation the year before, but now I wanted to delve much more deeply into the details of our annual budget.

In our years as a proprietary law school, the shareholders had claimed a privacy interest in the financial details of the law school. Budgetary information was closely guarded. The law school, however, was no longer the private property of the shareholders. It was a nonprofit organization, chartered and financed in the public interest. Except for individuals' privacy interests in their own salaries, no sound reason existed for maintaining the confidentiality of the law school's budget. Secrecy about the budget would only prevent accountability and thereby undermine sound institutional governance.

Accordingly, each year, beginning in 2002, I made an increasingly detailed presentation on the annual budget to the faculty. I made a similar presentation to the staff each year at a staff meeting called for that purpose. The presentation showed how the funds of the law school were budgeted and, in particular, how new revenues each year were allocated. In this way, I hoped to build a capacity for institutional governance and to increase the sense of communication and participation among faculty and staff.

I knew that a summary presentation at an annual retreat would not suffice to create a genuine capacity for budgetary oversight by the faculty and so I proposed that the faculty create a Budget and Planning Committee, composed of members who would have the time to develop a more intimate knowledge of the law school budget. After the faculty adopted my proposal in 2004, I appointed one of our most talented members of the faculty, Eric Mitnick, to chair the committee. I then met with the committee and asked it to advise me on what the budgetary priorities of the law school should be. I relied on the committee's advice to prepare the annual budget. Once the annual budget was approved by the board, I met again with the committee, showed the members the entire budget (excluding individual salary information), and then explained how the budget reflected the priorities assigned by the faculty. In this way, the faculty would participate in setting the budget priorities for each year. Over time, this process could create a pool of faculty well-versed in the details of the law school's finances and it could ensure that the faculty set the direction of the law school.

Shortly after its formation, the committee surveyed the faculty to ascertain the faculty's views regarding budget priorities. Eric drafted a memo reporting that, based on the survey, the faculty believed that our top priority should be to spend the funds necessary to raise our bar passage rate. I fully agreed with the faculty in that regard.

Our second priority, according to the faculty, was to increase faculty and staff compensation, which was well below that at comparable law schools. Again, I agreed with the faculty. I obtained board approval for a 5 percent raise pool for both faculty and staff, well above inflation, every single year that we were a nonprofit institution, enabling me to grant those faculty members who published regularly raises of $9000 annually. I believed that we should continue raises at no less than that level until we not only reached parity with comparable institutions, but had the ability to lure strong lateral and entry level candidates. Further, the faculty and staff had built the law school and deserved to share in its success.

Our third priority, according to the faculty, was to continue to reduce class sizes and to focus on the quality of the entering class. The faculty wanted fewer, stronger students. Once again, I agreed completely. Improving the strength of our entering class, of course, would solve our bar passage rate problem and thus the faculty's third priority was the means of achieving its first.

The committee, in short, reported that raising our bar passage rate, increasing salaries, and improving the quality of our entering class should be our top priorities. These priorities indicated that the faculty shared my view that the value of a law school rests on the people that it comprises. We had transformed the law school by transforming first the faculty and then the student body. The faculty wanted that process of investing in people to continue.

At a somewhat lower level of importance, the faculty called for funding improvements to our existing facilities and constructing a new building on the land that we had acquired. The faculty also attached a high priority to strengthening the reputation of the law school and thus it called for increasing the quantity of information that we sent to the community.

I drafted my proposed budget in accordance with the faculty's priorities. The budget that I proposed to the Board of Trustees that year called for an increase of a half million dollars in scholarships for students, an increase of $800,000 in salaries, and an increase of $100,000 for publications promoting the law school. Building construction would be funded out of our cash reserves and money generated through a later bond offering, described below. After witnessing the divisions of the faculty in the early years, I took great satisfaction in seeing the faculty so unified in setting the future direction of the law school and was pleased that we now had the resources to move us in the direction chosen by the faculty. Open communication had served to bring the faculty together.

One aspect of our planning required a specialized committee. As will be discussed below, we anticipated expansion of the campus in the near future. Indeed, we had discussed the construction of a new building as early as 1997. Accordingly, I established a Building Committee to begin to assess the law school's facilities needs and to set priorities for the use of such new space as we would be able to construct. I knew that our future construction would fall to my successor and wanted to ensure that the faculty was heavily involved in the design process from its inception.

One change that occurred during the last three years of my deanship may have weakened faculty governance. Ironically, it came at the initiative of a few faculty members. In March 2002, a member of the faculty proposed the abolition of the Faculty Executive Committee.

The argument was that the only function of the committee had been to appoint committees. In addition, the faculty chair presided at faculty meetings. The proponents thought that I was capable of presiding at faculty meetings and appointing committees and that the need for a faculty committee to perform those tasks had passed. Both of these tasks, especially presiding at faculty meetings, are typically decanal prerogatives at other law schools. I was sympathetic with the proposal because, in candor, I was already thinking ahead to my planned departure the next year and it was going to be embarrassing to tell decanal candidates that, at Thomas Jefferson, the dean did not even preside at faculty meetings. I thought we should make the change in order to render the job of dean more attractive to future candidates.

I also noted, however, in a memorandum to the proponents of the proposal that the disadvantage of their proposal was that the committee did serve as a conduit for faculty concerns, just as the Staff Liaison Committee served as a conduit for staff concerns, and that eliminating the committee could mean that some important faculty concerns would never be raised. I recommended to the proponents that any change preserve an elected committee to speak for the faculty. Ultimately, however, the proponents' motion was simply to abolish the committee and that was the motion passed by the faculty. At a personal level, I deeply appreciated the faculty's expression of confidence, but I still believe that the faculty should have retained some kind of elected committee to represent it.

Forging Links between the Board and Faculty

If the board was to work with the faculty in setting institutional direction, then we needed to forge links between the board and the faculty. I surveyed the deans of all of the ABA accredited independent law schools regarding the nature of the involvement between the governing board and the faculty. Based on the results of the survey, I told members of the board that the typical practice at independent law schools was for board members to meet on a regular basis with at least some members of the faculty, other than at social events. Because of the importance of staff participation, I wanted to build links between the board and the staff as well. The board met only quarterly and the first couple of board meetings were devoted to organizational matters. In June 2002, about nine months after the board assumed control of the law school, I proposed to the board an event at which members of the board would meet the faculty and the staff and begin a process of regular interaction to discuss the future direction of the law school.

One problem that my proposal encountered was that the board was very small and was shrinking. The board began with nine members, but the press of other commitments caused several members to resign so that, even though we periodically added new members, by early 2005, the number of board members had fallen to six. Two members of the board resigned at my final meeting with the board, leaving the board with only four members by June 2005. As the numbers dwindled during the years from 2002 to 2005, the board's responsibilities fell on fewer and fewer individuals and it became increasingly difficult to persuade the members of the board to agree to a firm date for meetings with the faculty and staff. Further, events after I left the dean's office persuaded me that at least some members of the board simply did not regard meeting with the faculty and staff as a priority.

After months of prodding, I was able to schedule a meeting of the board with the faculty and staff for March 13, 2003, almost a year after I had first sent my memo proposing such a meeting. I hoped to schedule meetings between the board and the faculty and staff on a regular basis, but I was able to schedule only one a year. After the initial 2003 meeting, we had a second meeting on December 9, 2004, and a third meeting on March 2, 2005.

The board decided that, following completion of the search for my successor, expansion of the board would become a major priority. The members assured me that, as their membership grew and the burden on each member decreased, they would schedule meetings with the faculty and staff on a regular basis.

Meanwhile, by the spring of 2003, the board was ready to think about long range planning. The members decided to organize a three-day retreat in Borrego Springs to discuss a number of key issues facing the institution, particularly the possible construction of a new library and conference center on the vacant land we owned in Old Town. I thought that it was critical that the faculty be involved in any long range planning discussions and I suggested that we invite some of the faculty to the retreat. The question was how to structure that involvement. It was not practical to have the entire faculty attend the retreat. Ultimately, we settled on inviting members of the faculty whose service responsibilities or committee assignments gave them special expertise in, or responsibility for, the kinds of issues that would be discussed by the board at the retreat.

The retreat was held on January 23-25, 2004. The board members scheduled one session during which they asked the four faculty members present to comment on the various issues on the agenda. Members of the board told me later that the participation of the faculty had been very useful and promised me that members of the faculty would be involved in all of the board's long range planning discussions in the future, whether involving building construction or other matters.

I also wanted to ensure a strong alumni presence on the governing board. When we created the Jeffersonian Law Foundation in 1995, I asked Denise Asher, one of our most distinguished alumni, to serve on the board. When the board was reconstituted in preparation for acquisition of the law school in 2001, Denise was the only member of the original board who remained. At that time, we added a second alumnus, former State Bar President Marc Adelman, another of our most distinguished alumni. Thus, at the beginning of our operation as a nonprofit institution, alumni constituted a fifth of the board membership. My intention was that, over time, alumni representation would increase. Because of their unique circumstances, alumni on the board can provide vital links among the students, the faculty, the staff, the community and the board. They often possess a keen understanding of the institution's strengths and its weaknesses and they can provide resources of expertise, time, money, reputation and energy that cannot easily be replicated.

21

Ensuring Financial Stability

Thomas Jefferson's history had amply demonstrated the law school's vulnerability to swings in the volume of law school applications. A decline in applications can tempt or force a law school to lower its admissions standards, with devastating effects on its academic quality, bar passage rate, reputation, and accreditation. In raising admissions standards, we would create an upward spiral. Higher admissions standards would raise our bar passage rates and improve our reputation, which would attract more students and allow even higher admission standards. A temporary decline in applications nationally could disrupt our upward movement, if it forced us to lower admissions standards.

In order to insulate the law school against a temporary drop in applications, I wanted to build a cash reserve. Such a reserve would also provide protection against the impact of some unforeseen event. Ultimately, a large cash reserve would serve as a shield for the quality of our academic program against whatever vicissitudes lay ahead. Thus, I planned to generate annual surpluses that could be set aside to create a quasi-endowment, much as we had begun to do in 1995. My initial goal was to set aside enough money to cover an entire year's expenditures, at that time about $20 million.

As it happened, however, the decision to build a cash reserve would have been forced on me in any event. In March, 2002, the Department of Education (DOE) notified us that we no longer satisfied the federal government's requirement of financial responsibility necessary to participate in federal financial assistance program. If we did not cure the problem, all of our students would lose their eligibility for federal financial assistance and the law school would close.

The root of the problem was that, under DOE accounting rules, a for-profit institution was allowed to include goodwill as an asset, while a nonprofit institution was not. When we converted the law school to a nonprofit institution, that very large asset simply vanished from our balance sheet. Ironically, by 2002, the law school was the strongest financially that it had ever been and it only grew stronger each year thereafter, but the change in the accounting rules applicable to us created a different impression. The solution was to accumulate sufficient cash to replace the goodwill and the DOE allowed us five years to do so, although we had to post an irrevocable letter of credit of more than $700,000 in the interim.

The members of the Board of Trustees were greatly troubled by this problem. They had been in control of the institution for barely six months and already it was being threatened with closure, which would result in a default on nearly $20 million in debt. I assured the board members that the law school was sufficiently profitable that it would have no trouble accumulating the necessary cash within the deadline. Still, the board members worried tremendously about the problem and it was an important distraction during the 2002-2003 academic year. Their preoccupation with the financial responsibility issue caused me to postpone by a few months my notice to them of my resignation and may have resulted in my remaining as dean for two more years.

The most important immediate consequence of the DOE notice was that we needed to generate a surplus whether we wanted to or not. The DOE notice in effect dictated the pace at which the law school created its cash reserve. It meant that I would have relatively little discretionary spending until my final year as dean. The need to build the cash reserve deprived me of the opportunity to alter significantly the law school's budgetary priorities.

One of the ways that I hoped we would use a portion of our surplus, once the DOE problem was solved, was to moderate tuition increases. In our years as a proprietary law school, the shareholders had argued that we needed to raise our tuition so that it matched or nearly matched that at California Western and USD in order to attract students. They believed that potential students would regard a low tuition rate at a private law school as an indication that its quality was poor, while a high tuition would signal that the law school was of high quality. Further, the higher the tuition, the fewer the number of students that we would need to admit in order to meet our revenue targets. Admitting fewer students would allow us to raise admissions standards. As we struggled to raise our bar passage rate, anything that would enable us to raise admissions standards, including tuition increases, merited serious consideration. Finally, the reality was that an extra couple hundred dollars per year of tuition charges would probably not deter very many students from attending or add significantly to their debt, but, multiplied by 750 students, it would generate an extra $150,000 per year that could be used to offer a variety of enticing and academically valuable programs. The corollary was that reducing tuition by a couple of hundred dollars probably would not attract many or even any additional students, but it would require us to eliminate programs that students wanted, causing a loss of good students and weakening our academic program. Thus, the irony was that a slightly higher tuition could render us more, rather than less, attractive to prospective students. This situation was not unique to us. Law schools nationally were locked in a perverse competition that forced schools to raise rather than lower tuition in order to be more competitive in the market.

For all these reasons, we allowed our tuition to rise to keep pace with that at the other law schools in the area, generally keeping our tuition about $1000 per year less than the average of the other two law schools. The additional revenue permitted us to offer more programs and to admit fewer students. I worried greatly, however, about the size of the debt that students were assuming and I believed that, once we had solved the DOE problem, we should consider using a portion of our annual surplus to provide financial relief. Indeed, one year, when the tuition increase at the other two law schools was especially large, we also increased our tuition rate significantly, but then offered every enrolled student a partial scholarship over and above any merit scholarships that we otherwise offered in order to reduce the financial impact of the sudden increase. Looking ahead, I believed that, if we did not cap our tuition increases, then we should at least increase our scholarship budget substantially in order to reduce the debt that our students were assuming. Even in the years that we were struggling with the DOE problem, the percentage of our revenue that we allocated to scholarships placed us in the top third of all private law schools in the country, something of which I was proud, and I wanted to see us devote an even larger percentage of revenue to scholarships in the future.

Our financial statements for the fiscal year ending June 30, 2004, demonstrated that our DOE problem had been solved during that year.

We had solved it two and a half years before the deadline imposed by the DOE. We would not receive the DOE's official acknowledgement of our compliance, however, until December 28, 2005, six months after I left the dean's office.

By 2005, two events had improved greatly our capacity to borrow. First, the law school's financial success had increased its credit worthiness, allowing us to borrow money on much more favorable terms. Second, interest rates had fallen. The result was that in 2005 we were able to refinance our debt to our considerable benefit. We issued a new series of bonds, this time for $28 million, compared with $15.75 million in 2001. While our 2001 bonds were unrated, Standard & Poor's gave our 2005 bonds an investment grade rating of BBB-. Because we were able to lower the interest rates from 7.75 percent on the bonds (and 8.25 percent on the subordinated notes) in 2001 to about 4.8 percent for the entire bond offering in 2005, the new bond issue, although about twice the size of the first bond offering, would not increase our interest payments. Yet, it would provide us with approximately $8 million that we could use to acquire land and to construct a new library and conference center. The second bond issue closed on September 15, 2005, almost four years to the day after our 2001 bond issue closed.

I would leave my successor with a law school that held a cash reserve in excess of $12 million, plus another $8 million from the refinancing of the bonds, and an annual operating surplus in excess of $4 million. With our DOE problem solved, the next dean would have an extremely rare and wonderful opportunity to use the surplus and bond proceeds to transform the academic program. I hoped that this circumstance would be a very attractive inducement for potential decanal candidates and would help us to attract a first-rate candidate.

22

Nurturing the Faculty, Staff and Students

The revolution at Thomas Jefferson School of Law had begun with an infusion of new faculty who changed profoundly the academic environment at the law school. It had also been assisted greatly by the hard work of our talented and dedicated staff. Ultimately, the revolution succeeded because of the stronger entering classes that we were able to enroll. These men and women – the faculty, staff and students -- were the law school and our success depended upon their success. The law school needed to nurture these critical human resources.

Much of the work of creating a more humane environment for students had been undertaken early in my deanship and grew out of my experience as associate dean from 1992 to 1994. As has been noted, we reformed many of our academic policies, established new channels of communication, created the position of academic counselor and, for the first time in the law school's history, began to diversify the faculty. After our receipt of ABA approval, we reduced our academic dismissal rate from approximately one third of the entering class to fewer than 10 percent of the class. We increased the percentage of minority students in the entering class to above the national average and lowered the academic dismissal rate for students of color below that for white students. By 1999, we were ranked sixth in the nation for the quality of life on campus and, after that, fifth in the nation. As my deanship drew to a close, I wanted to make some lasting changes in the quality of life for the faculty and staff.

On June 17, 2003, I announced that I was creating a new position of associate dean for faculty development. The purpose of this new position, as the title implied, was to promote the development of the faculty as teachers and scholars. This would strengthen the academic program of the law school and build our reputation. More generally, I wanted Thomas Jefferson to become the finest place to teach in American legal education. The creation of this position was particularly timely because we had six new full-time faculty members arriving in the fall. With the creation of this new position, Steve's title was changed to associate dean for academic affairs.

I appointed Julie Greenberg to this newly created position. Julie was highly accomplished as both a scholar and teacher. Thus, she excelled in the skills that she would be helping others to develop. Moreover, she had the vision, energy, organizational ability and commitment to the future success of the law school that were essential to the endeavor. In addition, Julie had served very effectively as acting associate dean during a semester when Marybeth was on sabbatical.

Over the next two years, we made tremendous strides in improving the working conditions of the faculty. During my first year as dean, I had unilaterally started a policy of awarding sabbatical leaves to the faculty, but at that time we had the resources to award only a couple of sabbaticals each year. Thus, we had a large backlog of faculty awaiting their first sabbatical.[8] I told Julie that I wanted to adopt a policy in which every member of the faculty would be able to take a sabbatical leave after every five years of teaching. Sabbaticals enable faculty members to have professional experiences that they could never have otherwise and thereby to enrich themselves as teachers and scholars. Allowing them frequent opportunities to gain new experience would only strengthen the law school. To accomplish this, we needed to eliminate the backlog and to create a schedule of leaves for the next several years. Julie put the entire faculty on a schedule intended to clear the backlog and move us toward the goal of a sabbatical after every five years of teaching. Having a published schedule also would allow the faculty to plan for, and thus make the best use of, their sabbaticals.

Very early in my deanship, I had also begun the practice of awarding research stipends to the faculty for the summer. Initially, I had no budgetary approval from the shareholders for the summer stipends and so I scraped together small amounts of money budgeted for other purposes, but unspent. Thus, when the new policy began, we were able to award each year only three or four stipends, each worth $3000. Over time we increased the funds available, however, and after our conversion to a nonprofit institution we had sufficient funds to award a summer stipend of $9000 to every faculty member every year, on the condition that he or she had an eligible research project.

---

8   The faculty had approved a college-wide sabbatical policy in January 1991, but the policy did not entitle anyone to a sabbatical. It simply stated the terms that would apply to a sabbatical leave, if one were granted. Bill Slomanson, in recognition of his strong publication record, was granted a sabbatical under that policy, but he was the only faculty member in San Diego to receive a sabbatical under that policy.

I sought to ensure that the faculty had other resources that would promote their scholarly productivity. Jack Monks had begun a policy of budgeting $500 a year for each faculty member to be used to purchase books. Very limited funds were available, upon request, for conference travel. A few members of the faculty received a couple of thousand dollars a year for this purpose, but most received less than that or nothing at all. Early in my deanship I started to increase funds for faculty conference travel annually. The problem was that the faculty was growing so quickly that a portion of each year's increase was needed simply to provide funds for new members of the faculty. Nevertheless, by 2005 we reached the point where members of the faculty could receive some $6000 a year for professional development. In 2004, we budgeted funds to permit every member of the faculty who so desired to have a laptop computer for research and teaching purposes and adopted a policy under which the law school would replace these computers on a regular basis. We hired a full-time academic events coordinator to assist the faculty in organizing conferences and other academic events.

Historically, every faculty member at Thomas Jefferson taught six courses per year, at a time when the norm in legal education was four courses per year. The heavier teaching loads put our faculty at a substantial disadvantage relative to the faculty at other law schools with respect to the production of scholarly research. In January 1997, I proposed to the faculty that we begin a process of reducing our teaching loads to the norm, which it appeared at the time would take three years. As the faculty grew, we were able to reduce the teaching load to five courses per year and finally, in 2003, to four courses per year.

I also wanted the faculty to sense the importance that the law school placed on their scholarly accomplishments. As I have mentioned, the annual merit pay letters that I sent to the faculty always acknowledged each of their publications. In addition, we purchased a cabinet that would display the faculty's latest publications and Steve Semeraro volunteered to keep the display current. With Bryan Wildenthal's very able editorial assistance, we compiled an annual booklet listing the faculty's most recent scholarship, which we mailed to every law school in the country. Julie Greenberg established an online journal through which faculty scholarship would be posted on the Social Science Research Network (SSRN) and Bryan assumed responsibility for editing the journal.

By 2005, we could look with enormous pride at what our faculty had accomplished. In that year, we learned that the Thomas Jefferson School of Law was ranked 55th among all law schools worldwide for the number of times that faculty publications were downloaded from the SSRN. This showed not merely that we were publishing, but that our publications were being read.

The law school had never had a parental leave policy for the faculty. In 1996, I sent a memo to the faculty asking that it form a committee and propose a policy, but nothing happened. I repeated the request in 1999, but again no committee ever was formed. Only one faculty member even responded to the request. In the absence of a faculty generated policy, I tried to address the issue on an *ad hoc* basis, but the results were not satisfactory. We needed a faculty approved policy. After her appointment as associate dean, Julie conducted extensive research on the policies at other law schools and led a lengthy discussion among the faculty. Eventually, on the basis of her research and the faculty discussion, she fashioned a very progressive policy, which the faculty approved just prior to the end of my deanship. I forwarded the policy to the Board of Trustees as I was leaving the dean's office, but the board and my successor apparently ignored it. Several years later, my successor promulgated a policy drafted by the administration that was less progressive than the policy approved by the faculty, but that was, of course, a major improvement over no policy at all.

I also wanted to improve the working conditions of our administrative staff. The Staff Liaison Committee had been a highly effective advocate for the interests of the staff. As a result of discussions with the SLC, for example, we increased the number of annual paid holidays for the staff from 10 to 14 and abolished the requirement that all staff members work at every graduation. I also decided that we should allocate some of our budgetary surplus to improving fringe benefits rather than raising salaries. Our salary increases were awarded on a percentage basis and thus disproportionately favored the highest paid employees. Fringe benefits were often of fixed value, which meant that they were of the greatest relative value to the lowest paid employees. We adopted a policy of providing health insurance for all full-time employees at no cost to the employee and free long term disability insurance that would pay 67 percent of the employee's salary in the event of disability. We also doubled the amount of the employer's contribution to the employees' 401(k) retirement plans. The quality of a law school is determined almost entirely by the people associated with it and I wanted ours to know that they were appreciated and that every position at the law school was deserving of respect and support from the institution.

23

Promoting Diversity

From its founding as a branch of Western State University, the law school had embraced the goal of providing broad access to a legal education and, in that way, diversifying the profession as well as promoting equal opportunity. Until Thomas Jefferson gained provisional ABA approval, the majority of its students were working adults attending law school part-time. In some cases, they were mothers of young children. As already noted, a large portion of the student body in the 1970s comprised military veterans. The law school took great pride in providing access to a legal education for those who otherwise would not have been able to enter the profession.

Diversity in the 1970s and 1980s

WSU's entering classes from the beginning were age diverse. In the 1970s, the mean age of the entering class typically ranged from 28 to 30. Not uncommonly, the oldest student was in his or her 60s and the youngest student was often about 19.

Women initially constituted about 20 percent of the class, but by the end of the 1970s they constituted about a third of the student body.

As has been seen, the college quickly noticed the superior performance of its female students and, by the mid 1970s, was actively encouraging women to apply, creating a Women's Law Institute in 1979 to promote women in the legal profession. By the mid 1980s, women constituted about 40 percent of the student body.

In the early 1970s, students of color constituted fewer than 10 percent of the class. For example, in 1976, just over 7 percent of the students were of color. As early as 1971, WSU initiated a Minority Assistance Program to assist students of color in pursuing their legal education. Starting with the spring 1972 semester, it began awarding minority scholarships. Four students received scholarships that semester and eleven more students received them the following fall. By 1981, 20 percent of the class consisted of students of color.

Superior Court Judge Lillian Lim, who graduated from the San Diego campus of WSU in 1977, became the first Filipina judge in the United States. Here, center foreground, she leads a group of students in a line dance at the 1994 Barristers' Ball.

The attempt to obtain ABA approval in the mid 1980s was accompanied by a reduction in the racial and ethnic diversity of the student body. For example, in 1986, the year that the law school submitted its application for ABA approval, students of color constituted only 12 percent of the student body. After the law school abandoned its accreditation quest, the percentage of students of color rose and, by the end of the decade, it again was approaching 20 percent.

In the early years, all members of the faculty were part-time. As the law school began to hire full-time faculty in the late 1970s, white males predominated. By the end of the 1980s, the law school had 11 full-time faculty members, of whom three were women: Karla Castetter, Joy Delman, and Mary Lynne Perry. All members of the full-time faculty were white.

Mary Lynne was the first woman to serve as the dean of the law school and her tenure witnessed a dramatic increase in the number of women on the full-time faculty. During her four years as dean, the number of women on the faculty grew from three out of eleven to nine out of seventeen. It was still the case, however, that all members of the full-time faculty were white.

Diversity in the 1990s and Beyond

As already described, among my first actions as dean during the summer of 1994 was to ask three individuals to assume special responsibility for increasing the racial and ethnic diversity of the faculty. Over the next five years, the law school hired the first African-American, the first Asian-American, and the first Latino full-time faculty members in its 30 year history. The law school continued to extend offers to applicants of color, but progress in achieving greater racial and ethnic diversity among the full-time faculty was slow. For example, our 2004

ABA site evaluation team noted that the law school had extended 9 offers to candidates of color over the prior three years without a single acceptance. By 2005, when I left the dean's office, four of the 31 members of the full-time faculty were of color.

In 1997, 23 years after the law school began to hire full-time faculty, K.J. Greene became the first African-American appointed to the full-time faculty.

We continued to enjoy great success, however, in promoting gender diversity among the faculty. By the late 1990s, Thomas Jefferson was second in the nation for the percentage of women on its faculty, behind only City University of New York. Nor were our women faculty relegated to a pink ghetto. Women constituted a majority of the tenured faculty and that remained the case at least through 2005. Although Mary Lynne's resignation as dean in 1994 meant that the law school no longer had a woman as dean, I appointed Marybeth associate dean that same year. In 2003, I appointed Julie Greenberg associate dean for faculty development. Thus, except for a single year, in 2002-2003, a female faculty member served as the dean or associate dean (or both) every year from 1990 to 2005.

By 1998, I was able to report that the associate dean, all assistant deans, the library director and the chief financial officer of the law school all were women, as were the heads of all administrative departments but one. The president of the Student Bar Association was a woman and six of the past nine class valedictorians had been women. We were the defending champions of the Roger Traynor Moot Court Competition and the team that won the competition was composed primarily of women and was coached by a woman. We also had conducted a study of the last four entering classes and found that the academic attrition rate for women was lower than that for men.

The mid 1990s also saw the appointment of the law school's first openly gay and first openly bisexual faculty members. By 2005, when I left the dean's office, the law school had appointed at least five members of the full-time faculty who were openly gay, lesbian or bisexual. In May 2001, Thomas Jefferson won the Friend of the Community Award from the Tom Homann Law Association, San Diego's lesbian, gay, bisexual and transgender law association, in recognition of our efforts to promote diversity with respect to sexual orientation, including not only our faculty appointments, but our extension of employment benefits to domestic partners and our course offerings. In 2006, Julie Greenberg would win the award individually for her own personal efforts.

Racial and ethnic diversity among the students increased gradually. At the time I became dean in 1994, the percentage of students of color was still only about 20 percent. I felt a personal commitment to the goal of increased diversity. My wife, Lidia, was born and raised in Mexico City, coming to the United States when she was 18. After we relocated to San Diego, she developed numerous connections to the local Spanish-speaking community and eventually she took a job teaching English to immigrant children at a public school near our home. We saw first-hand the struggles of these children and their families to succeed and I took pride in the fact that Thomas Jefferson provided a path for upward mobility.

In 1995, at the end of my first year as dean, I drafted and submitted to the faculty for approval a proposed policy on diversity in admissions that listed a number of concrete actions that I believed that the law school should take in order to provide opportunities for the study of law and to promote entry into the profession by members of racial and ethnic minorities. The faculty approved the policy, the first such policy in our history, without change. I revised the plan in 1998 to include additional measures that I thought we should take to increase student diversity and the faculty approved my revision, again without change.

As soon as we gained provisional approval and became eligible, Thomas Jefferson became one of only a small minority of law schools that made the large financial commitment necessary to join the Council on Legal Education Opportunity (CLEO) as a full member. We began to send students of color on recruiting trips in other cities and we established a mechanism whereby the names of newly admitted students of color were provided to the Black Law Students Association, La Raza, and the Pan Asian Law Students Association so that they could contact admittees and assist us in recruiting them to the law school.

By fall 1997, students of color comprised about 30 percent of our entering class, well above the national average and the highest percentage in the law school's history. The WASC inspection team that visited the law school in early 1998 noted the "striking increase" in the number of students of color and praised us for our "strong commitment" to diversity among the students, while the WASC commission itself praised our "very impressive record" of minority student recruitment. At the end of that year, as already noted, I hired a full time director of diversity affairs and academic support, whose responsibilities included assisting us in our efforts to recruit and retain students of color, the first time that the law school had employed a director of diversity affairs. By 1999, the ABA also was praising our successful efforts to diversify the student body. By that year as well, the dismissal rate for our students of color had fallen to below that for our white students. We were recruiting more students of color than ever before and we had created an environment in which they were succeeding.

Interestingly, our drive for ABA accreditation was itself not a significant factor in our efforts to improve the diversity of our student body. When Jack Grosse visited the law school for the first time in early 1995 and gave his report on our readiness for an application, he did not even mention diversity. When I asked him later whether we met the standards in that regard, he said that the ABA would not deny us accreditation on the basis of diversity. We might be encouraged to do more, but our accreditation would depend on other matters. Thus, our efforts to improve diversity ultimately were unrelated to our pursuit of ABA accreditation. Indeed, if anything, the drive for accreditation impeded our efforts to diversify. Faced with problems that could cost us our accreditation and potentially destroy the law school, as had almost occurred in the 1980s, we had to devote our major energies to issues critical to our survival, leaving the law school with fewer resources to apply toward increased diversification of the student body.

The law school long had allocated the great majority of its scholarship funds to the single goal of recruiting students with a high probability of passing the bar exam. Although the law school had created scholarships for minority students in the 1970s, by the time that I became the dean, all of our scholarship funds were awarded on the basis of LSAT scores or grade point averages, rather than to promote diversity. Beginning in the late 1990s, Jennifer Keller and I agreed that she would use a portion of the scholarship budget to attract students of color, but the amount available for that purpose was small. When the faculty became involved in setting budget priorities, after our conversion to a nonprofit, our pass rate on the July bar exam was still 20 to 30 percentage points below the statewide average for all ABA approved law schools. As already noted, the faculty's recommendation to me was that we use our available scholarship funds to strengthen our entering classes and to raise our bar passage rate, which is what we continued to do, eventually with tremendous success.

We knew that the best way to increase significantly the diversity of our student body was simply to increase substantially the funds available for scholarships for students of color. Our efforts to raise our bar passage rate, however, necessitated that we not reduce the funds allocated for scholarships to attract applicants who were likely to pass the bar exam regardless of race or ethnicity. At the same time, our need to build a cash reserve to satisfy the DOE financial responsibility requirements limited the amount of new money that we could add to the scholarship budget. Thus, we continued to use only very small amounts of our scholarship funds for promoting diversity.

Nevertheless, because of our aggressive recruiting efforts, the number of students of color in our entering classes continued to grow. Between 2000 and 2003, the number of students of color enrolled grew by about 25 percent. The number of white students enrolled, however, grew even faster. Thus, while we were bringing more students of color into the profession than ever before, the percentage of minority students in our student body actually declined in the years after we received full approval, dropping back toward 20 percent.

The increase in the absolute number of students of color nevertheless changed the character of the student body, a fact that the students noticed. For example, the September 23, 2004, edition of *The Informer* (as the student newspaper was by then named), published a front page story that was headlined "Diversity Is Strong at Thomas Jefferson School of Law," that described the growing number of student organizations for minority students, and that praised what the article called "the great diversity" at Thomas Jefferson. These various organizations began to coordinate their activities, which led to the creation of an annual event known as Diversity Week, featuring daily programs celebrating diversity, including a Diversity Lunch at which each organization served homemade food representing a different culture. The October 29, 2004, edition of *The Informer* featured another front page story headlined "Thomas Jefferson Promotes Diversity." The previous year I had appointed a Diversity Committee, the first in the law school's history, to promote a more multicultural environment on campus and the article described the activities of the committee.

As a result of our efforts to build a cash reserve, we achieved compliance with the DOE financial responsibility requirements by summer 2004 and would receive DOE confirmation of that fact in December 2005. Meanwhile, our bar passage rates began to increase dramatically in 2006, as the much stronger classes admitted from 2003 through 2005 began to graduate and sit for the bar exam. With the DOE and the bar passage problems both solved, my successor quickly reallocated large sums of money to diversity scholarships, resulting in substantial increases in the percentage of students of color in our entering classes. By 2007, the percentage was consistently above 30 percent.

24

Expanding the Campus

By fall 2003, we were actively exploring the possibility of constructing a new building on the two parking lots that we owned, adjacent to the Courtyard Building. The plan was to build a new state-of-the-art library and conference center above ground and a parking garage below ground.

Relocating the library to the new building would give us about 30,000 square feet of space in the Law Library Building, allowing us to provide all of the faculty with spacious window offices, which I hoped, along with our rising salaries and ever-growing support for research, would aid our efforts to attract outstanding entry level and lateral candidates. It would also enable us to add more classrooms on the east side of the Law Library Building and to provide better spaces for a clinic and other student activities. The renovation of our existing buildings would permit us to bring the latest information technology into both buildings. The conference center would give us the means to bring high visibility events to an attractive venue on campus. The parking garage would all but eliminate the parking problem.

Mel, Dick and Art had considered leaving Old Town on a number of occasions over the years, but they had never found a suitable alternative. After the sale of the law school to the foundation, Sandy Kahn in particular advocated that we move the law school to a new location, perhaps somewhere downtown. I noted in response that, if we remained in Old Town, we could construct a beautiful new building, renovate our existing facilities, and add the best technology for a fraction of the cost that relocating the entire campus would entail. Controlling these cost would permit us to keep our student body small and thus to maintain the high admissions standards necessary to strengthen the academic program, to ensure a high bar passage rate, and to build the reputation of the law school. Keeping our student body small would also render us less vulnerable to inevitable downward fluctuations in the size of the national applicant pool and other adverse changes in the environment in which we operated. The board was persuaded and, as we began to plan our campus expansion, we operated on the assumption that we would remain in Old Town.

In the spring of 2004, the Board of Trustees held a three day retreat, noted above, to discuss long range planning, including in particular the possibility of new construction in Old Town. We invited representatives of the faculty, who described some of the deficiencies of our existing facility. Everyone agreed that new construction was highly desirable, although we concluded that it would not be financially feasible in the immediate term. It would become feasible only after the 2005 bond refinancing.

A new building would have to await my successor, but we could start preparing for it. The board and I agreed that in the short term we should acquire more land to ensure that the new building would be large enough to suit our present and future needs. We should also put the law school in the financial condition where it could start construction within a couple of years, both by refinancing our existing debt and by planning a capital campaign in order to reduce to a minimum the amount of any additional borrowing needed for new construction.

Looking for Parking

Meanwhile, with construction of a new parking facility not possible in the immediate term, we needed to take steps to find more parking for our students. As has been noted, our enrollment soared unexpectedly in 2003 as a result of a sudden increase in the percentage of admissions offers that applicants were accepting. The growth in enrollment meant that far more students needed a place to park.

I scouted the area looking for commercial parking lots where we could rent spaces. I contacted shuttle companies to explore the cost of running a continuous shuttle from a remote parking lot to the law school. Finally, in February 2004, I discovered that the John C. Fremont Elementary School in Old Town, a short walk from the law school, had ceased operating as a school and housed only a few administrative offices. It had a large unused parking lot. I approached the San Diego Unified School District about leasing the lot from the district. Initially, the school district refused, but in August it relented and only days before classes started we found that we had 60 additional spaces available within a 10 minute walk from the law school.

The problem was to persuade students to walk 10 minutes to the Fremont school, rather than parking a block away in front of a neighbor's house. I tried to set an example by parking in the Fremont lot myself. After the lease went into effect, I never again parked in the law school parking garage or surface lots. I sent letters to the students urging them to park there, but the letters had little effect. The lot sat empty.

We began looking for some kind of incentive to encourage students to park in the lot. Steve Semeraro suggested that we conduct a lottery among students using the parking lot and award the winner a cash prize. In September, we announced the lottery. Each day, we would record the parking permit number of every student in the lot. At the end of the week, we would draw five winners and each would receive $200. The more a student parked in the lot, the greater his or her chances of winning.

The lottery did not work. Students told us that they did not want to walk the extra ten minutes for a mere chance of winning, even if the prize was significant. They suggested that more students would park in the lot if they were assured of some reward, albeit a small one. At that point, we announced a new policy. We would pay students $5 per day to park in the lot. That worked. The lot began to fill to capacity and we were keeping 60 cars off the street throughout the day. Although the incentives were expensive, the parking problem was the result of our unanticipated increase in enrollment attributable to the rise in the percentage of our admissions offers that applicants accepted. The excess students were generating a large financial surplus and we could easily afford to use a small part of that surplus to address the parking problems created by the higher enrollment. Our plan for the long term was to reduce the number of admissions offers we were making enough to shrink our enrollment by 100 students, which would greatly alleviate the parking problem. In the short term, we needed to find ways to reduce the number of students parking on the street.

I continued to search for unused parking spaces in the area. In January 2005, the owner of Heritage Plaza, which was less than a five minute walk from the law school, agreed to rent us 24 unused spaces in his garage. We announced that the lot was available to students, faculty and staff on a first come, first served basis.

In accordance with our conditional use permit, we hired consultants to perform annual parking surveys and these surveys indicated that the additional parking that we were providing as well as the other steps we were taking, such as Kay Henley's scheduling of classes to spread demand, were counteracting the impact of our larger enrollments. The empirical evidence was that, as a result of the additional parking that we provided, our increased enrollment had not worsened the parking situation, but some of the neighbors claimed that it had – perhaps an impression that was formed when enrollment first surged, before we secured the additional parking. A few neighbors told me privately that they knew that the parking situation had improved considerably since we began to rent the lot at the former Fremont Elementary School, but that they would never admit that publicly.

I reported to the neighbors frequently about the steps that we were taking to reduce the number of students who were parking on the street. I continued to try in every way that I could to build good relations with the neighbors. One day, a neighbor called and complained that a student, in trying to create a parking space on the street, had moved the neighbor's trash can off the street and the can had not been emptied by the trash collector. He wanted to know what he was supposed to do with a week's trash. I drove over to his house, emptied all of the trash into my car, drove back to the law school, and put the trash into our dumpster. Some of our students also tried to help. The Environmental Law Society, for example, held neighborhood clean-ups, walking through the residential areas collecting litter

Defending Our Conditional Use Permit

In 2002, our city councilman, Byron Wear, was succeeded by Michael Zucchet. In May 2003, the FBI arrested Zucchet on charges of fraud and extortion, arising out of allegations that he had taken money from local strip clubs in exchange for seeking to amend a city ordinance that prohibited patrons from touching nude dancers. Zucchet remained in office, however, pending trial. After some of our neighbors complained to him about our students' parking on the street, he apparently decided to intervene on behalf of the neighbors. One day, we found two city inspectors walking around our campus. They told us that, as a result of pressure from Zucchet's office, they had been ordered to scrutinize every aspect of our operation in search of any possible violation of any ordinance.

In April 2004, city officials finally found a violation. When our building contractor died unexpectedly in 1999, he had not yet called for final inspection of his work. We had a facilities manager at the time who was overseeing his work, but she too had died unexpectedly. So, no one at the law school knew that the final inspection had never been done. A city official searching through old records had found the five year old violation. We were sent a notice of noncompliance and directed to show cause why our conditional use permit should not be revoked.

With utterly invaluable assistance from Trish Butler, I had worked very successfully with the city in the past to obtain a conditional use permit without an enrollment cap and to obtain other accommodations, such as allowing us to use the second floor of the Law Library Building to shelve books without reinforcing the floor. I believed that Trish and I had very good working relations with the city officials and I wanted to call upon those relationships to resolve our current problem. Further, remembering how we had been able to enlist Councilman Byron Wear's support in the past, I thought it critical that we schedule a meeting with Michael Zucchet immediately to let him hear our side. Our legal violation was a technical one that could be easily remedied. To my mind, our real problem was political and should be addressed that way. We needed to resolve our differences with Zucchet. We had thousands of alumni throughout the city, more than 800 currently enrolled students, and nearly a hundred employees. We were providing education, creating jobs and bringing $20 million in revenue into the district annually. Zucchet needed to understand that we were an asset to the community, as Byron Wear had quickly recognized.

The members of the board were alarmed by the building code violation and decided to hire outside legal counsel. The board directed me to allow our attorney to deal with the city on our behalf. Our attorney told me that, because of the need to speak with one voice, he did not want me to accompany him to any of the meetings with the city or to have any contact with city officials. Except for brief remarks at a hearing in February 2005, I never again spoke to a city official about any of our permit issues. The meeting with Zucchet that I repeatedly urged that we schedule never occurred.

By November 2004, we had passed our final building inspection. On November 24, the city held a hearing on our permit. A large contingent of neighbors attended the hearing to complain about the parking situation. The hearing officer had the annual parking surveys that we had conducted as well as reports from city officials who had walked the streets to see the situation first hand. The objective evidence was that we had addressed the parking problem. Based on this information, the city found no violation of the permit with respect to parking. The city, however, did want us to provide additional landscaping on our surface lots and, at our own expense, to repair the city sidewalks that passed in front of both buildings. Another hearing was scheduled for February 23 to evaluate our progress on these requirements.

The board designated our attorney to represent us at the February hearing. A number of students, faculty and staff attended, as did I. Approximately a dozen of our neighbors testified against the law school, asking that our conditional use permit be revoked, notwithstanding that the city already had found that we were not in violation of it. Then the floor was opened to speakers in favor of the law school and the number of speakers in our favor roughly tripled the number of speakers against the school. More than two dozen members of the faculty and staff spoke, as did several students and an alumnus. I was enormously proud of the spirited showing we made that day and it reinforced my belief that, if we treated the parking problem as the political issue that it was, we could dwarf the opposition.

As already noted, I had been excluded from our attorney's discussions with the city. Before the hearing, our attorney informed us that the hearing officer would come to the hearing having already decided to impose some kind of cap on our enrollment as a means of reducing the amount of student parking on the street. The decision was astonishing because the hearing officer had already found that we were in compliance with our permit and that parking situation had not worsened since the permit was granted. It appeared that the hearing office was simply responding to political pressure.

At the time we conducted the 1998 parking survey that was required for us to obtain our conditional use permit, we had 3.28 students per parking space. The hearing officer decided at the February 2005 hearing that he would require us to maintain that ratio. In other words, we would not be permitted to have any more students per parking space than we happened to have in 1998. The use of that ratio was arbitrary. The process of obtaining our permit had stretched over a period of two years, during which our enrollment had fluctuated from semester to semester. At the moment that the city required us to conduct the parking survey, our enrollment was unusually low – 588 students -- because of our efforts to raise admissions standards. We had never intended to maintain an enrollment below 600 or indicated to the city that that was our target enrollment. Indeed, our long range planning called for an enrollment between 700 and 750 students, which was approximately the size of our enrollment when we had been allowed to occupy the Old Town site in 1983. Never had the city suggested that whatever ratio of students to parking spaces we happened to have at the moment we conducted our parking survey would someday be used as a cap. If the city wanted to reach back in history for a ratio, the only fair approach would be to use the ratio from 1983 when we moved to Old Town and invested in the campus in reliance upon our legal entitlement to operate in that location. In 1983, we had 5.6 students per space, almost twice the number that the city was proposing to allow us in 2005.

Then matters got worse. Suddenly, the hearing officer announced that, in addition to limiting our enrollment to 3.28 students per space, he would impose an overall cap on enrollment so that no matter how many spaces we added to the campus, we could never have more than a certain number of students. At first, having been told that our long range planning called for up to 750 students, he toyed with that number as a cap. But then remembering that our enrollment at one time had been just under 600 students, he began to speak about an overall cap of 600 students. Our enrollment at the time of the hearing was approximately 835 students and so he asked no one in particular how long it would take us to shrink our enrollment from 835 to 600 students.

Throughout the entire discussion of the overall cap on enrollment, our attorney had said nothing. He had acquiesced in the use of the 3.28 ratio and now it seemed as if he was prepared to acquiesce in the cap on total enrollment. Horrified at the idea that we would have a total cap regardless of the amount of parking that we provided, I jumped from my chair in the audience and rushed to the front of the room, where our attorney was at the microphone. Responding to the hearing officer's question about how long it would take us to reach 600, I told him, "I think we'd be in bankruptcy before we got that far down."

"Really?" asked the hearing officer, with surprise in his voice. I explained that we had issued some $16 million in bonds and that we now had to service the debt. I said that we would default on the bonds before we reached the 600 student figure.

"Well, what do you need?" he asked. Our attorney, unhappy that I had emerged from the audience and was now violating the policy of speaking with one voice, gave me a gentle shove away from the microphone. He then told the hearing officer that our business plan called for a total enrollment of between 700 and 750.

"I take it that you agree with that answer, 750?" the hearing officer asked, looking toward me.

I gave our attorney a gentle shove in return and resumed my place in front of the microphone, wondering whether the shoving match was apparent to the audience. "No," I said, "the school can't operate at that cap." I explained that we were trying to refinance our bonds in order to raise capital for construction that would include additional parking. If potential bond purchasers were told that our enrollment had been capped at below the current enrollment and that our revenue therefore was about to decrease substantially, they would not buy the bonds and our ability to create more parking and thereby solve the parking problem would be destroyed. I said that we could not live with a cap on total enrollment.

The hearing officer was convinced. "All right," he said. "I'll withdraw the decision on that." He required us to limit our enrollment to 3.28 students per space, but we could enroll as many students as we wished, as long as we provided enough parking to maintain the ratio. In other words, we had managed to avoid an enrollment cap, but now we had a new parking requirement.

One of my regrets as dean is that I acquiesced in the board's direction to allow the matter of the conditional use permit to be handled by outside counsel. It was frustrating to watch the negotiations from a distance and not to be able to deal directly with the city or with Zucchet. In the past, we had been very successful in dealing with the city directly and city officials had assured me that no enrollment cap would ever be imposed on us. Once outside counsel became involved, however, our relations with the city deteriorated.

As already noted, I believed strongly in the need for a governing board that served as a genuine check on the authority of the dean. Our board was new and the relationship between the board and dean was still being established. I wanted to set a precedent for effective board oversight of the dean. So, I deferred to the board with respect to its wish to allow outside counsel to speak for us, not realizing how ineffective our counsel would be.

The parking ratio was not a serious obstacle in the short run because it allowed us to have the enrollment at the levels that we projected in our long range planning. It was a nuisance, however. In any event, the permit would need to be revised in a couple of years, when we were ready to seek approval for the construction of our new facility. At the time of the revision, the city would likely reevaluate all of the conditions of the permit and so the particular terms imposed in 2005, in effect, were only temporary.

Zucchet eventually would be convicted of the criminal charges and would resign from office in July 2005. The federal district court later would set aside the convictions on seven counts and order a new trial on the other two counts. Prosecutors, however, would decline to prosecute on the two remaining charges. His political career finished, Zucchet would become the head of the Municipal Employees Association, a union for San Diego city employees.

Acquiring More Land

Meanwhile, we moved forward with our plans to expand the campus. During the 2004-2005 academic year, the owners of Olinda's, a Mexican restaurant immediately north of the parking lots adjacent to the Courtyard Building, offered to sell the land and building to us. The owners were a couple who had owned the restaurant since before the law school moved to Old Town. They were ready to retire and believed that we were the logical purchaser. After we acquired the property, we tore down the building and integrated the land into our parking lot.

For years, I had hoped that we could purchase the building immediately north of the Law Library Building, owned by Melhorn Construction Company, which, coincidentally, had built the Law Library Building. Periodically, I had inquired whether the owners would sell us the building, but had always been told that any such discussion was premature. By 2004, we had realized that constructing a parking garage under the proposed new library and conference center next to the Courtyard Building on the east side of San Diego Avenue would be very expensive. The Melhorn building, like the Law Library Building, rested on a slope on the west side of San Diego Avenue, where a parking garage could be constructed far more cheaply. I suggested to the board that, if we acquired the Melhorn building, we could build a parking garage on that site on the west side of San Diego Avenue and construct our library and conference center next to the Courtyard Building on the east side of the street, with perhaps one level of underground parking. This would reduce the cost of the new library and conference center substantially, while giving us more parking than we could have obtained underground.

As luck would have it, in June 2004, Melhorn finally offered to sell us its building. The board authorized Sandy Kahn and me to begin immediate negotiations, but these came to a halt when one of the principals of Melhorn suddenly became reluctant to sell. California law, however, allowed us to exercise eminent domain powers to compel the sale of the property, a fact that we brought to Melhorn's attention. That recommenced the negotiations, although the transaction was not completed until August 26, 2005, a few weeks after I left the dean's office.

In 2005, we acquired the Melhorn building, located immediately north of the Law Library Building.

We now had additional land on both sides of San Diego Avenue on which to build new facilities, the library and conference center on the east side of the street and a parking facility on the west side. In June, I learned that a 20,000 square foot building on Old Town Avenue, just a couple of blocks from the law school, was on the market. The building was well maintained and it had 69 parking spaces, which would allow us to expand our enrollment by almost another 250 students, bringing our total enrollment to about 1000 students, if we ever wished to do so, even without constructing a new parking garage. We had no intention of expanding enrollment to that level, but we could use a cushion in case of an unexpected surge in enrollment. With this additional building, the parking ratio would lose virtually all significance. Several of the trustees and I toured the facility and we agreed that it would be an excellent acquisition. On June 22, I sent a letter to the owner offering to purchase the building. My tenure as dean ended eight days later, however, and the transaction was never completed.

25

Enhancing Academic Quality and Reputation

The revolution at Thomas Jefferson entailed a process of radical internal reform and renewal. Yet, the ultimate success of the revolution would depend upon the relationship between the law school and the world beyond the walls of its campus. We could achieve academic excellence only by attracting talented faculty and students and we could do that only to the extent that others perceived that the law school was, in fact, a place of excellence. In short, the quality of our academic program depended upon our reputation, which in turn depended at least in part upon the quality of our program. In the years following our receipt of ABA approval, the law school devoted ever increasing emphasis on nurturing both the quality and the reputation of its academic program.

Reaching Out to the Community

With our transformation to an ABA approved, nonprofit, independent law school completed, I believed that in the coming years our most important tasks with respect to enhancing quality and reputation would involve our external relations. We needed to introduce this outstanding new law school to the community, build ties with those outside the law school, raise money, and use our higher bar passage rates to recruit stronger entering classes.

One group with whom I wanted very much to build relations was our alumni. I had been careful throughout my deanship to try to include the alumni in our transformation. Immediately after our decision to seek ABA approval, we sent the alumni a letter announcing the decision. Knowing that many of the alumni would want a diploma with our new name on it, I negotiated with the ABA an arrangement that would allow us to issue such diplomas for a limited period of time to any alumnus or alumna who requested one, as more than 700 alumni did. In 1996, I created our first office of alumni relations, headed by Jean Calvo, although I was able to obtain funding at that time only for a half-time position. As we completed each step of the process of gaining accreditation and converting to a nonprofit, we invariably sent letters to the alumni keeping them informed of our progress. In 2003, I proposed that we launch a new alumni magazine, *The Declaration,* that not only could be used to keep alumni apprised of the latest developments on campus, but that also could be sent to community leaders and prospective students. The first issue appeared in spring 2004. The magazine was published semiannually for the remainder of my deanship.

The law school launched its semiannual alumni magazine, The Declaration, in 2003.

I also wanted to raise the profile of the law school within the San Diego community. When Sue Tiefenbrun notified me that she believed that she would be able to persuade U.S. Supreme Court Justice Antonin Scalia, with whom she had worked in the past, to visit our campus, we decided that we would use Justice Scalia's visit to inaugurate the Jefferson Lecture series. The Jefferson Lecture was intended to be an annual lecture that would be a true community event. We held the first lecture in January 2001 at The Prado in Balboa Park and Justice Scalia spoke to a packed audience of alumni and community leaders, including one of the area congressmen. Because the lecture occurred not long after the Supreme Court's controversial decision in *Bush v. Gore*, public interest in the lecture was intense and a crowd of protestors picketed outside the auditorium. The lecture was even reported on the front page of *The New York Times*. Congratulatory letters and phone calls from alumni poured into the law school.

Joking with Justice Scalia, who delivered our Jefferson Lecture in 2001 and 2004. From left to right are Marybeth Herald, me, Bryan Wildenthal, Justice Scalia, and Sue Tiefenbrun. We were relocating a doorway at the time of Justice Scalia's visit, which explains the missing door jamb and carpet.

We had intended that Justice Ruth Bader Ginsburg, with whom Sue had also worked in the past, would deliver our 2002 lecture, but because of her schedule the lecture did not occur until February 2003. Again, the Jefferson Lecture was delivered to a packed audience. Like Justice Scalia before her, she also consented to teach a Constitutional Law class for our elated students. We were puzzling over whom we could invite as our third Jefferson Lecturer when Sue informed everyone that Justice Scalia had enjoyed his first visit so much that he had consented to a repeat performance. The 2004 Jefferson Lecture, the last of my deanship, was held in February 2004 and was as magnificent as the first two, demonstrating the ability of Thomas Jefferson School of Law to organize events of true significance on a consistent basis. Like the first lecture by Scalia, it drew considerable public attention and attracted about three dozen protestors. I hoped that the Jefferson Lecture would continue to serve as a moment each year when we were able to attract the community at large to a thought-provoking evening of discussion that would help establish a new image for us as a center of learning.

Justice Ruth Bader Ginsburg delivered our 2003 Jefferson Lecture.
She is shown here teaching a Constitutional Law class on campus.

For years, I had been rankled by the fact that the Interstate 5 highway, which ran past both California Western and Thomas Jefferson, featured a large sign indicating that California Western was located at the next exit, while we had no such sign. Although the University of San Diego was located several blocks from the I-5, it had a sign as well. Of the three ABA accredited law schools in San Diego, only Thomas Jefferson lacked a directional sign on the freeway. It was a small thing perhaps, but it seemed to symbolize the ways in which we had been marginalized in the past. Jeff Joseph, a member of our adjunct faculty who also served as legal counsel to the Department of Transportation, gave me the name of the individual in the Department of Transportation who was in charge of highway signage and I called him to request installation of the sign. He explained that our enrollment was too small to meet the criteria for a sign on the freeway.

Over a period of three years, I persisted in my quest for signage, arguing that we were seeking only parity with California Western, our chief competitor. After repeated denials of my requests, the Department of Transportation finally acquiesced. By the spring of 2004, we had a sign on the I-5 announcing that the Thomas Jefferson School of Law was located at the Old Town Avenue exit. It was, again, perhaps a trivial matter, but so many students told me later that finally having parity of highway signage with the other two law schools legitimized Thomas Jefferson in the eyes of their family and friends in some significant way. Most people know nothing of law school rankings, but they will assume that signage on a major interstate highway indicates that an institution is important to the community.

In 2004, after 35 years, Thomas Jefferson finally achieved parity of highway signage with the other San Diego law schools.

I hoped as well to raise the profile of the law school in the legal community, among both academics and practitioners. I have already mentioned our visibility on the SSRN and our annual scholarship brochure. We produced and distributed widely brochures for our Jefferson Lectures, our annual women and the law conference, described below, and other events of significance. Although I did not expect all of this material to be read, I wanted to keep the name of the law school in front of the leaders of the legal community in a context that associated us with scholarly productivity and significant law-related community events. I became a prolific letter writer, sending congratulatory notes to local attorneys and community leaders who

achieved some newsworthy accomplishment, taking every opportunity
to place our name in front of others.

Much of the burden for reputation enhancement fell on Lori
Wulfemeyer, who had been hired by Mary Lynne as a part-time director
of communications. Lori was an ideal candidate because she had
degrees in both law and journalism and even taught communications at
San Diego State University. In time, Lori sought more responsibility.
To justify to the shareholders the expansion of her position to full-
time, I promoted her to assistant dean of administration in June 1999.
In her new capacity, Lori oversaw communications as well as several
other departments and served as academic counselor to the students.
She juggled all of these new responsibilities with tremendous energy,
good cheer, and competence, while producing an ever increasing flow
of attractive brochures and other publications and overseeing publicity
for our events as well as our general relations with the news media.

The Board of Trustees was especially anxious to begin a fundraising
campaign. We had conducted a highly successful campaign in 1996,
raising more than $30,000 from our alumni in just six weeks, merely
to prove to the ABA that we enjoyed alumni support, something that
Jack Grosse thought was important to do. Throughout our many
accreditation inspections, however, alumni fundraising never emerged
as even remotely a concern and so, after that initial effort, we focused
on matters that were more critical to our accreditation.

The board believed that, before we began fundraising, we needed
a fundraising strategy. In 2002, we hired a consultant selected by
members of the board to develop such a strategy. While the consultant
worked on a strategy, the board approved funds to hire a director of
development and to expand to full-time the position of alumni relations
director. Our alumni relations director at the time, Lisa Kellogg,
could not work full-time and resigned, leaving us with two positions

to fill. The board asked our consultant to take the lead in filling these positions. The positions were filled by the spring of 2004.

Our new alumni relations and development directors immediately set to work on a blockbuster alumni event, a 35th anniversary celebration aboard the U.S.S. Midway, a decommissioned aircraft carrier that served as a floating maritime museum in the San Diego harbor. The highly successful event was held in October 2004 and was intended to be the first in a series of major alumni events in coming years. Unfortunately, our new director of development resigned shortly thereafter because she and her husband were relocating to another part of the state. Because my tenure as dean was at an end, the board and I decided to leave to my successor the opportunity to choose our next director of development, with whom my successor would need to work very closely. Our efforts to raise funds and develop alumni relations were largely suspended while we awaited the arrival of my successor.

Enriching the Curriculum

As we endeavored to build our reputation, we looked for ways to emphasize distinctive elements of our academic program. Almost from the moment that we assumed responsibility for the administration of the law school, Marybeth and I agreed that we wanted to strengthen the law school's instruction in professional skills. A stronger program in professional skills would improve the quality of our academic program, enhance students' employment prospects, and bolster the reputation of the law school among the members of the bench and bar.

The campus long had offered courses in Trial Practice and Appellate Advocacy and, when she arrived in 1992, Ellen Waldman added a course in Mediation. Those few offerings, however, were the extent of the law school's professional skills curriculum.

Very few disputes, of course, ever reach trial and even fewer are the subject of an appeal. We decided that we wanted to add a full range of courses that would give students a much broader array of transactional and dispute resolution skills. Marybeth aggressively recruited adjuncts and created an impressive list of skills courses. Many of these new courses were focused on dispute resolution, such as Civil Motion Practice, Criminal Motion Practice, Pretrial Preparation, Scientific Evidence and Expert Testimony, Advanced Trial Advocacy, and Advanced Appellate Advocacy. We also offered courses in alternative dispute resolution, including Ellen's course in Mediation Theory and Practice and an Arbitration course taught by Hadley Batchelder. Other new courses, however, were oriented toward a transactional practice, sometimes in a specific subject area, such as Legal Drafting, Business Drafting, Business Planning, Legal Accounting, Patent Claim Drafting, and Entertainment Law Transactions. Still other courses were broadly applicable, such as Client Interviewing and Counseling, Negotiation Theory and Skills, and Law Office Management.

When we obtained provisional ABA approval and began to recruit students nationally, we emphasized professional skills training as part of our marketing strategy. I soon discovered, however, that few prospective applicants were enticed by an emphasis on professional skills. So, we began to emphasize other aspects of our curriculum in our marketing, although our commitment to professional skills training remained as strong as ever and we continued to build our course list in that area.

One weakness in our professional skills curriculum was the absence of an on-campus live client legal clinic. The closest program that we had to such a clinic was the mediation program founded and supervised by Ellen Waldman. The clinic permitted students to mediate cases referred by the local courts, but it operated largely off-campus and Ellen obtained much of the funding by applying for grants.

On-campus, live client clinics are expensive and we simply could not afford one. Accordingly, to provide our students with experience in live-client settings, we tried to provide as many field placements as possible. Such placements offer students the opportunity to work in a completely authentic setting with practicing attorneys and to make useful professional contacts, although the risk exists that the field supervisor will treat the students as a source of free labor to perform menial tasks. Thus, constant monitoring by the law school is necessary. Our field placement program originally was supervised by a full-time faculty member as part of his or her regular teaching load, but in 2003 we decided that the program could benefit from a supervisor able to provide his or her undivided attention. Ellen was directing our field placement program at the time and she recommended that we hire Judybeth "J.B." Tropp, a very talented young attorney, as the director. Eight years after J.B. joined our staff, as a result of her very hard work, Thomas Jefferson was ranked fifteenth in the nation by *National Jurist* magazine for the number of field placements per student that we offered.

In my final year as dean, I decided that, with our DOE problem resolved, our large budgetary surpluses would enable us to establish a clinic. I had recruited Steve Berenson to our faculty with the promise that, when the time came for us to open a clinic, he would supervise it. Accordingly, I asked Steve to begin the process of designing a clinic. Soon after my departure from the dean's office, an anonymous donor would provide the law school with a grant to open a veterans' clinic, supervised by Steve.

Meanwhile, having discovered that an emphasis on professional skills did not seem to have strong appeal to large numbers of prospective students, I began to look for other ways to describe our program that would entice applicants. One day in the spring of 1999, I suddenly realized that a great deal of our faculty's research coalesced around three principal areas: the international community, information and communications technology, and the struggle for equal opportunity. All of these areas represented cutting-edge areas of contemporary importance.

On May 9 of that year, I sent the faculty a memorandum proposing that we create three new research and teaching centers that would signal to the legal community and to prospective students some of the special expertise that we possessed. The three proposed centers were the Center for Global Legal Studies, the Center for Law, Technology and Communications, and the Center for Law and Social Justice. The subject matter scope of the three centers, taken together, encompassed the vast majority of the research then being performed by the faculty. Thus, each center reflected a deep pool of faculty expertise and a genuine strength of the law school. Virtually every member of the faculty could see his or her research and teaching linked in some way to at least one of the centers. The faculty approved my proposal and the three centers have greatly enriched the law school.

The Center for Law and Social Justice, for example, spawned one of our most successful annual programs. In 2001, Susan Bisom-Rapp, Julie Greenberg, and Sue Tiefenbrun requested funding for a conference on women and the law that they were organizing. Susan was the director of the Center for Law and Social Justice, which was able to provide some of the funding. The three of them had already raised additional money through private donations, but it was not enough. They wanted to know whether the law school could supplement their funds. We had nothing budgeted, but I found a few thousand dollars for the conference. The conference was a tremendous success and became an annual event, which we soon were able to fund entirely from law school resources, allowing the organizers to concentrate on the substance of the event rather than fundraising. It is the only annual conference on women and the law west of the Mississippi and it has brought a tremendous number of distinguished speakers to our campus. After Ruth Bader Ginsburg's 2003 Jefferson Lecture, the organizers established an annual Ruth Bader Ginsburg Lecture, which is now the keynote event of the annual conference. One of the most impressive aspects of the conference, apart from the intellectual stimulation and the visibility that it has brought to Thomas Jefferson, is the collaborative spirit that it has fostered. The three founders readily welcomed the participation of other faculty members, allowing the role of chief organizer of the annual conference to be rotated among a significant number of the faculty.

Those who had served as an organizer for one or more of the first ten annual Women and the Law Conferences gathered together for this 2011 photograph. From left to right are Marybeth Herald, Linda Keller, Bill Slomanson, Julie Greenberg, Bryan Wildenthal, Julie Cromer-Young, Susan Bisom-Rapp, Kaimi Wenger, Lori Wulfemeyer, Claire Wright, Sandy Rierson, and Sue Tiefenbrun.

The Center for Global Legal Studies carried forward a longstanding tradition at the law school with respect to the teaching of international law. As already mentioned, during his presidency, Bill Lawless had founded summer abroad programs in Cambridge and Beijing and, in 1990, WSU had launched a third summer abroad program in Mexico City. Alan Berman, who joined the Thomas Jefferson faculty in 1994, proposed the creation of a summer abroad program in Australia and I was able to persuade the deans of the other campuses and Jack Monks to approve the program.

All of these programs used indigenous faculty, rather than American law professors. For example, in the Cambridge program, a course in comparative constitutional law was taught by a constitutional law professor from Cambridge University, while a course in international human rights law was taught by the head of Amnesty International, who was based in London.

ABA standards did not permit a law school to operate a summer program while seeking provisional approval. Accordingly, to my very great sadness, we discontinued all of our summer programs in 1995, following our decision to apply for provisional approval.

The students who participated in our Cambridge program during its final year, which I had the privilege of supervising, posed for the traditional photograph taken each year of the program, but decided to add an irreverent twist.

Soon, however, we had access to an excellent successor. When Sue Tiefenbrun joined the faculty in 1999, she was the director of a summer abroad program offered by Hofstra University in Nice, on the beautiful French Riviera. Sue asked me whether she could continue to manage the program as a faculty member at Thomas Jefferson and, believing that this program could become a wonderful asset for us, I agreed. The Nice program was a great success from the start. In 2003, Hofstra accepted Thomas Jefferson as a co-sponsor of the program and, in 2008, Thomas Jefferson would assume exclusive control over the program. By 2005, as I was leaving the dean's office, Sue was in China attempting to organize another summer abroad program, this one in Huangzhou. She would succeed in her efforts and would thereby become the director of two summer abroad programs, on different continents in different hemispheres.

Launching Our Graduates in Their Careers

Although some students attend law school because they want a legal education for use in non-legal careers, the majority attend law school because they wish to become lawyers. Ultimately, the entire endeavor is a success from their perspective only if they do become lawyers. Further, a law school's ability to place its graduates is important to building its reputation.

Mary Lynne had hired a career services director who provided career counseling to students and who arranged for a few employers, principally local public agencies, to conduct interviews through the office. After my appointment as dean, the position happened to become vacant and we started interviewing applicants. The first rounds of interviews did not produce an impressive candidate and so we continued to advertise. In December 1995, we received an application from a local attorney named Andrea Lamb. Andrea was a graduate of George Washington University Law School and had extensive practice experience. She had also served as the director of recruiting for a major national law firm and thus had a deep understanding of recruitment from the employer's perspective. I knew the moment that I met Andrea that she was the applicant for whom we had been waiting and we hired her immediately. Andrea was smart, energetic, and creative. In her dealings with employers at all levels, she was poised and confident. She knew how to win their trust. After a little more than two years, in March 1998, I promoted her to the new position of assistant dean for career services.

Assistant Dean Andrea Lamb built an outstanding career services office and opened to our graduates the doors of major law firms all over the country.

Andrea and I agreed completely on the direction in which her office should move. We needed to boost on-campus recruitment and we needed to place some of our top students in prestigious national law firms and judicial clerkships. Finding highly prestigious jobs for some of our students would dramatically improve our reputation and credibility in the legal community, thereby encouraging other employers to interview and hire our students. Further, the success of a few students in prestigious firms would encourage those firms to consider hiring more of our students.

Andrea worked tirelessly and with great success. She built a career services office that employers routinely told me was the finest in the area. By 1999, more than 300 employers were recruiting students through our career services office, compared with about 10 when Andrea was hired.

By 2005, the number of national law firms that had hired our students since Andrea's arrival was really impressive, particularly given that we were only provisionally approved for most of that time. A partial list of these firms included Arnold & Porter; Baker & McKenzie; Cadwalader, Wickersham & Taft; DLA Piper; Foley & Lardner; Howrey, Simon; Kaye Scholer; Pillsbury Winthrop; and Shearman & Sterling. Private companies that had hired our graduates by 2005 included Price Waterhouse Coopers, Qualcomm, Ericsson Wireless, Wells Fargo, the Houston Astros, Conoco and Union Oil. We had also placed students as clerks with judges of the United States Court of Appeals, the United States District Court, and at least one state supreme court.

In 1998, only two years after we received provisional ABA approval, our graduate Bryon Mulligan was hired by Shearman & Sterling in New York. He quickly would be followed by other graduates who landed jobs at top law firms around the country.

Contemplating a University Affiliation

Many of the faculty long had dreamed that Thomas Jefferson someday would become a nonprofit law school, a dream that had been realized in 2001. Even better would be a university affiliation, which, if it was with the right university, could give our students and faculty access to vast resources in other units of the university, enhance our reputation immensely, and promote a quantum leap in the quality of our academic program. In 1995, during the period when it appeared that we would not be seeking ABA approval, I had explored affiliations with Webster University, Point Loma Nazarene University, and USIU, any of which

I believed would make it possible for us to acquire ABA approval and convert to a nonprofit organization. In 2000, when the shareholders informed me of their desire to sell the law school, I contacted several universities in southern California before deciding that the only way to prevent a sale to a publicly traded company was for the Jeffersonian Law Foundation to purchase the law school.

I continued to pursue the idea of a university affiliation. During the summer of 2000, as I was negotiating with the shareholders for the acquisition of the law school by the foundation, news reports indicated that both the University of California at Irvine and the University of California at Riverside hoped to start law schools. I recalled news reports from 1992 indicating that a law school was part of the long range plan at the University of California at San Diego (UCSD). If California was prepared to fund another law school, I hoped that it would be at UCSD and that it might occur in the form of a merger with Thomas Jefferson. Such a merger would allow the university to acquire a law school without incurring the enormous costs associated with founding a law school and obtaining ABA accreditation. As a world class university, UCSD could do far more for our academic program and reputation than any other university with which we could affiliate. At faculty meetings, I began to speak openly about my hopes for an affiliation with UCSD at some time in the future, in order to measure faculty support. Many faculty members were enthusiastic about the idea and none indicated any opposition.

In August 2000, as I was negotiating on behalf of the foundation to acquire the law school, I sent a letter to Richard Dynes, the Chancellor of UCSD, inquiring about the university's interest in an affiliation with Thomas Jefferson. By then it appeared likely that we would soon be a nonprofit institution and I wanted to alert UCSD to our interest in an affiliation and to find out whether a basis for future discussions existed. If so, I wanted to begin to lay the foundation for those discussions.

Dynes referred my letter to Vice-Chancellor Marsha Chandler. In October, she replied that UCSD was in the midst of a multiyear strategic planning process and that it would be premature for the university to respond to my inquiry until that process was completed. Two years later, in October 2002, after our nonprofit conversion was completed, I sent a follow-up letter to Dynes, but UCSD still was not interested in pursuing the discussion further at that time.

It was clear that affiliation with a law school was not an urgent priority at UCSD at the beginning of the decade, but I believed that in time the university would want to affiliate with a law school. My goal became to create as many linkages as possible with UCSD so that, when that time came, affiliation with Thomas Jefferson would seem like a natural next step.

In January 2003, I contacted Robert Sullivan, the recently appointed dean of the new Rady School of Management, to propose that he incorporate a joint JD/MBA program into the long range planning for the school. Dean Sullivan responded that the school, which had not yet admitted its first class, was not ready to consider joint degree programs. The Rady School did not admit its first class until September 2005, three months after I had left the dean's office.

Our most visible linkage with UCSD was the presence on our Board of Trustees of UCSD Assistant Vice Chancellor Elazar Harel, whom we had recruited to the board because of his expertise in information technology and because of his connection to UCSD. As the board contemplated the addition of new members near the end of my deanship, I hoped to include other officials from UCSD as well. In spring 2005, for example, I recommended that the board invite Peter Cowhey, the dean of the School of International Relations and

Pacific Rim Studies at UCSD, to join the board. I left the dean's office a few weeks later and do not know whether the invitation was ever extended. Elazar resigned from the board at the last board meeting that I attended as dean. Since then, no representative of UCSD has served on our board.

Sue Tiefenbrun also worked hard to forge links with UCSD. As early as 2003, she had invited Peter Cowhey to present to our faculty. Peter accepted the invitation and we had a well-attended event. Afterward, Sue and I took Peter to lunch and spoke about our hopes for a closer affiliation. A few weeks later, Peter invited me to a conference at UCSD. Sue also invited a number of UCSD dignitaries, including Chancellor Dynes, Vice-Chancellor Chandler and Dean Cowhey to our Jefferson Lectures.

We forged other links. For example, Claire Wright, our expert in international trade law, taught a course on the World Trade Organization at the UCSD international relations school. Later, rather than offering different sections of the course at each institution, Claire taught a single section of the course that was cross listed at both campuses and that included students from both institutions in the same class.

Because of UCSD's great strength in the health sciences field, health law was a natural area of potential common interest between UCSD and the law school. In fall 2003, we appointed a health law specialist to our faculty, with the hope that she would develop linkages with UCSD in that area.

In June 2005, Sue traveled to China to lay the groundwork for a summer abroad program in Hangzhou. Sue noted that UCSD's international relations school has a particular focus on the Pacific Rim and that a summer program in China would be a logical basis for cooperation with UCSD.

Each of these represented only a small connection between the two institutions. If we could continue to multiply them annually, however, then we eventually would have a vast web of linkages between the two campuses. Even if no formal affiliation ever occurred, linkages between Thomas Jefferson and a world class university would only strengthen the law school.

Seeking AALS Membership

With ABA accreditation successfully attained, the faculty and I believed that we should seek membership in the Association of American Law Schools (AALS) at the first opportunity. Most ABA approved law schools are eventually admitted to membership in the AALS, although in 2001 there were approximately 20 ABA approved law schools that were not members. AALS membership would enhance the law school's reputation and create additional professional opportunities for the faculty.

The AALS membership rules require that, prior to applying for membership, a law school engage a consultant approved by the AALS to evaluate the law school's prospects for attaining membership. In fall 2002, I contacted Carl Monk, the executive director of the AALS, and asked him to recommend a consultant. He recommended several individuals, including our eventual choice, Professor Barbara Black. Barbara, who taught at Pace University, was a former deputy director of the AALS.

Barbara visited the law school on October 21 and 22, 2002. She conducted a kind of site inspection, touring the facilities, speaking with more than 20 members of the faculty, holding two fora with students, meeting with several administrators responsible for areas in which the AALS would be especially interested, and observing classes. She also reviewed an extensive compilation of documents, including recent ABA site evaluation reports, self-studies, budgets, bibliographies of faculty publications, minutes of faculty meetings, letters to alumni, and the catalog. At the end of her visit, she came by my office to discuss her findings. Her plane was departing soon and so she had no time for dinner, but she suggested that we talk over a drink instead. We headed to Kelly's Pub, located just down the street from our campus, where over the noise of billiard balls and televised sports she told me her impressions of the law school. Then I drove her to the airport.

Barbara told me that, when a law school applies for AALS membership, usually the greatest concern is the quality of the faculty. The AALS considers whether faculty members are good teachers and productive scholars and whether they work well together. She said that, in our case, there would be no such concerns. Our faculty was "terrific" in every respect. They took teaching seriously, were enthusiastic about all aspects of their responsibilities, and worked well together. Once again, our efforts over the past decade to build the strongest possible faculty would be the key to our advancement.

The gist of her report was that the law school was doing everything right, but that an application for AALS membership would be premature. She said that the law school had only a year's history as a nonprofit institution and that the AALS would want to evaluate a longer period than that to ensure that, in our new incarnation, we had adequate resources to meet AALS membership requirements. She also said that there would be only two major issues at the time that we applied. The first was the soundness of our financial management as a nonprofit institution. The second was our bar passage rate, now that we were fully approved. These were both issues with respect to which the AALS would want to evaluate our performance after one more year. She also said that the law school should increase the diversity of its faculty and perhaps intensify efforts to increase the diversity of its student body, but diversity would not be a concern that would preclude us from gaining AALS membership.

She suggested that we wait at least one more year and then apply in fall 2003, at which time she believed that our track record with respect to finances and the bar passage rate would be sufficient for us to gain admission to the AALS. The only problem with waiting was that I had already decided to resign at the end of the spring 2003 semester, meaning that, if we waited a year as she recommended, we would be in the midst of a dean's search at the time that we were inspected. Barbara, of course, had no way of knowing of my plans to resign. I knew that we should not apply for AALS membership while we were without a permanent dean. The only choices were to postpone my resignation for a couple of years or to leave the application to my successor. I wanted us to join the AALS as soon as possible. But I had already stayed in the dean's office far too long and seeing the entire process through to completion could require me to stay through 2005, two years longer than I planned to remain. On the one hand, I didn't like the idea that decisions about the future of the law school were being influenced by my personal considerations, but on the other hand I knew that I would never find a perfect time to leave the dean's office and that a delay of a couple of years in gaining AALS membership would likely have little long term impact on the law school. I very reluctantly decided that I would resign in spring 2003 as planned and leave the application to my successor.

Ironically, as it happened, I would remain in the dean's office until 2005 anyway. Had I known in 2002 that I was going to remain that long, we could have applied in fall 2003 as Barbara recommended and completed the process by 2005. In any event, we would successfully obtain AALS membership in 2008.

Epilogue

Late in the 2002-2003 academic year, as Marybeth and I had agreed I would do, I notified the Board of Trustees of my desire to leave the dean's office and to resume the teaching career that had been interrupted so soon after my arrival at the law school. The board entreated me to stay one more year. Jim White pointed out that we had an ABA inspection in spring 2004, which was the inspection routinely scheduled three years after a law school receives full approval. After that inspection, we would be visited by the ABA only once every seven years. Jim said that, if I resigned at the end of the year, the law school likely would still be in the middle of a dean's search when it was inspected and that this would result in an ambivalent report that might leave many open issues. If I remained, we would have a successful inspection that would leave us with no significant accreditation problems for the next seven years. After nine years in the job, they argued, surely one more year would not make that much difference. Jim suggested that I announce my resignation the moment that the site evaluation team left. I could be gone within a couple of months. I finally acceded to their request to stay through spring 2004. When spring 2004 arrived, I agreed to remain in the dean's office for one more year, during the search for my successor, so that the law school would not lose the considerable momentum that it had achieved.

As Jim had predicted, the spring 2004 ABA inspection went quite well and the ABA found no significant accreditation problems. During the exit interview, the team told the Board of Trustees that the transformation of the law school over the past nine years had been "miraculous." The team went on to refer to Thomas Jefferson School of Law as "one of the great success stories" of legal education. It said that no law school in the history of ABA accreditation had accomplished as much as we had in so little time.

The faculty's publication record was "incredible." Members of the faculty were "very happy" and "remarkably collegial." The law school had done a "great job of recruitment." The team found the teaching to be "excellent" and praised the appointment of an associate dean for faculty development. The open forum for students was attended by an unusually large number of students. The students told the team that they "loved the faculty."

The team commented on a number of aspects of the academic program. The three year academic support program was "very well thought out." The three centers had "enriched" the law school, but the team cautioned against allowing a proliferation of programs in the future such that resources would become too thinly dispersed. The team initially was concerned about the absence of a live client clinic, but said that Ellen Waldman's mediation program was, in fact, "a very well run" live client clinic. The librarians were doing "a fantastic job" and those managing the physical facility were "a dream team."

The Accreditation Committee found only three concerns. The first was insufficient diversity in our student body. As noted above, the law school would increase funding for minority student scholarships significantly in 2006 and would very quickly solve this problem. The second was our low bar passage rate. Again, as described above, this problem had already been solved by our higher admissions standards, although we would not see the evidence until our stronger entering classes sat for the bar exam, beginning in 2006. The third was that our catalog listed nine courses not offered during the past two years. That was easily remedied by a minor revision of the catalog. Thus, by 2004, Thomas Jefferson no longer faced any accreditation issues that it had not already solved or would not be able to solve very quickly. We could seek a new dean as a law school with tremendous resources and no significant barriers to our advancement.

At the end of the spring 2004 semester, I announced that the next year would be my final year as dean of the law school. By that time, of the approximately 190 deans of ABA accredited law schools, only eight had served longer than I had.

I urged the Board of Trustees and the faculty to commence a search for my successor immediately and to complete the search quickly, inasmuch as the best available candidates would likely have offers by December. I believed that we had the opportunity to attract an outstanding dean, if we moved rapidly. We were a law school in a beautiful location, with an incredibly productive and collegial faculty as well as a dedicated and highly competent staff, and more than 4000 applications annually for the fall entering class. Rapid increases in the quality of entering classes already admitted would soon push our bar pass rate above 75 percent. Higher bar passage rates would help to attract even more applications, allowing further improvements in the strength of the entering class and even better bar results. Major national law firms were hiring our graduates. We had a $12 million cash reserve, had refinanced our bond debt giving us access to another $8 million in cash for future construction, and were earning a surplus of $4 million a year. We had ample land for the construction of new, state of the art facilities. And, perhaps most importantly, we faced no significant challenges.

The law school was strong, on the move, and brimming with resources. The next dean would have the opportunity, if he or she chose wisely, to use these resources, in consultation with the faculty, to elevate the institution to new heights of academic quality and reputation. Over the next few months, as the faculty and the board discussed what they were looking for in the next dean, one phrase was heard repeatedly and more often than any other. We all wanted a dean who would "keep the momentum going."

Made in the USA
Las Vegas, NV
11 May 2021

22806338R00251